OTHER BOOKS BY TERRY PLUTO

Tall Tales: The Glory Years of the NBA

Loose Balls: The Short, Wild Life of the American Basketball Association

Bull Session (with Johnny Kerr)

Tark (with Jerry Tarkanian)

Forty-Eight Minutes: A Night in the Life of the N.B.A. (with Bob Ryan)

Sixty-One: The Season, the Record, the Men (with Tony Kubek)

You Could Argue but You'd Be Wrong (with Pete Franklin)

Baseball Winter (with Jeff Neuman)

Weaver on Strategy (with Earl Weaver)

The Earl of Baltimore

Super Joe (with Joe Charboneau and Burt Graeff)

The Greatest Summer

The Curse of Rocky Colavito

A Loving Look at a Thirty-Year Slump

Terry Pluto

SIMON & SCHUSTER

New York   London   Toronto   Sydney   Tokyo   Singapore

SIMON & SCHUSTER
Rockefeller Center
1230 Avenue of the Americas
New York, New York 10020

Designed by Irving Perkins Associates
Manufactured in the United States of America

1   3   5   7   9   10   8   6   4   2

Library of Congress Cataloging-in-Publication Data

Pluto, Terry, date.
The curse of Rocky Colavito : a loving look at a thirty-year slump
/ Terry Pluto.
p.   cm.
Includes index.
1. Cleveland Indians (Baseball team)—History.   2. Colavito,
Rocky.   I. Title.
GV875.C7P58   1994
796.357′64′0977132—dc20   93-46866
                                                  CIP

ISBN: 0-671-86908-6

PHOTO CREDITS

AP/Wide World Photo: 37; Cleveland Indians: 1, 2, 3, 4, 5, 10, 11, 12, 15, 21, 25, 27, 28, 31, 32, 34, 35, 36, Gregory Drezdzon/Cleveland Indians; 38, 39, 40; Paul Tepley: 6, 7, 8, 9, 13, 14, 16, 17, 18, 19, 20, 22, 23, 24, 26, 29, 30, 33

To Tom Pluto, my father,
who gave me the Indians

Acknowledgments

Thanks to the following for their interviews and input into this project: Rocky Colavito, Herb Score, Dennis Eckersley, Frank Robinson, Andre Thornton, Joe Charboneau, Duane Kuiper, Rick Manning, Gabe Paul, Bob Quinn, Hank Peters, Peter Bavasi, Mike Hargrove, Mudcat Grant, Vern Fuller, Larry Brown, Max Alvis, Ted Bonda, Bruce Fine, Rich Rollins, Sam McDowell, Ray Fosse, Mike Paul, Joe Tait, Pete Franklin, Greg Brinda, Nev Chandler, Sheldon Ocker, Dan Donnelly, Ed Keating, and Jimmy Dudley. A special thanks to Simon & Schuster's Jeff Neuman, the Rocky Colavito of editors, who came up with this idea that became so close to my heart. Also to my agent Faith Hamlin.

Photographer Paul Tepley supplied many of the photos, as did Bob DiBiasio of the Indians, who opened his files and gave me his time. Finally, to Roberta Pluto and Pat McCubbin, for being there as always to transcribe the tapes and smooth out the manuscript.

Contents

Introduction

Why would anyone be an Indians fan? There are no rational reasons. In my case, I blame my father. He grew up in Cleveland watching the Indians, loving the Indians. But those Indians were Bob Feller, Bob Lemon, Early Wynn, Larry Doby, and Lou Boudreau. Those Indians happen to be Hall of Famers.

My Indians were Jack Kralick, Mudcat Grant, Joe Azcue, and Chico Salmon.

Now there's a frightening thought.

It's time for a little history—Cleveland Indians baseball history.

• Fact Number One: The Indians last won the American League pennant in 1954.

• Fact Number Two: I was born in 1955, and I was born a baseball fan in Cleveland.

• Fact Number Three: The average age of the typical Clevelander is thirty-three. That means more than half of the city can't remember when they last had a decent baseball team because more than half of the people weren't born. This generation has married, had children, divorced, buried their parents, remarried, and had more children. They've learned nearly everything you can learn about life except what it's like to live with a winning baseball team.

• Fact Number Four: Being born a year after the last Indians pennant and being only four years old the last time they were in contention, I can honestly say this much: Boy, have the Indians been in a long slump.

The first baseball player's name I learned was Rocky Colavito. He was everything a ballplayer should be: dark, handsome eyes, and a raw-boned build—and he hit home runs at a remarkable rate. Best of all, he had a nickname. Baseball fans love nicknames, especially when they fit. In 1959 he led the American League with 42 homers. He drove in 111 runs, and no player signed more autographs.

Colavito was the Rock . . . the Rock of the franchise.

"Don't knock the Rock," my father would say.

"Don't knock the Rock" probably were not the first words I said, but they are the first I remember.

The Indians didn't knock the Rock, they just traded him. The date was April 17, 1960. It was the day Cleveland baseball died, or at least went into a deep, dark, seemingless endless coma.

Since trading Colavito, the closest the Indians have been to first place at season's end was eleven games out, except in the strike-marred year of 1981. In the last thirty-four years, they have finished no higher than third—and that was just once, in 1968.

But from 1947 to 1959 they finished above .500 every year but one. In those thirteen years, they won two pennants and finished in the top three spots *nine* times. Hey, they were a damn good team.

If you can, think back to the spring of 1960. Colavito was twenty-six years old. He already had 123 big-league homers and would hit 251 more. Yet the Indians traded him for thirty-year-old Harvey Kuenn, who would hit 87 homers in his fifteen-year career.

"The Indians traded a slow guy with power for a slow guy with no power," said Gabe Paul.

Paul knows a bad trade when he sees one because he made so many himself during his twenty-five years running the Tribe—some say running it right into the ground. One of those deals was in 1965. Colavito was thirty-two and three years away from retiring to his mushroom farm. To bring him back, Paul gave up Tommy John and Tommie Agee. John had won only 2 games as a rookie with the Indians. He would win 286 more after he was traded. Agee would become a solid center fielder and a World Series hero—with the New York Mets, not the Indians.

It was so typical of the Tribe: They trade a guy too soon, and then they get him back too late, both times giving up more than they should.

"I had to make the Colavito deal to save the franchise," said Paul. "We were dying at the gate. We needed to create some fan interest. If we didn't do something dramatic, the team would have moved."

Okay, so what was Frank Lane's excuse in 1960?

"I don't know," said my dad when I asked.

That's because with Lane there was no "why." He'd rather trade than explain. He traded everybody. He even wanted to trade his entire team for the entire Chicago White Sox, and Chicago was considering it until the American League said, "No you don't." Discovering that he couldn't trade the whole team and not wanting to fire the manager, as most general managers do in that situation, Lane became the first and last guy ever to trade managers. He sent Joe Gordon to Detroit for Jimmie Dykes.

A lot of good that did, especially in light of Lane's other moves. Lane had Roger Maris in the farm system, but he traded him. He had Norm Cash and traded him, too.

We Indians fans often seek refuge in flights of fantasy. We think of 1961, of Cash, Colavito, and Maris in the same Cleveland lineup. In 1961, Maris was setting a major league record with 61 homers—for the Yankees. Cash was batting .361 with 41 homers—for Detroit. Colavito had 45 homers and 140 RBI—for Detroit.

For those trades, all the 1961 Indians had to show were Vic Power and Woodie Held, who combined for more errors (35) than home runs (28).

But back to 1959. That was the last time the Indians went into September with even a chance to win a pennant. Boston Red Sox fans whine about the curse of the Bambino, about losing in the World Series. Losing in the World Series? You call that suffering? What Indians fans would give for a repeat of 1954—the Indians' last World Series—when they were swept in four games!

Chicago Cub fans gnash their teeth, go to the wailing wall, and compare themselves to Job because their team has not been to the World Series since 1945. But the Cubs almost got there a few times. They won the National League East in 1984. They're often in first place until the heat of August.

Cubs fans at least have some almosts and September swoons. Since 1959 and the Colavito trade, September may as well have been erased from the Cleveland baseball calendar. August, too. This team was usually out of sight in the American League by the Fourth of July. Since 1959, Cleveland has had eighteen managers and twelve ownership groups, and nothing has changed but the faces. The whole organization seems stuck in the dufus syndrome.

There was the Mother's Day promotion when the team gave out deodorant. What a way to show Mom that you care.

There was the game in 1984 when Smokey the Bear was supposed to throw out the first ball. He couldn't make it, so Bozo the clown filled in. Cleveland writers found the symbolism too good to be true.

There was the saga of Super Joe Charboneau. He was supposed to be the next Rocky Colavito, a good-looking, powerful outfielder. Super Joe was the American League Rookie of the Year in 1980. Nine months later he was banished to the bushes, sleeping on an army cot next to the dryer in the Class AAA Charleston Charlies clubhouse. Charboneau wasn't just napping there; he had moved into the clubhouse. He was the first player in major league history to be a Rookie of the Year one season and back in the minors the next.

Cleveland fans knew Rocky Colavito. Joe Charboneau was not Rocky Colavito, but he was a guy who had been stabbed four times, including once with a Bic pen. He also had eaten raw eggs, shells and all; opened beer cans with his eye socket; sewed up a cut with fishing line; and pulled his own tooth with a pair of pliers and a bottle of Jack Daniels.

You know these stories are true because who could possibly make them up? Who could imagine something like Beer Night when the team had to forfeit a game in 1974? Ah, yes, Beer Night. *Ten-Cent* Beer Night with no limit. Imagine what a buck's worth of beer would mean. Imagine drinking ten beers in an hour. Imagine the lines at the rest rooms. Imagine selling the beer behind the stadium fence during the game, the fans lining up, some of them simply unzipping and relieving themselves right there, not wanting to lose a place in line to buy ten more beers.

One of the Indians' old owners, Bill Veeck was the man who brought the last World Championship to Cleveland back in 1948. Well, Veeck would have known how to stage Ten-Cent Beer Night. He would have found the slowest taps in the world, and all the vendors would have arthritis. It would have taken five minutes to pour each cup.

Veeck was no fool. But Veeck, like the glory days of Indians baseball, is nothing more than a hazy, beery memory.

So the Indians got the crowd roaring drunk, and then the front office wondered why the fans poured out of the stands and onto the field, scaring the hell out of the players from both teams. Texas Rangers left fielder Jeff

Burroughs turned around and saw about twenty-five fans climbing over the wall and heading for him.

"I felt like Custer at Little Big Horn," Burroughs said later. But Little Big Horn was an Indian victory.

Around the nation, much is made of the miserable crowds at Indians games. But think about what they've seen when they've gone to the games. Sometimes it's a wonder anyone shows up. Would you go back to a restaurant that gave you ptomaine poisoning?

For their thirty-four sad seasons, the Indians have played in the worst stadium in the major leagues. It is a depressing, Depression-built structure of eighty thousand seats teetering on the edge of Lake Erie. It catches the brunt of every weather front that blows down from Alberta, Canada. Games have been called because of rain, sleet, snow, even fog. In July the bugs were thicker than the crowds, and players would rather step to home plate with a fly swatter than a bat. Pitcher Jim Kern once had to leave a game when he swallowed a moth.

The place had poles that wrecked your view—perhaps an act of mercy considering what Cleveland fans were forced to watch on the field. Some nights the stadium reeked of beer and stale hot dogs. Imagine working out next to a guy who was sweating out a three-day drunk; that's how it sometimes smelled at Cleveland Stadium.

No wonder this confused poor Herb Score. The voice of this franchise for thirty years and one of the symbols of its lost promise, in May 1993 Score said on the air, "Oh, my. The Indians have just walked the bases loaded on ten straight pitches."

Well, it was twelve, but after a while, who was counting?

The franchise has been the worst funded, the worst managed . . . the worst of the worst. The remarkable aspect of this franchise is not how few people have gone to the games over the years but that anyone bothered to go at all. That is why in my town they sell T-shirts that say CLEVELAND, YOU GOTTA BE TOUGH.

Well, we have been, but so have the times. And to think it all looked so promising once, only a lifetime ago.

Herb and Rocky

The news clippings are yellow and brittle. They belong to Nev Chandler, a longtime Cleveland broadcaster.

"I was never one to save much from when I was a kid, but I kept these," said Chandler. "It's hard for Cleveland fans to believe, but I remember going to games in the 1950s and the Indians *rarely* lost. I was eight years old when they won 111 games in 1954. Think about that— 111 wins in one season. The Indians owned the town. I was like a lot of kids in the late 1940s and 1950s. First thing every morning I'd pick up the *Plain Dealer* and check out the little Chief Wahoo cartoon on the front page. If the Indians won the night before, Chief Wahoo would be holding a lantern in one hand, and he would have his other hand up with a raised index finger. It was a sign of victory. If they lost, the Chief would be battered—a black eye, a couple of front teeth knocked out, and his feathers crumpled.

"Back then, the Chief was in great shape most mornings. That was because the Indians kept throwing those great pitchers at you—Bob Lemon, Bob Feller, Early Wynn, and Mike Garcia. The Big Four. The Yankees had the best team in the American League, but the Indians were always right behind them. And the Indians had better pitching."

That's why Chandler kept three newspapers dated May 2, 1955. Two of the papers no longer exist, but the lead story on all the sports pages was the same:

TRIBE'S TERRIFIC TWOSOME: MR. ROBERT, MASTER HERBIE
—*Cleveland News.*

FELLER AND SCORE JAR BOSOX TWICE
—*Cleveland Plain Dealer*.
"FELLER WAS BETTER THAN I WAS" —SCORE: ONE-HITTER BY BOB, 16 WHIFFS BY HERB
—*CLEVELAND PRESS*.

"Herb Score broke in with the Indians in 1955, and I vividly recall going to the Stadium to see a doubleheader against Boston," said Chandler. "Feller was in the twilight of his career. He pitched the first game and shut out the Red Sox, 2–0. It was a one-hitter (a single by Sammy White). Then Herb started the second game. I had heard a lot about him but never saw him until that afternoon. It was dusk, and Herb was throwing that fastball out of the shadows. It was awesome to see him get the ball up to home plate. I was just a kid, but I couldn't imagine anyone throwing harder. Herb struck out sixteen and won the second game, 2–1.

"I kept all the newspapers from the next day. Cleveland had three papers at the time. All that is left now is the *Plain Dealer*. But I thought I had seen something special, the passing of the torch from Feller to Score, from one great pitcher to another."

And everyone close to the Indians felt the same way.

On this Sunday afternoon in 1955, the Indians were still the defending American League champions. They still had the Big Four. Feller was "a trim-tailored 36 . . . still sneering at Father Time," according to Frank Gibbons in the *Cleveland Press*.

Now they had a fifth pitcher, a great pitcher, a twenty-one-year-old left-hander. This was his fourth big-league start, and all Score did was strike out the side in the first inning. He walked into the dugout and said to no one in particular, "Where did I get that curveball?"

Then he struck out the side again in the second inning, and in the third. By the fifth inning Score had 12 strikeouts. His 16 strikeouts put the Indians into first place and inspired veteran Boston outfielder Sam Mele to say, "Score is the fastest pitcher I've ever faced."

No one knew it at the time, but Cleveland baseball would never again be this good. The team would never be as confident, never be the defending champs, and never have a lefty quite like Score.

The *Plain Dealer*'s Harry Jones called him "the heir apparent to Feller's throne. A fading meteor and a rising star gave the Indians pitching of a heavenly magnitude."

The two pitchers allowed only three hits all afternoon. Feller needed only two hours four minutes to put away Boston, then Score did it in one hour fifty-five minutes. It was indeed another era.

In the *Cleveland News*, writer Hal Lebovitz enjoyed the fact that Score watched the first five innings of Feller's game, then went into the clubhouse and tried to fall asleep on the trainer's table but didn't quite make it.

"Too nervous," said Score.

The newspaper battled to find a nickname for the rookie. The *Plain Dealer* went with "Hasty Herb." The *News* suggested "Hurricane Herb."

That was Feller's first victory of the 1955 season; he'd win only three more games during the rest of his career.

As for Score, he took Feller's place among the Big Four. His record was 16–10, and he struck out a league-leading 245 in 227 innings. The Indians finished the 1955 season at 93–61, three games behind the first-place Yankees.

It seemed the next great milepost on a road that began with Bill Veeck and the 1948 season—an American League pennant, winning the World Series, and 2,620,627 fans, setting a major league attendance record.

The town was hooked on the Indians.

From 1948 to 1959 the Indians won two pennants and finished in second place six other times. That's eight out of twelve years in first or second place. The only big-league team with a better record during that time was the New York Yankees.

With a young Herb Score and Rocky Colavito, Herb's roommate in the Cleveland minor league system, not far behind, Indians fans thought that the 1960s would be just like the 1950s. Their team would be good every year, a contender.

"It's hard for this generation of Indians fans to understand that feeling," said Chandler. "I tell kids about the big crowds, the winning, and how the Indians were one of the most respected organizations in baseball. Kids look at me like I just got out of the Home. 'What do you mean, the Indians a good team? Is this guy nuts or what?' That's how it was in the 1950s, and with Herb and Rocky, that is how it should have been in the 1960s."

Today, most Indians fans know Score's voice after thirty years of broadcasting, but only some know he pitched. Or if they are aware that he was a former player, few realize that he was Sandy Koufax before there was a Sandy Koufax.

"If you hung around with Herb, you'd never catch on," said Chandler. "I was his radio partner for five years. He hardly said a word about playing. When he did, he talked about being a lousy hitter. That was it."

Herb Score was born in Rosedale, New York, on June 7, 1933. When he was a freshman in high school, his parents separated, and Score moved with his mother to Lake Worth, Florida.

"Herb was an instant phenom in baseball," said former Indians infielder Larry Brown. "We went to the same high school, but Herb was five years older. My brother, Dick Brown, was in Herb's senior class, and he was Herb's catcher. I remember seeing games where Herb pitched and people would make bets about what hitter could manage to foul one off. Not only was he the fastest pitcher anyone had seen, he had a great curve. He also was pretty wild, and that scared everyone to death. Herb pitched his team to the Florida High School state title. We all thought he'd be a star."

That included scouts, who romanced Score and his mother.

"There were sixteen teams, and all but Washington made me an offer," said Score of those free-for-all days before the amateur draft. "Washington told me they wanted to sign me, but they knew the price was too high for them. I usually struck out seventeen or eighteen in the games, which were seven innings. It was not uncommon for me to throw a no-hitter, but I also walked a ton, too. I signed for $60,000, which was a lot of money [in 1952], but it wasn't the highest offer. A couple of teams told me that they would give me $100,000. But I liked the Indians because of their scout."

Their scout was Cy Slapnicka, the same man who signed Bob Feller. Actually, Slapnicka had resigned from the Indians in 1941, planning to retire, but Bill Veeck brought him back in the late 1940s.

"Cy was at every game I pitched in high school for three years," said Score. "He was there before the games, watching me warm up. He took me to dinner. He had friends in town take me to dinner and tell me how great it would be if I signed with the Indians. He'd tell me stories about Feller and the other great Indians pitchers. He literally camped on my doorstep. When it came time to sign, it was inevitable that I'd sign with the Indians."

Score would be Slapnicka's last great find for the Tribe. The scout was sixty-six when he signed Score.

"Herb Score is also the reason my brother Dick signed with the Indians," said Larry Brown. "Dick was dating Herb's sister Helen, and planned to go to dental school. Helen told the Indians that they not only should sign Herb, they should sign his catcher. At the last minute they decided to do it because they needed catchers in the minor league system. Had Helen not put in a good word for Dick, I don't think he'd have gotten a contract."

Dick Brown made it to Cleveland as a backup catcher from 1957 to 1959, and he had a chance to catch for Herb Score in the big leagues. Score's career soared.

"When I came to the majors, I had it easy," said Score. "The pitchers were Wynn, Garcia, Feller, and Lemon. All I had to do was watch what they did and do the same thing. The pitching coach was Mel Harder, who was an excellent teacher. The manager was Al Lopez, a former catcher and a great handler of pitchers. I was with a very good team. Everything fell into place."

From 1948 to 1956 the Indians had twenty-game winners every year, sixteen in nine years. Three of the Big Four are Hall of Famers: Feller, Wynn, and Lemon. Garcia won twenty games twice and had a career record of 142–97 before retiring from baseball to operate the Big Bear Cleaners on the west side of Cleveland.

Then there was Score, who won twenty along with Lemon and Wynn in 1956. That's three twenty-game winners in one season. Since then the Indians have had only five—total. In the spring of 1957, the Boston Red Sox made an unprecedented offer of $1 million for Score. They also were willing to throw in some respectable players. It was as if the Red Sox wanted to redeem themselves for selling Babe Ruth to the Yankees thirty-seven years before. The Indians turned it down. They had to turn it down. Score was twenty-three and had already won thirty-six games in two big-league seasons. He was baseball's strikeout king. "Everyone thought Herb was destined to win twenty games forever," said Chandler.

Hank Peters agreed: "Herb threw as hard as anyone I had ever seen. But on top of it, he had a great mental makeup. He was a clean-living guy, a devout Catholic, and a hard worker. Sam McDowell may have thrown as hard as Herb, but Sam had none of Herb's maturity or good habits. Herb was the kind of guy you'd say, 'Give him fifteen years, see what kind of numbers he piles up, then elect him to the Hall of Fame.' "

But two healthy years was all there would be for Herb Score.

❖   ❖   ❖

If you want to know When It All Went Wrong for the Indians, look no further than what happened to Herb Score and Rocky Colavito.

Colavito signed with the Indians in 1951, Score in 1952. By 1953 they were friends and roommates with the Indians' Class AA Reading team. Score was going to be a twenty-game winner; Colavito was going to hit 40 homers. You hear that kind of talk all the time about prospects, but these guys actually did it. They were legitimate. Then add that they were best friends, clean-cut athletes, perfect images for the fans.

Rocky and Herb. When the Indians were winning 111 games in 1954, they also knew that they had Score and Colavito in the farm system, two young lions waiting for someone to open the cage door and let them loose in the majors. At this point the Indians were the envy of every team in the big leagues, even the Yankees. They had great players in the big leagues and a terrific farm system.

"I first saw Herb in the spring of 1953," said Colavito. "He was tall and thin and threw so hard. His motion was fluid. I was playing the outfield in a spring game at the minor league camp. Herb was pitching, and no one hit a fair ball to the outfield off him."

Score and Colavito both turned twenty in that summer of 1953. Both were Roman Catholic. Both were born in New York, and both knew they would one day be together in Cleveland.

"In 1953 we started the year with different roommates," said Colavito. "But my roommate liked to stay up all night playing cards, and so did Herb's. We talked about how our roommates were getting to us with all this card playing. Since neither one of us played cards, we just traded roommates. Then we found out that we had a lot in common in terms of our background. But the big thing was that we knew we would never B.S. each other. We also told each other the absolute truth even if it hurt."

Which brings up the car incident.

"In 1954 we both played in [Class AAA] Indianapolis," said Score. "By then we not only roomed on the road, but we shared an apartment in town. We needed a car and we pooled our money, coming up with $125. For that we bought a used two-seat coupe with a stick shift. Rocky knew how to use a stick, but I had no idea. He took me out to teach me a couple of times, but those lessons nearly ruined our friendship."

"Herb just couldn't get the hang of it," said Colavito. "Finally, I gave up and said I'd drive him anywhere he wanted to go."

"If I had a date, Rocky would drive me to the girl's house," said Score. "Then he'd drive us to the movie or wherever, then he'd come back and pick us up later and drive us home."

Sounds like the definition of true friendship.

Meanwhile, Score was 22–5 with 330 strikeouts in 261 innings at Indianapolis in 1954. Colavito hit 38 homers and drove in 116 runs.

"I made the Cleveland roster out of spring training in 1955," said Score. "Rocky didn't come to the big leagues to stay until 1956."

While Score was a legitimate, honest-to-Cy-Slapnicka phenom, Colavito did not have the endorsement of a legendary scout or even a pack of scouts staking out his Bronx doorstep.

"The three teams most interested in me were the Phillies, Yankees, and Indians," said Colavito. "I went to a Yankee tryout camp; then one of their scouts came to my house. The guy had a big, long cigar, and his attitude was 'Hey, everyone wants to play for the Yankees, so why would I even think about signing with anyone else? Just sign here.' He figured I was a New York kid and wouldn't sign with anyone else. All they were offering me was a chance to play. I'd get a bonus for each level I advanced in the minors but no money up front. The guy was really arrogant. I ended up letting my brother talk to him. The Phillies made what would have been the most lucrative offer to me, but then they started giving me a runaround about how they had to get the bonus approved first. Then there was the Indians."

The Tribe's offer was a $3,000 bonus, a first-year salary of $1,500, and more bonus money as he advanced in the minors. Colavito signed in 1951 and went to Daytona Beach, where he hit 23 homers and had 111 RBI as an eighteen-year-old outfielder.

"Rocky loved Joe DiMaggio," said Score. "I'm not sure if it was intentional, but growing up in New York, it was natural for Rocky to copy DiMaggio's stance. Rocky spread out at the plate. He sort of looked like DiMaggio, especially early in Rocky's career. He also had the same no-nonsense, hardworking approach to the game as DiMaggio. As a kid, Rocky had trouble hitting the breaking ball, but he also understood his weakness. He knew that he had to learn to hit curves, so he spent hours in batting practice learning how to do it. By the end of his career, he hit the breaking ball nearly as well as the fastball. But it took time. He also had no speed. He had inverted ankles. No matter how hard he ran—and he always ran hard—he just never got anywhere very fast."

But then there was Colavito's arm.

"Rocky had the strongest arm of anyone in the Cleveland farm system, and that included the pitchers," said Score. "In the minors, the players would make bets before the game. Then we'd make sure the manager was in the clubhouse so he couldn't watch. Rocky would stand at home plate and try to throw a ball over the center field wall on a fly. He could do it—four hundred feet. I saw it myself several times."

Former major league third baseman Rich Rollins was raised in Parma, a suburb on the west side of Cleveland. His father took him to Indians games, "and one of my most vivid memories is seeing someone hit a double down the right-field line. Rocky chased the ball into the corner, picked it up, and threw it to third base. Only he threw it from the right-field corner about fifty feet over the third baseman's head, and it landed halfway up the stands, right near where I was sitting."

"Everyone knew Herb would pitch in the majors," said Colavito. "There were some people who doubted I'd make it. They thought my lack of speed would hold me back. But I knew I had good power, a good arm, and I got a good jump on fly balls. I had excellent numbers in the minors, but it still took me a couple of tries before Cleveland finally made up its mind to stick with me."

Score was a regular member of the starting rotation in 1956. Colavito opened the season on the Cleveland roster but saw only spot duty in the outfield. "I started really slow; I was hitting about .150," he said. "Then we went on a road trip. By the end of it, I had my average up to .215. When we got home, Earl Averill, Jr., was at my house, and he had just been told he was going back to the minors. I was feeling really bad for him and his wife. But when we got to the Stadium that night, they had changed their mind and sent me out instead."

The Indians were bringing veteran outfielder Gene Woodling off the disabled list. Averill was batting only .156, but he was a backup catcher and all managers love to have an extra catcher. The Indians had just lost their fifth game in a row, and they had only 5 hits their last twenty innings. *Akron Beacon Journal* writer Jim Schlemmer could not understand why the Tribe decided to send Colavito to the minors. He pointed out that the

Indians claimed to be on a "youth movement." He mentioned that Colavito averaged over 30 homers and 110 RBI in his last three minor league
seasons, so what was left for him to learn in the bushes? He said that Colavito "possessed possibly the strongest throwing arm to come into the majors in the last quarter century on a squad known for its weak throwing
arms. . . . Here is a player, if given an opportunity, who might provide
both offensive and defensive power, and add much needed color to the
squad along with giving reporters a new theme for their typewriters and
microphones."

When told of the decision, Colavito wept openly in the clubhouse. "I
can't understand it," he told reporters. "No one else could, either," according to the *Akron Beacon Journal*.

Colavito's next emotion was that of betrayal, and he stormed up to General Manager Hank Greenberg.

"This isn't right," he said. "I'm starting to hit the ball. My wife is preg-
nant. You want to send me to [Class AAA] San Diego. I'm not going across
the country. I'm going home."

Greenberg asked Colavito to reconsider.

"Just go for three weeks," he said. "Rocky, I promise you. After three
weeks, I'll bring you back."

According to Colavito, the general manager of San Diego was a good
friend of Greenberg's. By sending him Colavito, he was doing the man a
favor and helping his team.

"After three weeks in San Diego, I was hitting .420," said Colavito. "I
called Greenberg and told him that it was time to bring me back, that he
had to keep his word. He asked me to wait a few more days so he could make
a move. The way I understood it, Hank was having lunch with [Manager] Al
Lopez at the time. When I hung up, Greenberg explained the situation,
and Lopez said, 'If you made the kid a promise, bring him back.' A week
later I was back in Cleveland. Back then, those were the high-caliber people running the team. If Al Lopez or Hank Greenberg told you something,
you could believe it. Later on it wasn't like that with the Indians."

Colavito had 12 homers and 32 RBI in thirty-five games with a .368
average at San Diego.

Lopez installed Colavito in right field, and he was in Cleveland to stay,
finishing the 1956 season with 21 homers and 65 RBI in 101 games. Score
was 20–9 with a 2.53 ERA and led the majors with 263 strikeouts.

Only Whitey Ford had a lower ERA, and only Frank Lary won more games.

The 1956 Indians had an 88–66 record and finished in second place, nine games behind New York. But they thought 1957 would be even better because they would have Colavito and Score in place for the entire season.

For Indians fans in the late 1950s, the question was "What were you doing the night Herb got hit in the eye?"

"I was going to the game," said Nev Chandler. "But we got a late start. We were driving to the Stadium along Lake Erie on the Shoreway, listening to Jimmy Dudley doing the game on the radio."

The date was May 7, 1957, and Chandler would be one of the 18,386 fans at Cleveland Stadium that night. The Indians were playing the Yankees, an early-season fight for first place between the two best teams in the American League.

For the Yankees, the leadoff hitter was Hank Bauer, who popped out. The next batter was Gil McDougald, who worked the count to 2 balls, 2 strikes.

"We heard the crack of the bat on the radio, and the next thing Jimmy Dudley was saying that Herb was down," said Chandler. "Herb had been hit in the face with a line drive."

McDougald later told reporters that he had been looking for a low fastball, and that was what Score threw. "I got all of it," he said. "When I hit it, it felt like a feather."

Dudley said, "When Herb pitched, he came right over the top, and he had a big follow-through. His fingers nearly scraped the ground after he let go of the ball. McDougald hit the ball, but Herb just couldn't get his glove up. It was as if Herb was stunned for a moment, like he couldn't believe that anyone would hit the ball that hard at him."

Score said, "I threw it straight, and he hit it just as straight. I didn't see the ball until it was right on me. All I know is the ball got big really fast."

The ball bounced off Score's head on one hop to third baseman Al Smith, who threw to Vic Wertz at first to retire McDougald. The stadium public address announcer asked if there was a doctor in the crowd and would he come down on the field. Meanwhile, McDougald never took a step toward first base. Instead, he went to the mound to check on Score. The players discovered that Score was bleeding. Towels were brought to the mound, but there was too much blood. Everything was red.

"I've never seen a man look so dead," said Indians catcher Russ Nixon. "He didn't even flutter, and his face swelled up like a beehive."

Score never lost consciousness. He wondered if he'd go blind, if he'd swallow his tongue, and even if he'd ever hear again because blood was coming out of his ears. He asked if he still had an eye or if it had been knocked out. He said, "Saint Jude, stay with me," as he was lying in the dirt on the mound.

Saint Jude was a vivid part of Score's spiritual life. According to a *Sporting News* story by Hal Lebovitz, Score had his legs crushed by a bakery truck when he was three years old. He was scheduled for surgery, and doctors feared he would never walk without a limp. The night before the surgery, Anne Score talked to a priest about her son. The priest brought a relic of Saint Jude to Score's bedside. The next day the bones had somehow slipped back into place, and there was no need for an operation. Doctors called it a miracle. Score would later credit Saint Jude, the patron saint of lost causes.

"When I walked into the Stadium in the second inning, Herb was already gone," said Chandler. "It was quiet, eerie. No one could quite comprehend what had happened. Everyone wondered about Herb, but everyone also knew they had just witnessed a tragedy."

As Jimmy Dudley recalled, "The crowd was in total silence, like a funeral parlor when the priest shows up."

McDougald was an emotional mess from the incident. He said he would retire from baseball if Score lost his eye. He continually called Lakeside Hospital for reports. When he wasn't satisfied with what he heard, he went to the hospital to speak personally with Score's doctor, persuading the doctor to give McDougald the doctor's home phone number so the Yankee shortstop could call from the road to keep track of Score.

Til Ferdenzi covered the game for the *New York Journal,* and this was his account:

> Blood flowed from Score's right eye. His mouth was ajar. . . . One quick look through my field glasses was enough to make me wonder, was he alive or dead? If alive, would he ever see out of that right eye again? . . . After sec-

onds that seemed like minutes, players on both sides swarmed the mound. Then a stretcher materialized, and the stricken Score was carried off the field. . . . A hard-nosed professional of enormous talent—McDougald played three different infield positions on three consecutive pennant winners. He was a soft-spoken man of great compassion and sensitivity. . . . So when McDougald's line drive hit Score in the right eye, it was like Sir Lancelot felling Sir Lancelot."

His teammates told McDougald that it could have happened to anyone, but he didn't buy it. "It doesn't help to say it was just one of those things," he told Ferdenzi. "I know it was an accident. It looked like the poor guy just couldn't get his glove up in time. . . . The nicest thing was that Herb's mother spent a long time on the phone with me. I'll never forget that. But I never felt the same about baseball after that."

Meanwhile, Score was in the hospital with a broken nose, a lacerated right eyelid, damage to the right cheekbone, and swelling in the right eyeball. That night Lakeside Hospital received a call a minute from fans wanting news of Score's condition. Amazingly, Score listened to the game on the radio, the same game he had started. He asked the doctors to call his mother and say he would be all right. Then he cheered when Rocky Colavito walked in the eighth inning with the bases loaded, forcing in a run to break a 1–1 tie. When the Indians won the game, 2–1, Score had some ice cream to celebrate. But he ate little, and the pain felt like a fist squeezing his head. He never had surgery; the treatment given was stabilizing his eye and not allowing his head to move much for two weeks.

As Score recovered, McDougald was haunted by the incident. Fans screamed "Killer McDougald" at him. A week after hitting Score, he lined a Frank Lary fastball up the middle that hit the Detroit pitcher on the hip, knocking him down. McDougald rushed to the mound, thinking, "Not again." Lary was not injured, but McDougald changed his stance so that he would pull the ball more often, decreasing his chances of hitting another pitcher. McDougald said that the injury to Score lessened his desire for the game. He retired after the 1960 season at the age of thirty, even though there was plenty of life left in his career. He batted .289 in the seven years through 1957, and .253 in his final three seasons after Score's injury.

"I talked to Gil and told him that it was something that could happen to anyone," said Score. "It's just like a pitcher beaning a hitter. He didn't mean it. I was in the hospital for three weeks, and I didn't pitch the rest of 1957. I had a tear in the retina of the right eye, but I could see out of my left eye. Today, my vision is twenty-twenty."

On the night of May 7, 1957, Score was still twenty-three years old. His big-league record was 38–20 with a 2.63 ERA and 547 strikeouts in 512 innings.

For the rest of Score's career, his record was 17–26 with a 4.48 ERA.

Herb Score was perhaps the greatest left-hander in the history of the Indians, but one pitch changed all that. Or so many would have you believe—but not Score. He disdains pity and considers his life to be one of triumph rather than tragedy.

"People want to make excuses for what happened to my career," said Score. "But what happened to me is what happens to a lot of pitchers."

Being hit in the eye?

"That wasn't it," he said. "My career went down because of an arm injury. I tore a tendon in my left elbow. It still hurts today when I hold my arm at a certain angle. I sat out all of 1957, but I went to spring training early in 1958 with Rocky. I was throwing to him, and throwing the ball pretty well. But toward the end of spring training I caught the flu and turned my ankle about the same time. I was scheduled to pitch the opener, and I wanted to very badly, especially coming off the injury. But I was physically weak from the flu, and my ankle was not 100 percent. Anyway, I got beat, and I didn't throw well at all. But I had a start not long after that, and I beat the White Sox. I was my old self, a three-hitter and struck out thirteen or fourteen. I had another good start after that, but I don't remember exactly what happened."

Then came a Sunday doubleheader in late April at Cleveland Stadium.

"Bobby Bragan was managing the team, and he wanted me to pitch the second game because my fastball would be coming out of the shadows," said Score. "Bragan said I didn't have to be there for the first game. I had an apartment in Lakewood [on Cleveland's west side]. When I woke up that morning and went to church, it was raining. The first game was on TV, so I stayed home to watch part of it. The rain was on and off, and by the fifth inning I decided to drive to the Stadium. They got the first game in, but by the end of it, the rain was coming down in buckets. I went to the bullpen and was warming up. It was still raining hard. [Indians general manager] Frank Lane was on the field, screaming at the umpires that we had to play no matter what the weather was because we had a big crowd. But the rain never stopped, and the game was called. Then we lost another game to rain.

"By the time I finally got to start, it was in Washington, and it had been about ten days since I had last pitched. It was a cold, wet night, but I got through the first three innings just fine. I was throwing the ball like I used to. In the fourth inning my forearm started to feel a little sore. But we had a 2–1 lead, and I figured I'd keep pitching and my arm would loosen up.

"In the seventh inning I threw a pitch, and it bounced about ten feet in front of home plate. I tried another pitch, the same thing. My elbow now was killing me, and I left the game.

"The Washington team doctor examined me and told me that he believed I had torn a tendon in my elbow. 'Wait a few days and see how it feels,' he said. That night my arm was so sore I couldn't get it through the sleeve of my sport coat. I waited a few days, then tried to throw. No good. A few days later I tried again, but my arm still hurt. Then I went to see a specialist in Baltimore, who told me that I had a torn tendon in my elbow and to rest for thirty days. 'Now, every time you throw, you just do more damage.' So I waited a month, threw, and felt pretty good.

"Bobby Bragan wanted me to test my arm in a game, and I felt I was ready. He brought me in for the final three innings against the Senators. Again, the game was in Washington. I was throwing great. I struck out five of the first eight guys I faced. But with two outs in the ninth inning, I wound up, and it felt like someone stabbed me in my left arm. I sort of lobbed the ball up there, and the hitter popped out to end the game. Bobby Bragan was shaking my hand, telling me how super I looked. I said, 'Bobby, I hurt my arm again.' He thought I was kidding."

Mudcat Grant remembers that night well: "I thought Herbie slipped as he threw the ball. I was in the dugout, and I swore that I heard something pop in his arm."

"I pitched on and off the rest of that [1958] season," Score recalls. "The crazy thing was that my arm hurt only when I threw my fastball. My breaking pitches were fine, so I threw a lot of curves."

Score pitched only forty-one innings in 1958 with a 2–3 record, while Colavito hit 41 homers and drove in 113 runs in his first full big-league season. Yes, 1958 was a rough year by the standards of these Indians. They finished fourth but still had a winning record of 77–76. There was reason for hope heading into 1959, especially from Herb Score.

"I rested over the winter, and by 1959 my arm problems were gone," he said.

But Score had other troubles.

"People would tell me, 'Herb, you're not throwing the ball the same way. You're stiff-arming it up to home plate.' I couldn't believe what had happened to me. I could throw for hours and my arm wouldn't get sore, but my mechanics were a terrible. I just wasn't throwing the ball the same way. I'd look at pictures of my delivery, and I'd say, 'That doesn't look like me.' Then I'd promise myself, 'Today, I'm going out there and throw like I used to.' But I couldn't find that motion. I could tell that my motion was different. Before I hurt my arm, I could go through an entire season and never scuff the toe plate. Later, I was ripping up a toe plate every game because I was dragging my foot on the ground. I couldn't get out of the habit of dragging my foot, and that wrecked my entire motion to home plate."

In the Cleveland newspapers it became known as the "Herb Score Problem." Years later it would be the "Steve Blass Problem." In each case it simply meant that a guy who had pitched and pitched well nearly all of his life suddenly couldn't do it anymore. A World Series hero with Pittsburgh, Blass degenerated to the point where he couldn't even throw a strike and had to retire. As for Score, Cleveland columnist Frank Gibbons wrote, "There is one school of thought, although a small one, which holds that most of Score's trouble is in the mind."

Veteran broadcaster Jimmy Dudley said, "I still insist Herb never got over the effect of that blow to the eye. That would change anyone, and he changed his motion so he would protect his eye. I firmly believe that."

Score firmly disagrees: "The reason my motion changed was because I hurt my elbow, and I overcompensated for it and ended up with some bad habits."

Regardless, on the mound it was obvious that Score had trouble getting his curve over the plate. But the real difference was his fastball.

"I didn't throw quite as hard as before my arm injury," said Score. "But what killed me was that my ball no longer moved. It went up to home plate straight as an arrow. Or else my fastball had a slider's spin to it, breaking

into right-handed hitters. It used to tail away. At one point in 1959 I believe my record was something like 8–3. Then I fell apart in the second
half of the season. Periodically, I'd throw a really good game. Then in my
next start it would be gone."

Score's final record in 1959 was 9–11. His ERA was 4.70. In 161 innings
he walked 115 and struck out 147.

"It was a struggle," he said.

If the 1959 Indians had the old Herb Score—the guy of whom Tris
Speaker said, "If nothing happens to this kid, he'll be the greatest left-
hander who ever lived"—if the Indians had *that* Score in their rotation
with Cal McLish, Mudcat Grant, Jim Perry, and Gary Bell, they would
have won the pennant by five games instead of finishing five games behind
the first-place Chicago White Sox. If that had happened, the cataclysmic
trades of the following spring would have been just someone's sick fantasy. Or maybe they'd have been made anyway.

You never can tell when it comes to Frank Lane.

Trader to the Cause

In many ways 1957 would be the turning point for the franchise. Before the season, Al Lopez resigned as manager to take over in the dugout for the Chicago White Sox. A former catcher, Lopez was known for his rapport with pitchers and for being just plain smarter than about any manager of his era. He ran the Indians from 1951 to 1956; they won one pennant and finished second five times. The Tribe averaged ninety-five wins under Lopez, and this was in a 154-game schedule.

But as 1957 approached, the front office was in a state of flux. Lopez left for Chicago. William Daley put a group together that bought the team from a group that was headed by Mike Wilson. On the field, the big change was that Kirby Farrell was named the new manager. Indians fans knew managers. They knew Al Lopez. They quickly knew that Kirby Farrell was no Al Lopez. He wasn't even another Oscar Vitt. Farrell was a skinny, dour man who wore a pained expression as if he were trying to pass a kidney stone. Maybe if you took over the Indians and the first thing that happened was that you lost Herb Score, you'd have a pained expression, too.

In 1957, the Indians tumbled to 76-77, sixth place.

Good-bye, Mr. Farrell.

Good-bye, too, to General Manager Hank Greenberg, who helped build the great teams of the 1950s.

And . . . oh, no . . . hello, Frank Lane.

No name invokes such utter, raw hatred among Indians fans as Frank Lane. If ever there was The Man Who Destroyed the Indians, Lane was it. Fans have suggested hanging, tar-and-feathering, or drawing-and-quartering Frank Lane. But none of that is bad enough.

For proper punishment, Frank Lane should have been forced to watch every Indians game since 1960. He should have had to watch Gus Gil try to play second base, Hector Torres try to hit, and Victor Cruz or Eddie Glynn try to pitch—or at least he should have had to sign Keith Hernandez's checks. He should have endured Joe Adcock as manager and Gabe Paul telling the fans, "The problem with this team is that we just haven't jelled yet," as if the Indians were a dessert requiring thirty-five years of refrigeration.

This was all Frank Lane's fault, and Frank Lane should have been forced to live with it—as we did. Instead, in his usual scorched-earth style, he did his damage, then he cut and ran. He left after getting a nice chunk of change to leave town, almost as if it were an extortion payment.

The real question at the end of the 1957 season was "Why Frank Lane?" One sixth-place finish after six years in an American League elite? That's a building that needs some plumbing and an electrical overhaul, not a wrecking ball.

Frank Lane was a wrecking ball.

"You have to understand this about Frank Lane: He could talk himself into any job," said broadcaster Jimmy Dudley. "He had a real knack for figuring out what people wanted to hear, then he would tell it to them."

Or as Hank Peters said, "Frank Lane was ahead of his time in some ways. He preached change, shaking up the status quo. If you had a team that was in the doldrums and you wanted something new, Frank Lane was your guy. He was the ultimate advocate of change."

That sixth-place finish in 1957 hurt the Indians' owners where they lived—at the bank. The Tribe drew only 722,256 fans, its worst gate since 1945 when there was a war on and the players were mostly graybeards or 4-Fs. Remember that the Indians were among the game's best draws. When Bill Veeck put more than 2.6 million fans in the Stadium in 1948 and 1949, the Indians were the first team to break the 2 million mark in attendance. So 722,256 was a problem.

Owner William Daley wanted to do something—and that something became Lane. And if that doesn't make you despise Daley enough, keep in mind that when Lane left in 1960, Daley turned to Gabe Paul. Some guys can really pick 'em, can't they?

"I'm sure that the Indians knew that Lane would keep the team in the newspapers and in the public eye," said Peters. "Fans love trades, and Frank Lane loved to make trades. The bigger the deal, the more controversial, the more he liked it. He made trades just to make them, to keep the pot at the boiling point. There was no off-season with Frank Lane. In the press he was 'Fearless Frank' or 'Trader Lane.' The media loved him, followed him, and wrote about him more than any other general manager. He loved those stories and his reputation for trades. He did make fans pay attention and wonder what he would do next."

Consider this background: In 1949 he was hired to run the White Sox. Chicago was truly dreadful in 1948. While the Indians were winning the World Series and drawing a record 2.6 million fans, the White Sox lost 101 games and lost them in front of a small circle of friends at Comiskey Park.

"The first thing I did in that job was put the entire forty-man roster on waivers," said Lane. "Only two guys were claimed—Howie Judson and Cass Michaels. That was when I insisted on a five-year contract."

Lane lasted seven years with the White Sox. The team did get better, finishing in third place in four of those seven seasons. Lane had a clause in his contract that paid him "a nickel a head for every fan over 800,000." In 1951 the White Sox set a club record with 1,328,234, and Lane cashed in.

But what Lane did best was trade. How about 242 trades in seven years? "I've dealt for the same fellow twice," he said. "If I think I make a mistake, I try to unmake it."

In 1955 he went to St. Louis. With Lane in charge, the Cardinals moved from seventh to fourth to second place.

"He got in trouble in St. Louis when he wanted to trade Stan Musial," said Score. "Stan was the most popular man in town. You couldn't trade Stan Musial for anyone. I also know that he proposed trading the entire Cardinal team for another team—I'm not sure which. None of those things made him popular with the St. Louis fans."

The Indians ownership viewed Lane as a quick fix. They romanced him, and Frank Lane was certainly a man who loved romance and attention.

"The Indians told me to write my own ticket. Well, I wrote it, and here I am," Lane said at the press conference the day he was hired.

The date was November 12, 1957.

It took Lane just three weeks to grab a headline with a monster trade, sending Early Wynn and Al Smith to the White Sox for Minnie Minoso and Fred Hatfield.

"The fans knew Minoso was a good player," says Nev Chandler. "He had even started his career with the Tribe [in 1949–50]. But trading Early Wynn? Early Wynn was supposed to end his career in Cleveland. You don't trade guys like Early Wynn."

Unless you happen to be Frank Lane. Then you don't care that Wynn won twenty games four times or that he was part of the Big Four. You see that he's thirty-six and that his last record was 14–17 with a career-high 4.31 ERA. You liked Minoso when you had him in Chicago. In fact, you made the deal with the Tribe to bring him to Chicago. You know it's a deal that will get everyone talking, so you do it. Of course, two years later you trade Minoso back to the White Sox in a mega-deal that brings you John Romano, Norm Cash, and Bubba Phillips. If only you had stopped there. If only you had kept Cash, a minor league first baseman with major power potential. But you're Frank Lane, and you can't stop. You trade Cash before he even plays a game for you. You trade him to Detroit where he hits 355 career homers. You trade him for Steve Demeter who the *Sporting News* said "swings a good bat but plays only third base and has trouble with his fielding." The *Sporting News* was right. Demeter indeed had trouble with his fielding. But his bat wasn't so great, either. While Cash was holding down first base for fourteen years in Detroit, Demeter's career with the Indians consisted of five at bats; naturally, he was 0-for-5.

And the deals kept coming.

In his first season, Lane engineered thirty-one trades involving seventy-six players. He also made some that didn't happen. In early June 1958 he tried to trade star pitcher Cal McLish, Mike Garcia, and Colavito to Washington for Eddie Yost, Jim Lemon, and Pedro Ramos. According to a report in the *Akron Beacon Journal*, "Colavito frizzled frightfully throughout the contest. Garcia entered the game in the eighth inning and only brought relief to the Senators, who hit safely every pitch that could be reached with a bat. By the end of the game the deal was called off."

Then Lane tried to deal Colavito to Kansas City for a package of Vic Power, Hector Lopez, Woody Held, Dave Melton, Bill Tuttle, and Duke Maas. That was seven for one. The A's decided it was too much.

Meanwhile, Indians fans were wondering, "Why trade the Rock?" In 1958 he hit .303 with 41 homers and 113 RBI. He was only twenty-five. But there was more to it than what was happening on the field.

❖   ❖   ❖

Frank Lane was not a nice man.

"I worked with Frank in Milwaukee in the early 1970s," said former Indians farm director Bob Quinn. "He had a favorite phrase. He'd say, 'Sympathy. You can find that in the dictionary, right between shit and syphilis.' That was what he said when he didn't want to hear someone's excuse."

In his book, *You Can't Hit the Ball with the Bat on Your Shoulder*, Bobby Bragan recalled Lane watching Minnie Minoso in a spring training game. Minoso was one of Lane's favorite players. He was talking up Minoso until Minoso took a called third strike. Then Lane screamed, "You look like a big sack of shit with a cherry on top." Nearly everyone at Tucson's Hi Corbett Field heard it.

Bragan was Lane's first manager with the Indians in 1958. He lasted sixty-seven games. In his last game the Indians lost 1–0 when Boston's Ted Williams beat Cal McLish with a home run. Lane summoned Bragan to his office and said, "Bobby, I don't know how we're going to get along without you, but starting tomorrow we're going to try."

Bragan had been hired by Hank Greenberg, who was fired as general manager and replaced by Lane before Bragan ever had a chance to manage his first game for the Tribe. After he was fired, Bragan told reporters, "It's tough when you have someone breathing hot and heavy on your neck all the time. When I walked into the clubhouse, there was Frank Lane. When I stepped into the airport limousine, there was Frank Lane. I walked out to the batting cage, and there was Frank Lane again." In spring training games, Lane even sat in the dugout next to Bragan.

Cleveland folklore has it that Bragan put a curse on the Indians after he was canned by Lane. Local talk show host Greg Brinda even persuaded a woman who claimed to be a witch to come to the Stadium and remove Bragan's spell. It didn't take.

"I didn't put a hex on the club," Bragan said in his book. "Having Frank Lane as the general manager was curse enough."

So true.

In 1958, Lane kept trading, and he made two monumental blunders. On June 15 he traded pitcher Dick Tomanek, first baseman Preston Ward, and a young outfielder by the name of Roger Maris to Kansas City for

Woody Held and Vic Power. This was after Lane's attempt to deal
Colavito to Kansas City for seven players collapsed. Then, on August 23,
he sold Hoyt Wilhelm to Baltimore.

Maris had not hit well in parts of two seasons with the Indians—.230
with 23 homers in 161 games—but he was only twenty-three when he was
traded. The Indians could have found room for Maris, a natural right
fielder. So what if Colavito was in right? Anyone ever hear of left field?
Two years later Maris would be the MVP for the New York Yankees. Three
years later he'd be the MVP again and hit 61 homers.

As for Lane's other brainstorm of 1958, Wilhelm had just a 2–7 record
with the Indians, but with a terrific 2.49 ERA. The day before the deal,
one of Wilhelm's knuckleballs had eluded catcher Russ Nixon, allowing
the winning run to score from third base for Kansas City. Lane blew his
cork, roared into the Cleveland locker room, and said the Indians would
never lose a game again because of "a damn knuckleball pitcher." Less
than twenty-four hours later, Wilhelm was gone. He would pitch for fourteen more years, ranking among the greatest relievers ever. All the Indians had to show for it was the $75,000 they received from Baltimore.

While Lane never had a manager he liked or a player he wouldn't trade,
the one player he simply couldn't stand was Colavito.

"It began when Frank was hired right after the 1957 season," Colavito
said. "I had to talk contract with him. I had hit 25 homers and had 84 RBI
in 134 games, and all Lane did was tell me how lousy I was. I wanted a
$3,000 raise. He offered me $1,500. I told him that I wouldn't sign for a
rotten raise like that. We went back and forth, and finally he said, 'Take the
$1,500 now. I'll give you the other $1,500 if you play well during the season. Don't worry, I'll take care of you.' I didn't know Frank Lane, but I will
take a man at his word until I find out that he can't be trusted. In early
September 1958, I hit my thirty-fifth home run. I had 102 RBI. I had been
waiting for a month or so for Lane to give me the $1,500 he promised me.
I made an appointment to talk to Lane, and I said, 'I've got 35 homers and
102 RBI. I've earned the other $1,500.' He acted like he had no idea what
I was talking about. He said he never promised me the other $1,500. I
called him a 'no-good liar.' He lied to me and he knew it, and I lost all
respect for him at that moment."

But the conversation wasn't finished.

"Then Frank tried to sign me for 1959," said Colavito. "He said, 'I'll give you the $1,500 if you take this deal.' It was really a paltry raise. I told him there was no way I'd sign that contract, and what was more, I expected the $1,500 because he knew he had promised it to me. I ended that year with 41 homers and 113 RBI and batted .303. We went back and forth all winter, and finally he signed me for double what I had made in 1958. Right then I knew I was in trouble with Frank Lane."

Herb Score sensed it, too.

"With Rocky, his word is his bond," he said. "If he says he will be there at five o'clock, he is there at five o'clock. He is the most honorable man I know. But if you promise to do something for him and you don't, you're off his list. He never forgets anything. There was a time when I was broadcasting, and Rocky was a coach with the Indians. I was talking to a guy who was a pitching coach. He had managed against Rocky and me when we were in the minors about twenty years before. Rocky walked right by us and barely said hello. I said, 'Rocky, you remember so-and-so.' Rocky said, 'Yeah,' then he walked away. I couldn't figure out why he acted like that. Later I saw Rocky, and I said, 'Roomie, what was all that about?' He said, 'Herb, don't you remember?' I had no idea what he was talking about. He said, 'In 1953 that guy had his pitcher knock me down.' I said, 'Rocky, that was twenty years ago.' But to him, it was still yesterday. So if he didn't forget something like that, you can imagine what he thinks of Frank Lane."

When the Indians arrived in spring training for 1959, no one had any idea that this would be their last legitimate run for a pennant *ever*, or at least for a long, long time.

The fans were happy with the new manager, former Indians second baseman Joe Gordon. He had once teamed up with Lou Boudreau to give the Indians their best keystone combination in history. When the Indians won the 1948 pennant, Gordon hit 32 homers and had 124 RBI—staggering statistics for a second baseman, especially one with a reliable glove. In 1957, Gordon was managing San Francisco, then a Class AAA franchise in the Pacific Coast League. He replaced Bobby Bragan in the middle of the 1958 season and finished with a 77–76 record. As the team went to spring training in 1959, the mood was upbeat, and the big reason was Colavito.

"As a kid, my favorite player was Rocky," said Nev Chandler. "Just about all the kids loved Rocky. We played a lot of pickup baseball back then, something you don't see much in Cleveland anymore. All the kids imitated Rocky's batting stance. Before he'd step into the box, Rocky would lift the bat over his head and put it behind his shoulders. Then he'd stretch left, stretch right, then bend around. As he stepped into the box, he would meticulously adjust his cap so it was just right above his eyes. For his practice swing he would point the head of the bat right at the pitcher, as if he were aiming a rifle. You'd watch kids' games, and you'd see most of them pointing that bat, just like Rocky. He was young, handsome, and hit a lot of home runs. They talk about being like Michael Jordan today. In Cleveland in 1959 it was 'be like Rocky.' "

Colavito's image in the community was impeccable. Former major leaguer Rich Rollins recalls attending Saint Francis DeSales Church in Parma as a teenager and seeing Colavito at Mass.

"Rocky signed a lot of autographs after games," said Herb Score. "But he had rules. If he was going to sign for one kid, he signed for everyone so no one would be disappointed. But he also would make the kids line up single file, and they had to say please and thank you. The parents loved to see Rocky teaching their kids manners."

Veteran *Cleveland Plain Dealer* baseball writer Gordon Cobbledick wrote, "He's handsome, boyish, and he doesn't smoke or drink or use violent language."

Or as Score said, "Rocky had tremendous charisma. Fans gravitated to him not just because he hit home runs, but Rocky never took a short step on the field. I never understand when someone says that a guy gives 110 percent. You can't give more than 100 percent, and Rocky always gave 100 percent. He was a courageous clutch player. With the winning run on second base and two outs in the ninth inning, Rocky wanted to be at the plate. Some guys get all their RBI early in the game; Rocky relished the clutch situations. He didn't always come through, but he wanted to be the guy who took that burden on his back."

Colavito trivia became important to the fans, such as learning that Lou Gehrig was his first favorite player, before Joe DiMaggio. Or learning that Colavito never went to a movie during the day when there was a night game. He preferred to take a nap instead. "What he does is hit so many homers and perform so effectively in the outfield and on the mound, and pull so many fans through the turnstiles, and some say he's already won the title as the New Babe Ruth," wrote Cobbledick.

Yes, Cobbledick did utter the "R" word, as in Babe Ruth. And he meant that Colavito could also pitch. In two exhibition innings against Cincinnati, Colavito struck out five. The first time Joe Gordon used Colavito as a reliever in a regulation game was August 13, 1958; he came in from right field to relieve Hoyt Wilhelm. Knowing that Detroit had geared its swings to Wilhelm's fluttering knuckler, Gordon put some heat on the mound in Colavito and his ninety-mile-per-hour fastball. In three innings he faced twelve batters; none got a hit, and he struck out one.

"As a pitcher, Rocky could have been a twenty-game winner," Gordon was quoted as saying several times. But the Indians didn't want to risk Colavito's getting hurt on the mound, so the experiment was junked. The only other time he pitched was in 1968 with the New York Yankees. For his career, Colavito worked 5⅔ innings, allowing one hit and no runs.

But what made Colavito a true Cleveland cult hero was the night of June 10, 1959, in Baltimore. Colavito had been in a 4-for-30 slump with one home run in his last ten games. The Indians had lost 7–3 the previous night, with a throwing error by Colavito being a key play. Rocky also was 0-for-3 at the plate. Before that June 10 game, Gordon met with Colavito and told him to ignore newspaper reports that Lane was about to trade him to Boston for Jackie Jensen.

In his first at bat, Colavito walked and later scored on Minnie Minoso's 3-run homer.

In the third inning, Colavito faced Baltimore's Jerry Walker and pulled one left, 360 feet down the line into the left-field bleachers. Walker said the pitch was a change-up. Colavito said it was a fastball down the middle.

In the fifth inning, Arnold Portocarrero was pitching, and Rocky crushed an outside slider over the fence in left-center, about 420 feet.

In the sixth, the pitcher was still Portocarrero, and Rocky smashed another slider, this one for a 410-foot homer.

In the ninth, Colavito went to the plate. Score told him, "Don't fool around, Roomie. Go for that fourth homer." Colavito said he was just thinking about getting a fourth hit of some kind, especially since Baltimore was considered the most unforgiving park for home-run hitters in the late 1950s. Until this night of June 10, 1959, no player had ever hit more than 2 homers in a game in Baltimore. The Orioles pitcher was Ernie Johnson, a right-hander who hadn't coughed up a homer all season. Having watched Colavito hammer outside breaking pitches, Johnson tried to slip an inside fastball past him. No chance. The ball landed in the left-field bleachers, 415 feet away.

> The fans gave Rocky a standing ovation, [said the *Akron Beacon Journal* account]. Ironically, earlier in the game, one of them had poured a beer on Rocky after he made a catch in right field. Rocky was so angry that he nearly threw the ball at the beer pourer, but managed to control himself. He left the field to boos. With each homer, more boos changed to cheers, and Rocky tipped his cap each time. When Rocky reached the dugout after his historic blow, he leaped into the crowd of teammates awaiting the conquering hero. The Rock let out several yells of "Yippee!" and "Wahoo!"

Somehow you get the feeling that the Rock didn't actually say *wahoo* and *yippee*, but it made for a good story, right? Anyway, Colavito became only the eighth player in history to hit 4 homers in a game, just the third to do it in four consecutive at bats, and he was on his way to a year in which he would hit 42 homers and drive in 111 runs.

Colavito's season wasn't the only excitement in town. The Tribe was in an actual pennant race. Considering the way Frank Lane behaved during it, maybe the gods simply decided not to risk giving Cleveland another one for the next three decades.

"The [first-place] White Sox came to town for a four-game series over Labor Day," says Nev Chandler. "The Indians were right on their backs. There were huge, seventy-thousand-some crowds. That was when they would let fans stand behind the outfield fence. There was no padding, just chicken wire. Early Wynn won a big game in that series, and it was hard for Indians fans to watch Early pitching for another team. But I also think it was the start of a trend where the Indians traded a guy and he ended up playing for someone else in the World Series."

The Indians lost all four of those games to the White Sox and were outscored 24–10. Lane had been questioning Joe Gordon's judgment all season, but this series was worse. When the Tribe followed shortly thereafter with a doubleheader loss to the Yankees, Lane blasted off: "Finishing second isn't good enough for a team that could be on top except for its own mistakes, mechanical and managerial. Go back through the games. You'll find we gave most of them away by faulty fielding, boneheaded base running, and stupid or stubborn strategies. You'd think that Gordon never heard of the bunt." Lane added that Gordon had "a fifty-fifty chance of winning reappointment."

Nice thing to read in the middle of a pennant race, isn't it? At this point the Tribe was still within five games of first.

Lane contacted Leo Durocher about managing the team, then denied it when asked about it. No one believed him. Gordon responded with a statement that said, "It is obvious that harmony can't be achieved between Frank Lane and myself. . . . I have enjoyed being in Cleveland and wish to thank the fans for their loyalty . . . but I can't return as manager in 1960."

Lane was delighted. Everyone else was dismayed. There were two weeks to go in the season, and the Indians still had a shot at first, but the manager and GM were too busy taking shots at each other.

Two days later, on September 20, Lane told Gordon to forget about quitting at the end of the season; he was fired as of now. When the team returned home from a game in Chicago, several hundred fans met them at Cleveland Hopkins Airport with signs reading DOWN WITH LANE . . . WE WANT JOE. Lane was swamped with telegrams demanding that he support his manager, not stab him between the shoulder blades. After two more days, Lane rescinded the firing—for now.

On September 23, Wynn beat the Indians for his twenty-first victory, and the Tribe was eliminated from the pennant race. The *Akron Beacon Journal* reported the subsequent events as follows: "At 11:15 P.M. Tuesday night, Lane fired Joe Gordon and named [coach] Mel Harder as manager pro-tem. At 10 A.M. Wednesday, Lane called Gordon, and the two men had breakfast. At 3 P.M., Lane called reporters to his office and said, 'After summing up everything, I decided that the best man to succeed Joe Gordon was Joe Gordon.' . . . Gordon was given a two-year contract and a $10,000 raise."

At the offices of American Shipbuilding in Cleveland, young George Steinbrenner had to be taking notes. But even at his worst, he never got this bizarre. Around the country, the Indians—especially Lane—were a joke. And keep in mind that this would be the best Indians team in thirty-five years.

They finished at 89–65, five games behind the White Sox. Despite the insanity with Lane, the fans were hopeful for 1960.

Meanwhile, ownership rewarded Lane with a new three-year contract. It was the same deal he had before: a $60,000 base with the five-cent bonus for every fan over 800,000. With the Indians drawing 1,497,976 in 1959, that bonus was worth $34,898 to Lane. Indians owner William Daley said, "Frank has done a tremendous job here. We are delighted with his performance. . . . He is a credit to the rebirth of baseball in Cleveland." Ownership especially liked the fact that attendance doubled in Lane's two seasons.

The worst part of this is that instead of learning something from his debate with Gordon, Lane was actually rewarded for it. Hooked on headlines, he never had as many that were as big as in September 1959 *when his team was blowing the pennant!*

Lane celebrated trading nineteen-game winner Cal McLish, second baseman Billy Martin, and a prospect named Gordy Coleman to Cincinnati for Johnny Temple, a former All-Star who was an old thirty-one. This was a great deal—for Gabe Paul. Only Gabe Paul was in Cincinnati, not with the Indians.

This deal was just a warmup for what was coming in April 1960.

For the third time in three years, Colavito and Lane engaged in their winter contract ritual. Colavito wanted dollars that seemed fair, given the feudal state that was baseball of the pre–free agency era. Lane was trying to put his foot on the face of his young star, grinding Rocky's image into the dirt by portraying him as greedy.

What you are about to read will tell you why today's players have agents—mean, nasty, money-grubbing, gouge-the-owners, grab-the-last-penny agents.

In 1959, Colavito made $28,000. He tied with Harmon Killebrew for the American League lead with 42 homers. His 111 RBI were one behind league-leader Jackie Jensen of Boston.

"Yeah," said Lane. "But Rocky hit only .257. He batted .303 the year before. I'm not even sure he deserves a raise."

Colavito mentioned his 42 homers and his 111 RBI.

"Yes," said Lane. "That was the same as you did in 1958 [41 home runs, 113 RBI], but you needed a hundred more at bats this season. So, really, you had a worse year no matter how you look at it."

Naturally, this didn't play very well at the Colavito household in Temple, Pennsylvania.

Lane pointed out that the Yankees had cut Mickey Mantle's salary. In

1959, Mantle made $70,000. He hit .285 with 31 homers and 75 RBI. New York's first offer was $55,000. After a two-week spring holdout, Mantle signed for $66,000. That was $4,000 less than the year before, but he remained the highest paid player in the American League.

Colavito said none of that mattered:

1. He had a better year than Mantle.
2. He wanted $45,000, far less than Mantle made. "I didn't even want that much," Colavito told reporters. "But Lane's offer was so ridiculously low, I came up with a ridiculous figure of my own."
3. In 1958–59, Colavito hit 83 homers, more than Mickey Mantle (73) and Willie Mays (63). More homers than anyone else in those two seasons, period.
4. He drew fans, and with Lane's attendance bonus, that meant more money for the general manager.

Lane countered by floating a rumor with writers that he might be willing to trade Colavito for Mantle.

"If the Yankees offered Mantle for Rocky, I'd scratch my head," Lane told New York writers. "If they offered Art Ditmar and Mantle for Rocky, I would not have to scratch. The deal would be made. Don't forget that Rocky is Italian, and with the number of New York fans who are Italian and want a successor to Joe DiMaggio, Colavito would mean an extra 300,000 fans. Also, Rocky is three years younger than Mantle. Another thing, Rocky is going to beat Ruth's record of 60 homers."

But Yankee GM George Weiss made Lane look foolish by saying, "I'm not trading Mantle. I'm not looking for a trade. I don't know what he is talking about."

Colavito was still holding out as spring training began. So was another star, a Detroit outfielder by the name of Harvey Kuenn.

Kuenn had led the American League by hitting .353 in 1959 when he made $35,000. He asked for $50,000. The Tigers laughed. He asked for $47,500. Then Frank Lane showed up in the Tiger spring training complex at Lakeland, Florida, peddling a Colavito-Kuenn rumor. Kuenn and his wife liked Detroit. At twenty-nine, he had spent eight years with the Tigers. He felt loyal to the team and didn't want to move. The trade rumor scared him.

Kuenn signed for $42,000, only a $7,000 raise for winning the batting title.

Then the Tigers GM Bill DeWitt and Lane met the writers together, announcing that any trade talks involving Kuenn and Colavito were over. They "were clearing the air. . . . The deal is off by mutual consent," said DeWitt.

"The Tigers had enough trouble [signing Kuenn] without taking on Rocky," said Lane who could never resist taking a cheap shot at Colavito.

Colavito signed in the first week of March for $35,000; like Kuenn, he had received a $7,000 raise. He also would receive a $1,000 bonus if he hit *fewer* than 40 homers because Lane wanted a higher batting average from Colavito and thought that swinging for the fences was killing Rocky's ability to make contact. Fewer strikeouts would mean more hits, Lane reasoned.

"I can look back now and see that Lane had a vendetta against me," said Colavito. "In our contract talks, he lied to me in 1957. Then he just downgraded everything I did. He tried to blame me for not winning the pennant in 1959 because he said I had a slump in September. He kept dwelling on my strikeouts, but I never struck out a hundred times in a season, which is really good for a power hitter."

Colavito wanted to be a team player in 1960. "I signed because I didn't want to hurt the team's pennant chances," he said.

So these two stars—two good people—made what appear to be financial sacrifices for the good of their teams. They made no threats. They demanded no trades. They wanted to play ball, and they wanted to stay with their teams and play for their fans.

Yet even after Colavito signed and the Kuenn deal was supposedly dead, Lane still talked about it.

"Sure I'd like to have Kuenn," he said. "Who wouldn't? I'm a Kuenn man. I like him. But I got to thinking of Harvey's 200 hits, of which maybe 40 would be doubles. The 150 hits for Colavito, well, 42 would be homers. I like the present margin in my favor. Also, Jimmie Dykes wanted to make the deal. That scared me. He's pretty smart."

Jimmie Dykes. Keep that name in mind. He was the Detroit manager in the spring of 1960, but he wouldn't be for long. Of course, when Frank Lane was involved, nobody was anything for long. In the spring of 1960, the only Tribe players left from the forty-man roster Lane had inherited two years earlier were Score and Colavito.

❀   ❀   ❀

Rocky Colavito said that Frank Lane was a "lying S.O.B." Rocky was right. That's because after saying he would not trade Colavito to Detroit for Harvey Kuenn, he did it—the day before the 1960 season was to open at Cleveland Stadium—against Detroit.

"We were playing an exhibition game in Memphis," said Colavito. "It was our last spring game before the regular season opened. We were playing the White Sox, and in my first at bat, I hit a home run to left field. In my next at bat, I was at first base [on a force play]. Joe Gordon came out to me and said, 'That is the last time you'll bat in a Cleveland uniform.' I looked at him, not really wanting to hear what he was going to tell me. Gordon said, 'You've been traded to Detroit for Harvey Kuenn.'

"There I was, still standing on first base, and this guy is telling me that I'm traded. Then Gordon said, 'I want to wish you all the luck in the world.' All I could think to say was, 'The same to you.' But Gordon spread the story that I said, 'Kuenn and who else?' That was the biggest lie ever. It implied that I didn't think Harvey was good enough to be traded for me. That wasn't it at all. I just couldn't believe they did it. It caught me totally by surprise. I heard one rumor in spring training, but that had died down [when the two teams said there would be no trade]. But I never said anything negative about Harvey Kuenn. After that, I never had any stomach for Gordon or Lane."

Colavito was removed from the game for a pinch runner. He went into the dugout and sat down.

"I was in the right-field bullpen," said Score. "Rocky came down to talk to me. This was right after he left the game. We had heard for a while that we both might be traded in a package. Lane wanted to trade us both, probably because we were the only two guys left from before he got there. But in my last start at Daytona Beach, I got murdered. Until then I heard the Tigers were going to take me, too. But after seeing how I pitched, they changed their mind. No matter what anyone says, Lane was determined to trade Rocky. He just didn't like Rocky as a person. Part of it was that Lane believed ballplayers should be rowdy, hard-living, hard-drinking guys. But that wasn't Rocky or myself. I believe that Lane resented the fact that no matter how many trades he made or how much the Indians improved while he was general manager, Rocky would still be the most popular Indian. I know for a fact that Nate Dolin [a vice president and one of the Indians' owners] did not want Lane to trade Rocky, and he told that to Lane. But Lane did it anyway."

Several newspaper accounts proved Score correct.

"Toward the end of spring training, Lane called me about the proposed trade," said Dolin. "I said, 'But Frank, what we need most is pitching.' He said, 'I guess you're right. It won't help us.' The next day I heard on the radio that he had made the deal."

They liked it in Detroit. The headline in the *Free Press* was: 42 HOME RUNS FOR 135 SINGLES.

Lane insisted that Gordon was all for the deal, and Gordon enthusiastically backed his boss: "Kuenn is an all-around player. He can run, he can throw, and he can shag a fly ball. He's probably the toughest hitter in the league, and I'm glad we've got him. I'll take full responsibility. There hasn't been a deal made since last September that I didn't completely approve."

A Cleveland headline was: COLAVITO FANS OUT FOR LANE'S SCALP: REACTION VIOLENT AS TRADE STIRS MAN IN THE STREET. The newspaper held a poll, and the fans voted 9 to 1 against the deal.

A *Cleveland Press* editorial read: "The Colavito-Kuenn swap has at least put baseball back on the tip of everyone's tongue. Just about everyone has an opinion, and just about everybody rates it as a major calamity. Colavito was a hero, even when he struck out. His departure for Detroit is about as popular as moving the Indians out of town."

Lane explained the deal like this: "Joe and I believe that the home run is overrated. Look at Washington. They almost led the league in home runs, yet finished last. I don't want to knock Rocky. He is a fine player and a fine man. He may hit 50–55 homers in Detroit . . . but we've given up 40 homers for 40 doubles. We've added 50 singles and taken away 50 strikeouts. . . . I'll probably make bobby-soxers mad at me, but they've been mad at me before. . . . I realize that Colavito is very popular. There were many people who came to the park to see him hit a home run, whereas they wouldn't come to the park just to see Kuenn hit a single. But those singles and doubles win just as many games as home runs. . . . Rocky's best year was 1958 when he batted over .300 and hit 41 homers, but our attendance was only 650,000 because we didn't have a contending club."

Where do you begin to shovel through this pile of public relations pap spewed out by Lane?

1. What about age? Lane didn't mention it. Colavito was twenty-six, Kuenn twenty-nine. And Kuenn was an "old twenty-nine" because he had a distressing injury history. In the spring of 1960, he had pulled muscles in both legs while in camp with the Tigers. From 1955 to 1959 he missed an average of twelve games per season with a variety of muscle pulls, leg bruises, and other problems. In 1959 he sat out fifteen games. Colavito had played every game in the 1959 season and never had a major injury with the Tribe.

2. About home runs: By the time Colavito was twenty-six, he had 129 homers. In his last two seasons, he hit 41 and 42, more than anyone in the big leagues. For all the discussion of Colavito's strikeouts, we're not talking Bobby Bonds here; he fanned 89 and 86 times in those two seasons. He was a great power hitter in the American League, even better than Maris and Mantle in 1958–59. Kuenn had only 53 homers in eight seasons. As Hal Lebovitz wrote in the *Sporting News*, "Last time I checked, a single doesn't count as much as a home run."

3. About doubles: Kuenn did lead the league with 42 doubles in 1959, but Colavito had 24. All right, Kuenn had 18 more doubles than Colavito, but Colavito had 33 more homers and 40 more RBI than Kuenn.

4. About the gate: This was pure Lane babble. First he said that fans came to the park to see Colavito hit home runs, and no one would make a special trip to watch Kuenn hit a single. Then Lane said that when Colavito hit .303 with 41 homers in 1958, the Indians didn't draw nearly as well as when he hit 46 points less a year later. What does that mean? The higher Rocky's average, the fewer the fans? Does it mean that trading a gate attraction should not be an issue? Didn't Lane have an attendance clause in his contract?

5. Maybe it's best not to apply any logic to what Lane did. As Mudcat Grant said, "You want to know why Lane traded Rocky? That's easy. Lane was an idiot."

In the *Plain Dealer*, Gordon Cobbledick wrote,

Many are aware of Rocky's limitations. They know he is an indifferent out-fielder. They know he is a slow and uninspired base runner. They know he is capable of long spells when his bat is a feeble instrument. But they love him because he's Rocky Colavito. . . . No more than a half-dozen players in the history of Cleveland baseball have been accorded the hero worship he enjoys. . . . Rocky was our boy. We raised him. He first came to our attention as a seventeen-year-old who won the Class D Florida State League home run championship at Daytona Beach in 1951. We followed his career through a disappointing season at Spartanburg, and another home run title at Reading and still another at Indianapolis—knowing that someday he would be hitting them for the Indians. We saw him, finally, and almost at once, took him to our hearts.

And now the object of that devotion would be opening the season in Cleveland, but in the uniform of the Detroit Tigers. Maybe the most astonishing thing is that, as gigantic a public relations blunder as that was, trader Frank had one more move up his sleeve: One day after trading Rocky Colavito, Frank Lane sent Herb Score to the Chicago White Sox for Barry Latman.

"Had Score been traded away as recently as a month ago, it would have been press-stopping news," wrote Gordon Cobbledick. "Yesterday, it was anticlimactic. The citizens were still so enraged over the departure of Colavito that they hardly noticed the end of the Cleveland phase of a career that seemed destined three years ago to be one of the greatest in the game's history."

Since the night of May 7, 1957, Score's record with the Tribe was 11–14 with a 4.44 ERA. In the spring of 1960, Score had a 7.61 ERA. He had an ankle injury, the flu, and an ear infection. He said his arm was fine, but most everything else seemed to bother him.

It was a nightmarish spring. The Indians hired veteran pitching coach Ted Wilks to tutor Score. In his first spring appearance, Score pitched three scoreless innings against the Chicago Cubs, striking out six.

"Herb had been able to do what he couldn't in 1959, get his curve over the plate," wrote Cobbledick. "But no mention was made of the fact that he didn't appear fast. . . . When he pitched again and again, relying on his curve, whispers began to be heard. Where was his bread-and-butter pitch, the fastball? . . . In Tucson, some of the players denounced what was interpreted as special coddling of Score. Only Colavito spoke in his defense."

So Score would be traded. The only question was where.

Three days before the deal was announced, Lane said he probably would deal Score, but the one team that wouldn't get him was Chicago. The fear was that reuniting with manager Al Lopez would somehow revive Score's career. Score positively, absolutely worshiped every word that came from the mouth of Al Lopez. For that reason, Al Lopez wanted Score. He didn't care about Herb's eye injury, his arm injury, his ear infection, or anything else. Al Lopez believed in Herb Score.

"The day after Rocky was traded, we had our Meet the Tribe luncheon in downtown Cleveland," said Score. "[Indians vice president] Nate Dolin came up to me and said, 'Al Lopez wants you. Do you want to be traded to the White Sox?' I told him that it would be the best thing that could happen at this point in my career. Al Lopez had caught more games than anyone in major league history until Bob Boone broke his record a few years ago. Al Lopez had had as much success with pitchers as any manager ever. I knew if anyone could help me, it was Al Lopez."

Dolin went to Lane. He said something like, "If you have just one ounce of compassion in that bucket of venom you call a heart, you'll send Herb to the White Sox." Lane knew that because of the Colavito trade, Dolin still wanted to tear his limbs off and feed them to a family of hungry grizzlies. He also knew that Dolin was a power among the owners.

When it came to making trades, Mudcat Grant was right: Lane could be an idiot. But when it came to saving his own butt, Lane knew when it was wise to follow an order. A deal was struck—Score for Barry Latman.

"Latman was known as 'shoulders' because he had the widest ones I had ever seen," said Nev Chandler. "He was shaped like a triangle, with his shoulders the widest part and then the rest of his body really tapering down." Lane said the best thing about Latman was that he was twenty-three and healthy, which was meant as a rap at Score, but actually it was a statement of fact. In four years with the Tribe, Latman was 35–37.

Meanwhile, Lane continued to snipe at Score.

"Herb's troubles are more psychological than physical," Lane said after announcing the deal. "Maybe a change of scenery will help him." Then Lane implied that Score was a hypochondriac and a prima donna, explaining, "Lopez won't be any more sympathetic toward Herb than Gordon was. But Herb will think he is and that may make a difference. Herb has a great imagination."

It would be nice to say that Lane once again stuck both feet down his throat. And it would make for a wonderful story if Score joined the White Sox and Lopez saw something that everyone else missed, that he had an answer for what was now called by everyone the "Herb Score Problem."

Lopez and Score certainly tried. Believing that Score had lost arm strength because of his elbow problems, Lopez had Score throwing every day, as well as fifteen minutes of batting practice and another fifteen minutes in the bullpen. The idea was that the arm was a muscle, and the only way to strengthen it was to use it.

"For a while I thought I was coming around," said Score. "I threw a couple of very good games after the trade. I wasn't totally my old self, but I felt I was getting there. On some pitches I threw as well as I ever did."

Early in the season, Score took a pounding. There was a night in Kansas City when he walked five in 3⅔ innings. There was a game in Baltimore when he struck out the first two batters, walked the next four, gave up a hit, and lasted only one inning.

But Lopez stuck with him. For his third start of the season, Lopez inserted Dick Brown, Score's catcher in high school, into the lineup for star Sherman Lollar. It worked, for one night anyway. On May 6, 1960, nearly three years to the day since his eye injury, Score beat Washington, 3–0. He went six innings, walked two, and allowed three hits.

He was only twenty-six years old. There was hope.

Score would produce a few more good games in 1960. He beat Boston, 9–1, but struck out only one. On August 1, he lost to Baltimore, 2–1, but it was the first time in his career that he didn't walk a batter. He started twenty-two games, completed five, and had a 5–10 record with a 3.72 ERA.

But he would win only one more big-league game. His elbow acted up. His fastball never really came back. The frustration and failures clung to his back like a sweat-soaked T-shirt. But Score kept pitching, bottoming out at Class AAA Indianapolis in 1963.

"I saw Herb pitch in the minors," said Larry Brown. "In high school and early in his career, he used to kick his leg high over his head, and his arm was like a whip. That was gone. He still threw fairly hard, but it was very stiff-armed and awkward, and his ball had no movement."

Score was thirty when he finally retired and became an Indians broadcaster.

"People asked me why I went to the minors to pitch," he said. "I still believed that my arm might come back. I was only thirty. I didn't want to be sitting somewhere when I was sixty and wondering, 'What if I had pitched one more year, would I have found it?' Now I know. I have no doubts. I tried everything, and I pitched until they pretty much tore the uniform off my back."

Score's career is a seldom-mentioned subject, at least by him.

"In my five years working with Herb in the radio booth, I never asked about it, and he never talked about it," said Nev Chandler. "I felt uncomfortable about the subject. Fans would bring it up. In Milwaukee, I remember a fan leaning into the radio booth and saying, 'Herb, let me see your eye. Is it okay? How well do you see?' I would wonder how I'd handle a question like that. But Herb was nice. He told the guy that his vision was normal. Then he said, 'Nice to see you. Thanks for stopping by.' But that's Herb. He is a man of no bitterness, no regrets. He says that the game has been great to him, so what does he have to complain about?"

Those who know Score admire this about him: He won't spend a moment reliving the past, and he truly seems to revel in the present.

"There has to be some private moment when he no doubt thinks back and wonders 'What if?' " said Score's close friend, Hank Peters. "But Herb is happy with his life. He enjoys his work. There is nothing phony about him."

Or as Score said, "People tell me that I was unlucky. Me? Unlucky? I started with a great team in the Indians and played under a great manager in Al Lopez. Then I went from the field to the broadcasting booth at the age of thirty, and thirty years later I'm still doing the games. If you ask me, that's not unlucky. That's a guy who has been in the right place at the right time."

3

A Slump of a Thousand Years Begins with One Loss

Comedian Bob Hope, a minor investor in the Indians for years, summed up the mood well: "I'm afraid to go to Cleveland," said Hope. "Frank Lane might trade me."

If Lane had been president, he would have visited a rest home—right after he cut off the funding. Then he'd wonder why the old people wanted to leave tire tracks all over his body with their wheelchairs.

"The Indians can win the pennant with Kuenn playing center and the Tigers can finish sixth with Rocky in right field, but the outcome wouldn't satisfy the thousands who want to boil Frank Lane in oil," wrote Gordon Cobbledick.

Before the opener, the war of words continued.

Frank Lane: "Colavito will hit a home run once in every 14 at bats. It's the other 13 at bats that are frustrating."

Joe Gordon: "I was pleased with the trade. I wanted to make it for some time. I asked Kuenn here if he wanted to play center or right. It didn't seem to matter to him where he played. He's a complete ballplayer."

Rocky Colavito: "I hate to leave Cleveland because the fans have been so good to me. I really love those people and always will. But as long as I had to be traded, I'm glad it's Detroit. I always said if I couldn't play in Cleveland, I'd like to play in New York, Boston, or Detroit. The ball carries well at Tiger Stadium. . . . But I just can't figure the trade. It really surprised me, but I guess you never know what Frank Lane will do. If he did hold our [contract] disagreement against me, it's not right. It's the American way to fight for what you think you deserve."

Frank Gibbons of the *Cleveland Press*: "It's possible that Lane likes Kuenn because he chews tobacco and doesn't drink chocolate sodas. Lane doesn't like 'chocolate soda' players."

"I went to that opener and sat in the upper deck behind home plate," says Nev Chandler. "I saw Rocky in a Tigers uniform, and I couldn't believe it. I actually cried. I was fourteen years old."

Revisionist history has taken hold, and the story goes that the Cleveland fans burned Lane in effigy and most of the 52,756 fans at the Stadium were carrying a rope, looking to hang Lane from the upper deck. Not true.

"A lot of people complained to the newspapers," says Chandler. "But most of the fans felt like I did—stunned. They were like someone after an accident when you know something terrible has happened but you can't comprehend it. You don't react."

Newspaper accounts support Chandler's memory.

"Rocky Colavito fans did plaster signs in the right-field stands. One read, LOST: ROCKY AND PENNANT. But Kuenn received more cheers than Rocky when the lineups were announced, and by the end of the game the cheers for Kuenn far outnumbered those for Rocky," reported the *Plain Dealer*.

"People who call newspapers to register complaints don't follow through. The demonstrations for Rocky and against Lane were comparatively mild. It seemed that Rocky was booed as much as cheered. As Lane toured the stands, nobody threw a blivit at him. A *blivit* can be anything from a brick to a squash," reported the *Cleveland Press*.

If you want to see when trouble set in for the Indians, consider their 1960 opening day lineup:

Johnny Temple 2B	Russ Nixon C
Harvey Kuenn RF	Woodie Held SS
Walter Bond CF	Bubba Phillips 3B
Tito Francona LF	Gary Bell P
Vic Power 1B	

What is wrong with this picture? Compare it to the typical Indians lineup in 1959:

Jimmy Piersall CF	Vic Power 2B
Tito Francona 1B	Jim Baxes 3B
Minnie Minoso LF	Russ Nixon C
Rocky Colavito RF	Cal McLish P
Woodie Held SS	

Question: Why did Francona hit a career-high .363 in 1959?

Answer: Because he had three established power hitters batting behind him in Minoso, Colavito, and Held. Francona could do what came naturally—swing for singles and doubles.

"Both Kuenn and Francona changed their hitting styles, trying to make up for the power we lost in Rocky and Minnie Minoso," said Mudcat Grant. "All hell broke loose in the minds of the players when Rocky was traded. We knew what he meant to the lineup. Pitchers were scared to death of him. My God, Rocky looked like a young Joe DiMaggio to me. And don't ignore the Minoso trade. Pitchers respected Minnie. Without those guys, we just weren't the same team."

The middle three men of the order—Minoso, Colavito, and Held—combined for 102 homers in 1959. The entire 1960 Indians lineup—minus Minoso and Colavito, and with Kuenn and Temple—hit only 83.

In 1959 the Indians stayed in contention because they led the league in batting average, runs scored, and home runs. They didn't come close in 1960 because Lane's trades gutted the lineup.

"What I remember most about opening day in 1960 was being in the Indians' dressing room before the game and seeing Harvey Kuenn with his shirt off," said veteran Cleveland photographer Paul Tepley. "He had a potbelly, an old-looking body. I couldn't believe that this was the guy they got for Colavito."

At the start of the game, the temperature was in the high sixties. By the end it was in the low forties, and there was a twenty-mile-per-hour wind swirling around the Stadium. The first of many strange sidelights to this game was that Detroit manager Jimmie Dykes misspelled Rocky's name on his lineup card: "Covolita."

This game would chew up four frigid hours and fifty-four minutes, ending at 7:59 P.M. Up to that point it was the longest opener in major league history.

Naturally, the Indians lost. The final was 4–2 in fifteen innings.

Colavito fans were disappointed as their hero struck out four times, grounded into a double play, and lofted a soft fly ball. Make it 0-for-6. He also botched a fly ball in right field.

Kuenn had a double and single, and made some nice catches in center, but even his performance was a bit of a downer as he pulled a hamstring beating out an infield hit in the twelfth inning, and he limped off the field at the end of the inning. He played the rest of the game on one healthy leg.

Those who stayed to the end froze their asses off. This, my friends, was the birth of the Indians baseball that our generation knows so well.

"That opening day was the worst game of my career," said Colavito. "I never struck out four times in a game before or after that. My family was there. The fans were cheering me. I saw the banners. Every time I came to the plate, I wanted to make Frank Lane eat every bad word he'd said about me. I was trying so hard, overswinging. And that game just went on forever. But the next day I got back at them."

Did he ever.

Just as ex-Indian Early Wynn knocked the Indians out of the 1959 pennant race by beating them five times as a member of the White Sox, so Colavito went to work on his old team.

In the second game of 1960, Colavito hammered a Jim Perry pitch off the facing of the upper deck in left field. One swing, three runs. That's what a three-run homer does for a team, in case Lane forgot. The game was 4–4 in the eighth inning when out of the Tigers dugout to pinch-hit came Norm Cash. Frank Lane had probably forgotten all about Norm Cash. He traded for him, then traded him without Cash's ever playing a game for the Indians. That deal was only six days before the Colavito trade.

Young Mr. Cash went to the plate with a slight crouch, an open stance. A left-handed hitter with an uppercut swing, he lofted a fly ball deep to right center. Walter Bond ran for it. So did center fielder Jimmy Piersall. No one called it. Bond ran full force into Piersall, and they both crashed into the fence as the ball hit the top of Piersall's glove and somehow fell over the fence for a home run.

The Indians lost, 6–4. They had blown a three-run lead.

The Tribe, this is my team.

After the game, the Indians were bitter. They would become very good at being bitter after games. It came from years of practice. Manager Joe

Gordon didn't like how Jim Perry threw to Colavito. "Rocky will hit some homers, but he can be pitched to," said Gordon. Kuenn played but was noticeably limping. The Indians announced he would rest his leg for at least a week. Naturally, it got worse.

The next time Colavito came to Cleveland, he beat the Indians with a tenth-inning home run off Dick Stigman one day, and came back twenty-four hours later to deliver a game-winning double off Gary Bell.

But Colavito actually had a rough start in Detroit.

"These fans gave Rocky a standing ovation on opening day for merely trotting out to right field," wrote the *Akron Beacon Journal*. "Three weeks later, they are riding him unmercifully."

Colavito was handcuffed by a 7-for-57 slump in the middle of May. Tigers manager Jimmie Dykes wasn't thrilled with his new power hitter. "Don't ask me about Colavito. [At least Dykes had learned to spell Rocky's name.] I don't have any comment about Colavito. I've only seen him in twenty-one games."

Dykes then benched Colavito for nine games; Detroit won six of them. Colavito pinch-hit twice in that span, striking out both times.

While he wouldn't admit it, Colavito seemed staggered by the deal. For any player, the first trade is the worst. "But for Rocky, it had to be devastating," said Mudcat Grant. "None of us ever expect to be traded, but the last guy anyone thought the Indians would give up was Rocky."

Colavito regained his swing in July and finished with 35 homers, 87 RBI, and batted .249. Not great by his standards, but it still was more homers and RBI than any member of the 1960 Indians.

As for those Indians, Kuenn played well when he was well, but his body kept breaking down. He had the pulled hamstring early in the season, then a wrist injury and a broken foot later in the year. He batted .308 with 9 homers and 54 RBI, but injuries cost him twenty-eight games.

"I felt bad for Harvey because he caught some of the public backlash from the deal," said Colavito. "Harvey was a helluva player, and he could really run when he was younger. He once got five infield hits in one game. I don't know if I got five infield hits in my career. If I could run like Harvey, I would have been a lifetime .300 hitter. But Detroit wanted to trade Harvey for me because they weren't sure how much longer his legs would hold up. That was a big factor in the trade, and no one talked about that until long after the deal had been made."

✦   ✦   ✦

After trading Colavito and Score, Lane wanted to do something else, something even bigger.

Part of working for Frank Lane is knowing anything was possible and anyone could be traded. Joe Gordon knew he'd go. Lane's managers usually had the life span of a caterpillar. But Gordon never thought he'd be traded. You'd think a manager would be spared that indignity—even one working for Frank Lane.

More remarkably, this trade wasn't even Lane's idea.

"It began [on July 25] when [Tiger GM] Bill DeWitt and I were talking about a trade for catchers [Hank Foiles for Red Wilson]," said Lane.

According to Lane and DeWitt's accounts, the conversation went like this:

DeWitt: While we are talking about deals, let's talk about a big one.
Lane: Like what?
DeWitt: Let's trade managers.
Lane: Hey, we're only one game out of first place, why would I do something like that?
DeWitt: Just think about it.

Lane thought about it, especially as he saw the Indians lose fourteen of eighteen, falling seven games behind the Yankees on August 3. At this point Lane had decided to fire Gordon—now there's an original thought. Then he remembered his conversation with DeWitt and called the Tiger GM.

At first Lane and DeWitt talked about more trades.

DeWitt: Frank, we're getting nowhere on this. Let's trade managers instead.
Lane: Your team isn't going anywhere [Detroit was fourteen games out of first], and neither is my team. That wouldn't be a bad idea.

At this point it should be noted that neither man discussed the merits of the two managers. Jimmie Dykes and Joe Gordon were just names on lifeless pieces of paper, stocks to be bought or sold. Actually, you can't trade managers. It had never been done before, for the good reason that their contracts are nonassignable. So both men had to be fired, then hired by the new teams.

DeWitt told Jimmie Dykes, "A lot of funny things happen in this game."

Dykes said, "Yes, and they've all happened to me."

DeWitt said, "Well, here's a new one even for you."

With that, DeWitt explained the deal to the sixty-three-year-old Dykes. The Indians would be the sixth team he had managed, his first being the 1934 White Sox. When he came to the Indians, he had been managing for nineteen years and had never finished higher than third place. If that wasn't an omen of what was to come . . .

Dykes was happy about the move. His contract with Detroit was going to expire at the end of the 1960 season, and he had been around long enough to know that he wouldn't be back in 1961, not with the Tigers in sixth place. "Frankly, I was already shopping around for next year, and I had a couple of things lined up," he said. "Let's face it, this is no trade. It's just a couple of guys getting fired and getting fielded on the first bounce by other teams."

Gordon had a contract through 1961. He was weary of Lane and glad to leave as long as the Tigers would honor the deal he had with the Indians. They did and he moved.

On August 5, both managers put on their new uniforms. At least the two teams weren't playing each other. The reaction in Cleveland was subdued; Lane's constant deals had blunted much of the baseball interest.

"Fans took it with remarkable calm," wrote Hal Lebovitz in the *Sporting News*. "Unlike last September when they screamed mightily when Joe resigned—only to be rehired a few days later—there were no sharp outcries. Several said, 'So what, this won't bring Colavito back.' "

"I remember asking my father if managers got traded," says Nev Chandler. "He said, 'In this town they do.' We figured Lane had something with Detroit. He traded them Norm Cash, Rocky, and then Gordon."

Nonetheless, Lane insisted this was an "inspiring deal." Maybe to the general managers, but not the players or fans.

The Indians were 49–46 under Gordon, 26–32 under Dykes.

The Tigers were 44–52 under Dykes, 26–31 under Gordon.

"It just proved that in most cases managers don't mean a lot," said Mudcat Grant. "When Lane traded managers, most of the players just thought it was silly."

The Tribe finished 1960 in fourth place with a 76–78 record, and the 1960 season finished Lane in Cleveland.

As soon as the 1960 season was over, Frank Lane was talking trade. Of course, as long as Lane could talk, he talked trade.

"Milwaukee came to me and wanted Harvey Kuenn," said Lane. "A lot of teams want Kuenn, but he's special to Milwaukee because he lives there."

Kuenn batted .308, fifth best in the American League in 1960. But he missed much of September because of injuries.

"I told Milwaukee that if they wanted to talk Kuenn, we had to talk [Hank] Aaron or Eddie Matthews," said Lane.

Milwaukee told Lane to go to hell. It wasn't the first time he'd heard those words.

In November, Lane signed Kuenn to a new contract. Then he proclaimed that his newest favorite player was "untouchable" on the trade market. No one believed it, least of all Kuenn. The Cleveland papers were savaging Lane. Ownership was very nervous because attendance dropped from 1.5 million in 1959 to 950,985 in 1960. The *Plain Dealer* quoted a fan as saying, "With all the trades, I don't even know this club well enough to get sore at it."

That is the worst sin of all: apathy.

Realizing that his end was coming, Lane was shopping for another job. But before he left, he made one final deal. On December 3, 1960, he traded the untouchable Harvey Kuenn to San Francisco for Johnny Antonelli and Willie Kirkland. Not exactly Hank Aaron.

Antonelli had been a twenty-game winner twice in the 1950s, but in 1960 his record dropped to 6–7, his arm hurt, and he was finished.

And Kirkland? Well, he was a power-hitting outfielder who hit 21 homers for the Giants in 1960. "This was just a case of walking the cat back," Lane said strangely. "When I traded Rocky to Detroit, I didn't think I'd be spreading the power too thin. Then Woodie Held got hurt, missed over fifty games, and he was a 30-homer man."

Actually, Held was never a "30-homer man." He hit 29 in 1959, and 21 in 1960 even though he missed forty-five games. But why ask why—at least rationally?

"Some deals can be explained only on the grounds that Lane was a compulsive trader the way some men are compulsive drinkers or compulsive gamblers," wrote Gordon Cobbledick in the *Plain Dealer*.

So there you have it. Colavito was traded because the Indians didn't need his power as much as they needed Kuenn's singles. Then Kuenn was moved on because he didn't hit enough homers. Add it up, and it means the Indians traded a guy who had averaged 40 homers a year from 1959 to 1963 for a guy who averaged 22.

This is progress? That was what the Indians' board of directors asked Lane when he went to them after the 1960 season and asked for a new contract. Talk about gall. He still had two years left on his old deal, and he had traded the team right into mediocrity. Now he wanted an extension.

If the situation hadn't been so heartbreaking, the Indians owners might have broken out laughing. Instead, they told Lane that he should continue under his old contract. But Lane resigned on January 4, 1961. It was the third time he had quit in the middle of a contract, jumping to another team because he feared he would be sacked. All three times he had worn out his welcome and worn down his roster. Yet, all three times, he got a better deal elsewhere.

He had two years left on his contract with the Tribe at $50,000 annually, but he talked his way into a new four-year deal with Kansas City—where his manager was, of all people, Joe Gordon. Furthermore, the sixty-five-year-old Lane got a raise to $80,000 a year.

Lane lasted two years in Kansas City. Then he became general manager of the old Chicago Zephyrs of the National Basketball Association. It seems he could talk his way into nearly any job in sports. He later worked in the front office for both the Milwaukee Brewers and the Baltimore Orioles, where he was relegated to scouting.

When he retired, he boasted that he had made more than four hundred trades involving at least one thousand players. But none would be remembered like the Colavito deal.

"To this day Cleveland fans still talk about that trade and why Lane made it," said Gabe Paul. "I know of no other trade that people discuss as much thirty-five years later as they do the deal for Rocky. I've even asked myself why he did it."

Right after leaving the Indians in January 1961, Lane said, "People say that the best deal I made was Larry Doby for Tito Francona. That turned out sensationally, but that was a shot in the dark. I would have traded

Doby for a dozen bats. The best deal I made for Cleveland was Roger Maris for Woodie Held and Vic Power."

Earth to Frank Lane: You said *what* was your best deal?

Granted, he said this right before the 1961 season when Maris hit 61 homers, breaking Babe Ruth's record. But Frank, in 1960 the MVP in the American League was a guy named Roger Maris. How in the name of Rocky Colavito can you watch a guy you traded hit 39 homers, win the MVP award, and then say that was your best deal?

By 1964, Lane was admitting that the Colavito trade "was the most unfortunate I ever made—not from a baseball standpoint but from the fans' standpoint. The gals loved that boy with his boyish grin." Maybe they liked his 41 homers, too.

Lane died in 1981 at the age of eighty-five. In his book, *You Can't Hit the Ball with the Bat on Your Shoulder,* former Indians manager Bobby Bragan said he was asked by former commissioner Bowie Kuhn to represent Kuhn at Lane's funeral. That was the last thing Bragan wanted to do, but he was working in the Texas Rangers' front office and believed he couldn't turn down the commissioner, especially with the wake being held in nearby Dallas. The service was held by an open grave. When Bragan arrived, he found only a preacher and a woman who was Lane's second wife. Finally, a Dallas city councilman showed up, as did Lane's daughter and her family. Counting the minister, there were eight people at Lane's gravesite; he had left few friends behind.

As for the Indians, Lane left them in such a state of chaos that Gabe Paul looked like the answer. God only knows what was the question. Anyway, Paul was named general manager on April 27, 1961. He would control the Tribe for twenty of the next twenty-five years.

My Indians

The first ballplayer I ever asked for an autograph was Mudcat Grant. He had a first name—Jim. Actually, his family called him James, but I didn't find that out until just recently.

But this was 1963, the last day of the season, a season like most others for the Indians: a 79–83 record and a staggering 25½ games behind the first-place New York Yankees.

When an Indians season ended, it was like a fire drill in the dressing room. Guys scattered, plane tickets in one hand and a suitcase in the other. That was how I saw Mudcat. My father and I were walking out of the Stadium, and Mudcat was coming right toward us. He was wearing a nice dark suit. He carried a suitcase in one hand, a garment bag in the other, and had a third bag hanging from his shoulder.

"That's Mudcat Grant," my dad said. "Go ask him for an autograph."

I hesitated for a moment. I didn't know *how* to ask for an autograph. My father handed me the Indians scorecard—they were ten-cent scorecards back then, no five-dollar glossy programs. Then he gave me a pen.

"Go ahead," he said. "Go ask Mudcat to sign."

I was eight years old. As I took a couple of steps in his direction, Mudcat stopped, put down all of his bags, and said, "How you doing, little man?"

I knew who Mudcat was, and I knew he was a good pitcher. I also was too scared to say a word.

"Want me to sign that for you?" he asked, taking the scorecard out of my hand.

"What's your name?" he asked.

I told him, in a whisper.

He signed the program "To Terry, best wishes, Mudcat Grant."

I whispered a thank-you.

That was it. That also was Grant's last full season with the Indians. In the middle of 1964, they traded him to Minnesota, where he won twenty games and pitched in the World Series a year later.

But that really isn't what I remember about Grant. Instead, I remember his kindness to a young fan. Thirty years later I told Mudcat about his being my first autograph.

"I try to be nice to everybody," he said.

Then we started to talk. I remember Mudcat as an Indians broadcaster in the middle 1970s, and I remember the running joke he had with his partner, Harry Jones, about growing up in Lacooche, Florida. It was a funny name for an exotic little town in the middle of Florida. When I asked Mudcat about being young and being in Lacooche, I found out it was no joke. This was the Lacooche that Mudcat never talked about on television.

"There was a lumber mill in Lacooche," said Mudcat. "We lived in the quarters, which were houses put up by the sawmill company. They gutted out two of the old houses in the quarters, and those were a schoolhouse. Working in the lumber mill was tough work. You come home bone tired. You can get fingers, arms, and legs cut off. You can get buried in sawdust. You could even get killed. I had relatives who were hurt, but none died in the mills. But people did die. When it happened, there was a chilling sound of a whistle coming from the mill. It was a whistle between shifts, which wasn't supposed to sound. That was when you knew something bad had happened.

"If you got hurt, you went to see Dr. Walters in the mill office. We didn't have any insurance or anything like that. But Dr. Walters was a good man. For two generations in that town, if anyone did get medical attention, it came from Dr. Walters, who was the mill doctor. Most of the time we just took care of ourselves with home remedies."

Mudcat went to work in the mill when he was thirteen.

"You were supposed to be eighteen," he said, "but no one asked questions. If you said you were eighteen and could do the work, you got hired. I wanted a mill job because my family was very poor. I used to cut firewood for people so they could put it in their stoves and fireplaces. I also had a paper route. I delivered the *Pittsburgh Courier*, which was a black paper from up north that most of the black people liked to read back then. I had to be creative to help my family."

Mudcat was born in 1935. His memories are of the post–World War II segregated South.

"Our town had a railroad track down the middle," he said. "The blacks lived on one side of the tracks, the whites on the other. I never went to school with white kids. When I was in high school, the team from the white school would play practice games against us. But the sheriff found out about it. He came in the middle of a game, broke it up, and ordered us not to play against each other again. I never played on the same field as another white boy until I went to spring training with the Indians in 1954."

Mudcat said that most of his friends wanted to be like Jackie Robinson, who broke the color line with the Brooklyn Dodgers in 1946.

"But my hero was Larry Doby," he said. "Some of the kids in town didn't even know who he was. That made it more special for me to want to be like him. Larry was the second black player in the majors when the Indians signed him. In the back of my mind, I wanted to play for the Indians because of Larry Doby."

Fred "Bonehead" Merkle was a "bird dog" for the Indians, which is a nice term for an unpaid, part-time scout. If a bird dog sniffed out a player, he would receive a bonus based on how far the player progressed through the Indians farm system.

The reason I know about baseball bird dogs is that my father was one for the Indians in the sixties. He was a friend of farm director Paul O'Dea. Being a bird dog meant having a Cleveland Indians business card with your name on it, designating you as a scout. It also meant having a free pass for two to every Indians home game. If you recommended a player to the Indians and he signed and eventually made the big leagues, you could make up to $7,500.

So Grant was discovered by Fred "Bonehead" Merkle, bird dog, a man who earned his nickname with a base-running blunder in 1908. He was born in 1888, making him sixty-six when he brought Grant to the attention of the Indians.

"I was scouted in what amounted to the Florida Negro high school base-ball tournament," said Grant. "The only thing I remember about those games was that I had to be throwing pretty hard and wild because our catcher couldn't handle me. Actually, I was a third baseman, and I thought I was signed as an infielder. I went to spring training in 1954, and Spud

Chandler was a scout for the Indians. He said if I signed a contract, he'd give me $500 in an envelope. I signed but I never saw the $500, and I was too scared to ask for it. I didn't want to antagonize anyone."

His career was nearly over after the first few days.

"The Indians minor league camp was in Daytona Beach," Grant said. "When I arrived, there was a practice game going on, and Herb Score was pitching. He threw harder than anyone I had ever seen. Herb had just come down from the big-league spring training in Tucson. After the game, I was taken to meet Mike McNally, who said, 'And what do we have here?'

"One of the coaches said, 'This is James Grant. You guys were looking for him. He's the boy Fred Merkle recommended.' McNally said, 'Tell you what, bring him back next month. Right now we have all these AAA guys, and we need to work with them.'

"Then Hank Greenberg walked by. He was the Indians' general manager. He asked who I was, and McNally said, 'This is the Grant kid that we wanted to take a look at, but I told him to come back next month with the rest of the young kids.' Greenberg looked at me and said, 'Where is he going to go? Do you have anywhere to go?' I said I didn't.

"Greenberg told them to let me stay in the spring training barracks with the older black players. I ended up being a go-fer for Sam Jones and some other veterans who always had poker games going. There was a place near camp called Toby's that sold groceries. During their games, they sent me out for beer and sandwiches. They tipped me. For a month about all I did was hang around with those guys. I wore the same clothes I came to camp with. I was just glad to be there, even if I wasn't playing.

"Then the day came when the young players came to camp. They took us to the far end of the field, walking past five diamonds where the older minor leaguers were playing. A guy named Leroy Bartow Irby saw me, decided I was from Mississippi, and called me 'Mudcat.' I didn't know him very well, and I didn't pay attention to what he called me.

"The old Yankee pitcher Red Ruffing was the coach in charge of making the minor league assignments. He read off names and the fields where the players were supposed to report. The first day I heard him say, 'Mudcat Grant, field number two.' I thought there was another Grant in camp, that I'd be the last one standing there. I wouldn't hear my name, so I'd just float around the different diamonds or go back to the barracks. There were five hundred-some players, and all of them knew where to go but me.

"After three days Ruffing said to me, 'When they brought you in here, they said you were an aggressive ballplayer who had ambition and worked hard.' I said I was. Ruffing said, 'Well, hell, you don't show it. You act like you don't want to be a ballplayer. I call your name every morning, but you just ignore it.' I said, 'You never called my name.' Ruffing said, 'It's right here on the list, Mudcat Grant.' I said, 'That's not my name.' Ruffing said, 'It is now.' "

Mudcat said he was a third baseman.

"Red Ruffing told me that they were going to let me go, but if I went to the manager and told him that I could pitch, they might let me stay around a little longer," he said. "So I said I was a pitcher. I wanted to do anything to make it."

In the 1950s, the Indians knew pitchers, and Mudcat Grant could pitch. In 1954 he went to Class D Fargo, North Dakota. Grant started thirty-one games and won twenty-one of them. Not bad for an eighteen-year-old kid who had never been out of the state of Florida.

The next season it was Keokuk, Iowa, and Mudcat was 19–3. By 1957 he was 18–7 with a 2.32 ERA at Class AAA San Diego.

Mudcat faced other tests in the minors.

He remembered Fargo, where no barber would cut his hair. Other than the few baseball players, there were hardly any blacks in Fargo, and the barbershops were not about to touch a black man's head. In Keokuk the black players stayed at homes of black families. No hotel or apartment would rent to them.

His four-year minor league record was 70–28. By 1958 the Indians knew he was ready for Cleveland.

"I was twenty-two when I got to the big leagues," he said. "Sam Mele was a veteran outfielder at the end of his career, and I remember that he gave me a new pair of spikes. That meant a lot because in the minors you didn't make any money, and no young players got free shoes. Larry Doby had come back to the Indians in 1958, and he took me under his wing. There still weren't that many black players. You figured because you made the majors, you now were on equal terms with the other guys, but that wasn't the case. And Larry Doby schooled me real well that first spring in Tucson. In Arizona there were restaurants that would not serve us. We were allowed only in one section of the team hotel. Even in the big-league clubhouses, they always put the black players together in one corner. I remember when we played in Baltimore and Kansas City, the blacks could use the elevators in the hotels but not the stairways. Don't ask me why, but that was the rule. I was from the South, so it didn't bother me as much as it did some of the black players from the North. I saw the racism just eat up some guys, turn them so bitter that they ruined their careers because they let themselves get sidetracked by all the hatred and ignorance."

Mudcat was a right-hander with a good arm and a better head. He could start or relieve, and from 1958 to 1963 he was 49–54 with a 3.86 ERA. The Indians saw him as a fourth or fifth starter—not bad but not real good, a .500 pitcher.

Early in the 1964 season, GM Gabe Paul traded Grant to Minnesota for Lee Stange and George Banks. No one said much at the time except that Mudcat would be missed, he was a great guy.

"The Twins were in town when the deal was made," said Mudcat. "I went from our dugout across the Stadium field to the Minnesota dugout. Getting traded really hurt because in my heart I was a Cleveland Indian. I wasn't one of these guys who couldn't wait to get out of Cleveland. I wanted to stay. I was making about $12,000 at the time. I heard that they got some money [about $25,000] kicked in as part of the trade, and that was the real reason they traded me—to cut my salary and help make the payroll."

In 1964, Grant was 11–9 after the Indians traded him. A year later he was 21–7, and he was a World Series hero, winning two games and hitting a three-run homer.

Mudcat won exactly one hundred games after leaving the Indians and became a relief pitcher who racked up twenty-four saves with Oakland in 1970.

And Stange? He went 13–12 for the Tribe in parts of three seasons, then was traded along with Don McMahon in another cement-headed move to Boston for a sore-armed Dick Radatz. (In his two seasons with the Tribe, McMahon saved twenty-seven games. But he was thirty-four, and Gabe Paul was worried about his age. Well, McMahon pitched ten more years after Paul traded him, while Radatz retired two years after he came to Cleveland.)

As for George Banks—don't even ask.

"People always asked me why I was so successful after I left the Indians," said Mudcat. "I was like a lot of guys who did better after they were traded. We wanted to play well with the Indians. A lot of us loved the

Indians. I still remember that first year in spring training, living in those barracks, and how the players and the organization took me in. The Indians felt like parents to a lot of us. But I was like a lot of guys who left. We were traded too early in our careers and went to better teams. I just wish I could have won twenty games and pitched for the Indians in a World Series."

It wasn't until Grant retired that Cleveland really began to hear from him. Right before spring training in 1973, former Indians TV broadcaster Harry Jones called his old friend Mudcat with an idea.

"Are you interested in broadcasting?" Jones asked.

"Of course I am," said Mudcat.

"I recommended that they hire you to be my partner on the TV games, and I think it will work out."

Grant joined the division-winning Pirates in September 1970, too late to be eligible for Pittsburgh's postseason roster. He did some color analysis of the playoffs with Bob Prince, the legendary Pirates broadcaster. But that was the extent of his experience. While Jones gave Mudcat an enormous break by hiring him—especially in 1973 when blacks in the broadcasting booth were nearly as rare as black managers—he didn't exactly prepare Mudcat for the job.

"Harry told me that we'd get together in Tucson during spring training to practice," said Grant. "We went to an exhibition game, talked for two innings into a tape recorder, and then Harry said, 'You sound fine to me. Did you bring your clubs?' I said I did, and we went out and played golf. That was our only trial run before we went on the air for real."

Grant's dialect was that of a rural southerner. Veteran Cleveland broadcaster Nev Chandler is a very good mimic, and one of his subjects is Mudcat Grant.

"Mudcat loved the game and got very excited when the Indians did something," said Chandler. "When George Hendrick or Charlie Spikes hit a home run, Mudcat would just scream 'Yeeaah!' into the microphone. He had a fishing net that he used to scoop up foul balls that hit the screen and bounced near the broadcast booth."

What made Grant famous—or infamous—was that he loved to read his mail on the air. Mudcat assassinated the names of Cleveland suburbs. Massillon was pronounced mas-silly-on; Fostoria was Fost-tor-ree-a.

Chandler recalled, "The moment I'll never forget is when Harry Jones said to Mudcat, 'Why don't you dig into the mailbag and see what we have?'

"Mudcat came up with a letter and said on the air, 'We have this letter here from Mas-silly-on. Harry, it from the two sisters, the Cunt sisters.'

"Harry said, 'Mud, I think that's the Kuntz sisters. The Kuntz sisters from Massillon.'

"Mudcat said, 'Well, maybe you be right. Well, anyway, these two Cunts be writing us, and they say . . .'

"Harry Jones just sat there, speechless, knowing Mudcat was talking about cunts on television. Mudcat didn't mean it. It was just his southern accent. But Harry was stunned. Finally, he just decided to go on with the game and pretend it never happened."

Grant was on the air from 1973 to 1977. He was let go when the local TV station hired a new manager who wanted to bring in his own announcer. He then worked for a few years for the Indians in the community relations department, making appearances and speeches for the team. In the 1980s he moved to Los Angeles.

"A lot of people made fun of Mudcat's grammar and how he butchered names," said Joe Tait, "but I heard his work and liked it. I thought he could have been another Dizzy Dean. The average fan related to Mudcat, but he never worked with a strong partner. Harry Jones was a very nice man, but he had no idea how to use Mudcat, to play to his strengths, which were his knowledge of the game and his personality. It's too bad that Mudcat could not have gotten another crack at broadcasting. I know that I would have enjoyed working with him. He would have been better than some of the guys I worked with on TV in the 1980s."

Grant has his own promotional company in Los Angeles, where he enlists the help of a few of today's players to give clinics for schools and youth groups.

"It's more than just baseball," said Grant. "It's a company called Slugout, and our goal is to slug out illiteracy and drugs."

Mudcat also returns to Lacooche, where he has been a longtime community activist and advocate for minorities.

"I look around and see that we have running water, paved roads, and electricity," he said. "We had none of that when I was a kid. It was all outhouses and oil lamps. Now there are trucks to pick up the garbage. We have a new park for the kids, and the street going into the park is named after me. I think a lot about growing up in Lacooche. That is also why I like to go there, to stay involved. It's good for me to remember where I came from. Then it means even more to me when I see what I've been able to accomplish in my life."

As I write now about the Indians, I wonder why I cared so passionately about them. It is true that Rocky Colavito was my first favorite player, but that was because I was four years old and I liked the sound of the name. But *my* Indians were Gabe Paul's first teams in Cleveland.

Compared to Frank Lane, Gabe Paul was . . . well, at least the man was sane. And when he first came to the Indians in 1961, that counted for a lot.

No one was sure exactly what qualified Gabe Paul to be a general manager. He had never played for pay. He had never managed. His first job at eighteen was as a public relations man for the minor league team in his hometown of Rochester, New York. Most of his early career was spent with the Cincinnati Reds, as a publicity man, as a traveling secretary, and then as ticket manager.

But one day in 1949 members of the Reds' front office looked up and discovered that Gabe was running the whole show. Vice President and General Manager was his official title. Not long after that he ended up with 11 percent ownership.

Is this a great country or what? You just know all the guys who worked with Gabe in the front office wondered, "How did he manage to pull this off?"

"But that was Gabe's true secret," says former Cleveland talk show great Pete Franklin. "Gabe was a master of working the room, of getting to know everybody and knowing where all the bodies were. The thing about Gabe was that while he did work for an owner, he always found a way to get a piece of the team himself. Then it became damn near impossible to fire him because he was a part-owner. Gabe's greatest gift was the ability to take care of Gabe."

By the simple fact that he was following Frank Lane, Gabe had the longest honeymoon of any general manager in baseball history. Some insist it lasted twenty years.

Gabe was shrewd enough to be the opposite of Lane. He appeared under control, like a man who was born without sweat glands. "Gabe had a

Mona Lisa smile," said Nev Chandler. "He didn't want you to know what he was thinking. He also was a master of finding out what you thought."

By saying little, Gabe gave the impression that he knew all or at least a helluva lot more than Frank Lane. He never publicly second-guessed his manager and seldom did it privately, but he always had his finger up, testing the winds. When it was blowing in the wrong direction for the manager, Gabe didn't say much—he just blew the guy right out of town.

But the manager was not his first problem when Gabe came to the Indians.

"I got to town and discovered that the owners were not about to put any real money into the team," said Paul. "They were talking about moving it, first to Minnesota, then to Seattle."

At this point, this much must be said for Paul: He busted his ass to keep the Tribe in Cleveland in the early 1960s. If it hadn't been for Paul, the Indians would have been some other city's heartache.

Hate him or not, Paul convinced owner Bill Daley not to move. When Daley wanted to sell out after the 1962 season, Paul put together a few of his own coins. He then found Other People's Money (his favorite kind), and suddenly Gabe Paul was listed as the owner of the Indians from 1963 to 1966. But Paul knew this couldn't go on forever.

"I had to find a real owner," he said, "one with some cash to really keep the team as a viable product in Cleveland."

That assumes the Tribe was a "viable product" to begin with. Because of those money problems—and remember, we're talking about the days when a ballplayer's take-home pay wasn't all that different from a factory worker's or a cab driver's—the team's struggles to make the payroll were matched by their struggles on the field.

But they were still my team.

It may have been after Rocky was traded, after Herb Score was hurt, and after 1959. It may have been after any hope of a pennant was gone. These were the teams of Sam McDowell, Sonny Siebert, Vern Fuller, and Leon Wagner. Need I say that these were not good teams? Nor would a discerning baseball fan even consider them to be interesting teams. But I loved them anyway.

For this, blame my father. Cliché or not, the fact is that baseball is passed down from fathers to sons. My father grew up in Cleveland. He talked about taking the streetcar to watch games at old League Park on the corner of East Sixty-sixth Street and Lexington Avenue. He was a member of the Indians "Knot Hole Gang," which permitted kids to watch the games for a dime. This was the 1930s.

When he came back from World War II, the Indians were playing at the Stadium. They were winning games, even pennants. Bill Veeck was the owner. My father loved Veeck, with his wooden leg, his signing Satchel Paige, and his sense of baseball as theater.

Greg Brinda understands.

Like me, Greg Brinda was born in 1955, and like me, Brinda has waited a lifetime for the Indians to at least pretend to be a contender. I write for a newspaper, Brinda does radio talk shows. When we were growing up in the 1960s, the Cleveland sports scene was simpler. There were the Indians and the Browns. No Cavs. No cable TV. No color TV in most homes.

But there was the Stadium, which seemed like a cathedral to us.

"You would walk through the tunnel, and then the field would unfold in front of you," said Brinda. "I couldn't believe how big the outfield was, and I couldn't believe that any batter could hit the ball over the fence. As a little kid that fence looked nine miles from home plate to me. Then there were the colors: the infield so green, the seats yellow and orange. You could look beyond the bleachers and see Lake Erie, which was a deep blue. The colors seemed so much sharper compared to today."

I thought about what Brinda had to say about the colors at the Stadium. He was right. They were remarkably bright. Then it hit me: black-and-white TV. We were used to watching games in shades of gray on TV. We were of the three-channel, black-and-white TV generation.

Years later I learned why that infield grass was so green. I arrived at the park very early for an afternoon game in April. The grounds crew was out there spray-painting the grass green. The Cleveland winter had blown into April and the grass hadn't grown, but Gabe Paul wanted the field to at least look like an infield, even if they had to paint it.

That paint job would serve as a symbol of the franchise in the 1960s—trying to gloss over the real problems with cosmetic solutions.

But I didn't know or care about those bigger issues. Neither did others of my baseball generation such as Brinda.

"My father was a huge Indians fan," he said. "He talked about the Cleveland teams of his youth, the ones from the 1930s and early 1940s at League Park with Bob Feller, Joe Vosmik, and Hal Trosky. In his mind those were good teams, but if you look them up, they weren't that much better than our Indians of the 1960s."

Those teams also were my father's teams. Actually, they never were closer than twelve games out of first place in the 1930s. But they did have winning records in nine of ten years.

I can't remember when I went to my first Indians game. It seemed like my father took me to Indians games from the moment I took my first step. Through grade school he took me to the home openers even though it was an afternoon game on a school day and the weather was cold enough to freeze your jaw shut. On those frigid April afternoons, we would follow the sun as it moved from spot to spot in the park. We would move from section to section, trying desperately to stay out of the shade.

But my first game? I don't know.

"I do," says Brinda. "I was seven. Minnesota beat the Indians, 3–2. I really did cry after the game because they had lost. As a Little Leaguer, my favorite player was Vic Davalillo. He was five feet seven, had a great arm, and played center field. His nickname was Mighty Mite. I was small and batted left-handed like he did, although he stepped in the bucket when he swung. I think that's what cements a relationship between a young fan and a team—when a kid picks out a favorite player that he believes belongs only to him."

Actually, Davalillo didn't always pull away from a pitch. He was hit by Detroit's Hank Aguirre in 1966. Put it this way: Davalillo batted .301 when stepping into the pitch in 1965 but fell to .250 in 1966.

As for my favorite player, it was Jack Kralick.

The year was 1964 and Kralick was a scarecrow left-hander, six feet two, 165 pounds. As he pitched, his face contorted as if he were being forced to eat mud. His nervous habits were an art form: grabbing an ear, tugging a sleeve, pulling at a pants leg, taking off his cap and running his hand through his hair, stepping off the mound, picking up the rosin bag and then throwing it back down.

I was mesmerized by Kralick. He did the same thing every time—the ear, the sleeve, the pants, the cap, the rosin bag. He had a jerky windup with all the grace of a drunk bouncing down a flight of stairs. But there was something about Kralick's vulnerability—although I didn't know the meaning of that word. Probably I just felt sorry for poor Jack who knew he was in trouble every time he had to pitch to anybody holding a bat.

My father presented me with the Indians sometime in 1964 in a game in which Jack Kralick pitched. I accepted them, failings, warts, and all. Kralick became my first favorite player for no rational reason. I would eventually find out that Kralick should have been much more than a .500 pitcher. He was a chain smoker, a guy riddled with self-doubt, and not much fun to be around. That was fine. I never had to meet him. Baseball was better that way, as I was to discover fifteen years later when I began covering the Indians for the *Plain Dealer*. That's when I learned that knowing the players was really knowing too much.

It was better when I was a kid in the 1960s and early 1970s.

Or as Greg Brinda said, "Baseball just seemed more important back then. It was a big deal to go to a game. The old *Cleveland Press* used to give out seven free tickets to any kid who got straight A's in the fourth quarter. I always made a point of studying extra hard to get those tickets. The *Plain Dealer* used to run a Grandstand Manager's Poll, where fans voted on things such as moving the fences in or back or whether there should be a designated hitter. For voting you got a free general admission ticket. I probably found a way to get ten free tickets a year, and I don't think kids scrape around today to do that. My favorite games were on Friday nights. That was fireworks night, which is still a great draw today. But in the 1960s, they often gave away a car. That seemed like an amazing deal: You got a baseball game, fireworks, and a chance to win a car. Of course, this was back when there were hardly any promotions, except maybe bat day and ball day. Now everything is promoted. Every night something is given away, and after a while it loses that special feeling."

Brinda and I talked about baseball cards. We collected them, but not like many kids do today. We didn't see them as junk bonds or a quick way to get rich; they *were* the players to us.

"There would be a game on the radio, and I'd have my cards out," said Brinda. "When someone like Vada Pinson came to bat, I'd pull out my Vada Pinson card. I always liked Vada Pinson because he had the shiniest baseball spikes I had ever seen. I used to try to shine my spikes like Vada's because I thought they were so cool."

I don't know if today's kids imitate how a guy stands at the plate or how he wears his shoes, the way we did. I know they try the same moves as Michael Jordan, but I just don't think baseball players have the same hold on kids that they once did.

"I wonder if they have favorite games they remember," said Brinda. "There was this Indians game in the early 1960s where Al Luplow made this great catch. The Indians were playing in Boston, and someone hit a drive deep to right field. Luplow went back, caught the ball on a dead run, leaped over the small wall in right field, and landed in the bullpen, hanging on to the ball. I never saw the play; I just heard it on the radio, and I remember where I heard it—I was sitting on my grandmother's porch."

Like Brinda, I had baseball cards. I invented games with them, throwing a rubber ball off the wall in my basement; depending on where it hit, how many times it bounced, and if I fielded it cleanly, then the player had a hit, out, or error. The cards were my lineups, and I managed both teams and played for both teams.

"I never got a player to sign a baseball card," said Brinda. "Really, I never even thought of it. I certainly didn't know that would increase the value."

I felt the same way. I would trade my doubles for cards that other kids had, but I never considered what the cards were worth in terms of dollars. I just liked them because they had the faces and the statistics of my favorite players. Like the game itself, baseball cards were fun.

After talking with Brinda, I started to wonder about Jack Kralick. That is the reporter in me coming out. He was my favorite player, and I wanted to know more about him than the image in my head from one of Kralick's baseball card photos. The card is long gone, but I can still see it. Kralick has just followed through, with his left arm extended and his right glove-hand up as if he expected the ball to be smashed directly back at him. But I know that Kralick had to be more than just that image.

John Francis Kralick was born in Youngstown, Ohio, in 1936, and he signed with the Chicago White Sox in 1955. He was cut and then signed with the Washington Senators, who became the Minnesota Twins. He came to the majors in 1960, and his records for his first three seasons were 8–6, 13–11, and 12–11. He was a lefty with control who threw about 220 innings a season.

Gabe Paul liked that, especially the left-handed part. If you want to find the source of some of Paul's most abominable trades, just check his quest for left-handed pitching. There was Mudcat Grant for Lee Stange; Jerry

Mumphrey for Bob Owchinko; Juan Bonilla for Bob Lacey; and Jim Perry for Jack Kralick.

"Jim Perry just wasn't pitching all that well," said Paul. "Kralick had thrown a no-hitter [in 1962], and he got the ball over the plate. Besides, we needed left-handed pitching." So Paul traded twenty-six-year-old Perry for twenty-six-year-old Kralick.

In his first season, Kralick got off to a fast start, made the 1964 All-Star team, and ended with a 12–7 record. But in the next two years he would be 8–17, and Paul would sell him to the New York Mets for $25,000 in May 1967.

"The night we traded him, he wrecked his car on the Shoreway," said Paul. "He got beat up very badly in the accident, and he never pitched after that."

As for Jim Perry, he pitched for a long time after the trade, long enough to win 118 games for the Twins—including twenty-game seasons in 1969 and 1970. He even returned to the Indians in 1974 and was 17–12 at the age of thirty-seven.

"Perry had more lives than a cat," said Paul. "It was hard to know he'd have a career like that."

I still wanted to know more about Kralick, but I couldn't find him anywhere. The Indians didn't have his address or phone number. Nor did the Major League Players Alumni Association. Nor had any of his former teammates seen or been in contact with him. With the proliferation of old-timers' games, fantasy camps, and baseball card shows, the players from the 1960s usually run into each other somewhere. But no one had heard about Kralick for years. In the towns where Kralick supposedly lived, there were no telephone listings under his name.

So what kind of a guy was he?

Broadcaster Jimmy Dudley: "Not a bad person but in a world of his own. He was a loner. Different from most players, and with all that fidgeting he did on the mound, it drove you crazy just to watch him."

Larry Brown: "Jack was a loner, a guy with a dry, sarcastic personality. Not real likable or fun to be around."

Rich Rollins: "Jack was the kind of guy who laughed at things that no one else did. While he was kind of a loner, I thought most of the guys got along with him when we were teammates in Minnesota."

Vern Fuller: "He was a loner, a nervous guy. Not a happy camper. My only memory of him was one day he went jackrabbit hunting outside of Tucson, and he brought the dead rabbits back and put them in the toilet by the dugout. That was Jack's idea of humor."

When veteran *Plain Dealer* baseball writer Russ Schneider made up his team of the worst guys he had to deal with in his twenty years with the Indians, he picked Kralick as the left-handed pitcher. (For those who are wondering, Wayne Garland was the righty.)

Meanwhile, the newspaper files revealed little.

His no-hitter in 1962 was 1–0 over the Kansas City A's. He had a perfect game for 8⅓ innings before he walked George Alusick. If you don't remember good old George Alusick, don't feel bad; I didn't either. When I looked him up, I discovered he was an outfielder who played 298 games between 1958 and 1964, and there wasn't much worth remembering.

Kralick lacks an overpowering fastball, wrote United Press International of his no-hitter. "But Sunday he threw mostly fastballs because he had trouble controlling his curve. Bob Allison, Bernie Allen, and Rich Rollins turned in fine defensive plays in support of Kralick."

The only interesting story about his three years with the Indians was on August 25, 1965. "Scarcely 24 hours after being knocked out by a single punch thrown by his roommate, Gary Bell, Jack Kralick had 10 counted over him again, this time at Chavez Ravine," wrote Jim Schlemmer of the *Akron Beacon Journal* in a game story of the Tribe's 8–2 loss to the Angels.

On Sunday the Indians played in Washington. Kralick and Bell went to dinner together and then returned to their room. Bell had pitched four scoreless innings and picked up the win. In their room "there were angry words, and both of us swung," Bell told reporters. Kralick missed. Bell punched Kralick in the mouth, and Kralick lost a tooth and had facial cuts that needed nine stitches to repair. Bell had cuts on his right hand and knuckles. Originally, the Indians said that Kralick was simply suffering from "a dental discomfort." Well, that was part of the truth, but it didn't fool reporters, especially when they got a look at Bell's hand.

"Both battlers were unable or unwilling to recall what the argument was about, but both said they would continue to room together on the road," reported the *Beacon Journal.* "Manager Birdie Tebbetts said, 'These are the dog days in late August, and fights are inevitable. My rule is that it's okay for players to fight so long as it doesn't interfere with their play.'"

Well, at least Birdie Tebbetts made that very clear.

Later there was an unconfirmed report that Bell and Kralick were debating about what to watch on TV when the punches were thrown, but who knows? Or who even cares twenty-nine years later? But somehow I believe it, especially after my experience with ballplayers later in my life.

When I was a kid, I was once in the same car as Gary Bell. My brother worked for the recreation department in the Cleveland suburb of Parma. He drove Bell to speak at a baseball clinic, and I got to sit in the backseat. All I recall is that Bell wasn't in the car more than five minutes when he was hanging his head out the window like a basset hound that wanted wind on his nose. Then I discovered that the reason for his preoccupation with the window was that he was chewing tobacco but making sure he spit the juice outside. How appetizing to a nine-year-old baseball fan. Bell also was known as "Ding Dong"—ah, those clever ballplayers and their nicknames.

I asked Ding Dong one question: Who is the toughest hitter you ever faced?

"Young fella," he said, "the one with the bat."

Then he spat out the window.

I can look back now and see that even at the age of nine I was preparing for my life's work as a sportswriter by asking dumb questions. And today Bell is a sporting goods salesman in his hometown of San Antonio.

The final news story on Kralick was from April 11, 1971. The *Beacon Journal* had a "Whatever Happened To?" column, and the subject was my favorite player. The headline was: FINDS BASEBALL EASY TO FORGET. EX-INDIAN HASN'T SEEN GAME SINCE RELEASE.

Kralick was living in Watertown, South Dakota, working for a school supply concern. He said that the night he was traded, the auto accident cracked a rib, "but the worst outcome of the accident was that I suffered from double vision. The Mets put me on the temporary inactive list, and I was to report to the team as soon as my problems cleared up. But the double vision continued through the [1967] season."

His vision eventually cleared, but Kralick simply quit.

"I haven't missed baseball at all," he said. "I've found other things to do, such as hunting and fishing."

Wherever he is, Kralick probably knows that baseball doesn't miss him, but he should know that he is responsible for making one kid into a Cleveland Indians fan. So thanks, Jack—I guess.

5

Here Comes
Sudden Sam

Question: How hard did Sam McDowell throw?

Answer: Hard enough to break two of his own ribs on one particularly swift delivery to home plate.

At that moment the Indians should have known that this kid was not going to be another Bob Feller or even Herb Score.

The year was 1961. McDowell was eighteen years old and had just pitched six scoreless innings against the Minnesota Twins in his big-league debut. He struck out nine, walked five, and allowed three hits. To open the seventh, he reached back for a little something extra and *bam*, broke two ribs while throwing a pitch!

Most guys break ribs when they are hit *by* a pitch, but most guys aren't like Sam McDowell.

Frank Lane takes credit for the Indians signing McDowell. Well, perhaps we should say that at least Lane didn't stop his scouts from giving McDowell a $75,000 bonus in June 1960. Nor did Lane immediately trade McDowell for Pumpsie Green. So you have to say, yes, Frank Lane did one bang-up job when it came to McDowell.

In his own way McDowell was terrific for the Tribe, but like most Indians there will be a "What if?" question attached to his name. Namely, what if McDowell had not tried to drink Cleveland dry? The bottom line is that McDowell was one of the best pitchers in the history of the franchise—sometimes in spite of himself.

"My high school [Pittsburgh Central Catholic] was only two blocks from

Forbes Field, but I never saw the Pirates play," said McDowell. "In fact, I never saw a big-league game until I played in one."

Wait a minute. There are newspaper stories about McDowell pitching a batting practice for the Pirates while he was still in high school.

"I did," said McDowell. "But I'd leave right after I was done. I never stayed for the games. I was one of those kids who always had a bunch of part-time jobs. I had a paper route with 129 stops. I figured throwing batting practice was just another one of my jobs. I never thought much about being a pro baseball player. In high school I played everything—football, basketball, baseball, and track. Every day I was going to a practice of some kind."

But in later interviews McDowell told a story of being befriended by a man who was a bird-dog scout with the Indians.

"In my junior year of high school, he took me to Cleveland for a three-game trip," he said. "I got to see the Indians play, and he took me into the clubhouse."

So McDowell either never saw a big-league game while in high school or he saw three of them. It depends on when he's telling the story. You'll get used to it. When he was with the Indians, McDowell was known as a latter-day Dizzy Dean: He had a different story for every writer who had a free ear.

No matter. This much is fact: As a seventeen-year-old high school senior, McDowell was six feet five, 190 pounds, and he may have been the greatest high school pitcher in the history of Pittsburgh. He struck out 152 in sixty-three innings. That means that in those sixty-three innings, while 152 kids fanned, only 37 made outs in other ways. And in those sixty-three innings, he allowed no earned runs. That's right—none. His record was 8–1.

"I pitched three consecutive no-hitters in my senior year, and that earned me some notoriety," said McDowell recently. "There were about fifteen scouts at every game I pitched, but none from Cleveland. My understanding is that the local Indians scout had been told that I was a problem, that I didn't throw hard and not to waste his time. In the Cleveland front office, Bob Kennedy and Hoot Evers were reading these newspaper stories about me, but they had no scouting reports. So they came to watch me in the state high school championship game. It was a nine-inning game. I struck out eighteen, the other kid struck out fourteen. We won the game, 1–0, and I hit a home run. I batted nearly .500 in high school. Immediately after my graduation, the Indians tried to sign me."

This was 1960, before the amateur draft. Players were free to sign with any team they wanted, and McDowell had been romanced by a Detroit scout named Cy Williams.

"For three years he was at every game I pitched," he said. "We had him to the house for dinner. He knew everyone in my family. He had taken my parents to dinner, even my sister to dinner. My sister really liked him, and when I signed with the Indians, she was so upset with me that she didn't talk to me for three months."

While every team tried to sign McDowell, the Indians' offer was the highest.

"But there was another consideration," McDowell said. "My parents and I both believed that I should start at the bottom of the minors, Class D. Other teams thought it would be a selling point by saying they would start me at Class AA or even send me right to the majors. But my dad was adamantly against that. Cleveland said they'd do what I asked."

After signing McDowell, the Indians brought him to Cleveland Stadium to work out in front of the brass. They also wanted reporters to watch him throw so that their $75,000 investment at least bought some free publicity. He was immediately pegged the next Herb Score. The front office told reporters that McDowell had thrown forty no-hitters in Little League. That sounded a bit excessive, but it was reported anyway. Why not? It made for a good story, and even Frank Lane could see that McDowell already had a better fastball than anyone on his 1960 big-league roster.

Lane got into the act, saying, "Sam has a good fastball, but I really like his curveball. He has a nice loose wrist. You have to have a loose wrist to throw a good curve. You have to give Hoot Evers and Bob Kennedy credit. They signed Sam right as there was a Yankees scout sitting on the doorstep waiting to make his pitch. Hoot told Sam, 'We don't care what the other clubs are offering. We're not going to pussyfoot around. Here's our best offer.' And Sam took it."

Actually, McDowell said that the Indians offered about $25,000 more than the Yankees. He doesn't remember the New York scout being on his doorstep as he signed, but it made for a good story. With McDowell there were always good stories.

"What scared me in that three-day workout in Cleveland was that I was throwing for [pitching coach] Mel Harder," said McDowell. "Harder told Hoot Evers, 'You can't teach this kid anything about mechanics. He has it all. There isn't a pitch he doesn't know how to throw. He's going to be a great one. All he needs is experience.' That's pretty heady stuff to hear when you are seventeen."

As promised, McDowell went to Class D, and he was 5–6 with a 3.35 ERA at Lakeland, Florida. But the Indians put him on their winter Instructional League team, where he was 7–2 with a 1.02 ERA in Florida. Farm Director Hoot Evers said McDowell's early problems were maturity. In 1960 he told the *Akron Beacon Journal:* "The boy had a bad temper. If an umpire called one wrong or if an infielder booted one behind him, he'd blow up. Then he'd get so wild the manager would have to yank him out of there."

Evers said McDowell would start the 1961 season at Class A Reading. Instead he opened at Class AAA Salt Lake City, where he was 13–10 with a 4.45 ERA in the Pacific Coast League. He came to Cleveland in September, made one start, and broke two ribs.

In the spring of 1962, McDowell earned the nickname T-Bird because he arrived in Tucson driving a new Thunderbird, purchased with his bonus money. Seeing a nineteen-year-old rookie who had done so little driving such a big car didn't endear him to some of the veterans. McDowell bounced between Cleveland and the minors for 1962 and 1963. "A million-dollar arm and a ten-cent head" was how Indians broadcaster Bob Neal characterized McDowell. All Neal did was repeat what many scouts were whispering.

A spring training story in the 1964 *Akron Beacon Journal* reported,

When Sammy signed, he suddenly thought he was opulent. He bought a Thunderbird. When Deborah Ann was on the way, he bought a Cadillac. He bought the finest Western clothes, black with white trim, including a white leather belt and a holster with pearl-handled pistols. . . . When he learned a resident's hunting license in Arizona cost less than one for an out-of-stater, he bought land in Arizona to qualify for a cheaper permit. He discovered the thrill of hunting javelinas. . . . Sam thinks he has it made. He became adept at pepper practice because it's fun, but he goofed off during regular training exercises. And he quit throwing hard. Pitching coach Early Wynn said, "Sam still has his fastball, he just won't throw it."

To this day his teammates rave about his ability:

Vern Fuller: "I can't imagine anyone ever having better stuff than Sam. He loved to throw batting practice, but no one wanted to bat against him. He threw so hard and was just wild enough to scare you to death."

Max Alvis: "The thing most people didn't realize about Sam was that he was a great athlete. He was so agile, and he could really run and hit for a pitcher."

Mike Paul: "Sam McDowell. Great fastball. Great curve. Great slider. I'd watch him warm up, and I'd wonder how anyone could ever hit him. You know, he was a real workhorse. Look at how many innings he pitched before the Indians traded him. Year after year he threw over 250 innings."

Ray Fosse: "Sam had the four best pitches of any pitcher I'd ever seen. He even experimented with a spitball and a knuckleball, and he had a quality knuckleball even though he didn't use it in a game. It's hard to believe that he won twenty games only once."

As was the case throughout his career, McDowell fought himself as much as opposing hitters.

"My problem was not the great expectations," he said in 1993. "I never worried about being the next Herb Score or Bob Feller because I never saw them pitch. What bothered me was my own frustrations, sitting there watching game after game where guys who didn't have one-tenth of my talent were winning games and I wasn't. Take Whitey Ford. He couldn't break a pane of glass, but he pitched like he was painting a Mona Lisa. I realize now that I had very low self-esteem as a young pitcher. I'd hear everyone say that Sam McDowell had the greatest fastball, the greatest curve, the greatest everything. Then I'd go out there and get my ears boxed in. I had no idea how to pitch. With Cleveland, Birdie Tebbetts called every one of my pitches. I mean every single pitch. I wasn't learning anything by him doing that because he never sat down with me after games or between innings to tell me why he wanted me to pitch a certain guy a certain way. Really, I didn't have to take responsibility for how I pitched. If I lost, I could always just blame Birdie Tebbetts. Another thing was that I knew in my early years that I didn't earn my way to the majors. Then they started to treat me like it was 1910, and they wanted me to throw nothing but fastballs. I don't care who you are or how hard you throw, if you throw nothing but fastballs, you are going to get hit. By the end of the 1963 season, I was so frustrated I was thinking of quitting."

McDowell opened the 1964 season at Class AAA Portland. The Indians decided just to leave him alone. He wasn't listening anyway. In McDowell's words, "I started to take responsibility for my career."

At Portland he was 8–0 with a 1.18 ERA. He struck out 102 in seventy-six innings. He threw two no-hitters. He joined the Indians for the second half of 1964 and was 11–6 with a 2.71 ERA.

For that season McDowell was a combined 19–6, and he wouldn't turn twenty-two until September. And, no, drinking was not the reason McDowell needed time to make the majors.

"I never drank at all in high school or the minors," he said. "Guys would sneak out for a keg party, but that wasn't me. I was kind of a health nut. During my first few years in the big leagues, I still didn't drink. I also felt like an outcast because veterans weren't very friendly to rookies. That was just how the game worked back then. I really wanted to be accepted by the veterans. In my third year I pitched a great game in Chicago. Gary Bell and Barry Latman took me to dinner. I respected them because they were established pitchers, and I appreciated the fact that they were paying attention to me. Whatever Gary Bell ordered, I ordered. He ordered a drink, and so did I. He ordered another drink, so I did. But when they stopped eating and drinking and went back to the hotel, I just stayed there and drank some more. It was the first time I had been drinking, and I didn't want to stop."

If you are an Indians fan, think about the year 1965.

That year, twenty-three-year-old Sam McDowell was in his first full big-league season, and all he did was lead the American League with a 2.18 ERA. He led the league with 325 strikeouts in 273 innings. He also led the league with 132 walks, but that really wasn't so bad—slightly under four per nine innings. He started thirty-five games and finished fourteen of them.

His record? A solid 17–11.

He should have been 22–6 [wrote Jim Schlemmer in the *Akron Beacon Journal*]. Some of the defeats were Sam's fault, but more were due to poor fielding, poor catching, and poor guessing on the part of Manager Birdie Tebbetts. . . . For example, there was a game in Baltimore where the score was 0–0 after ten innings. Sam had allowed only two hits and struck out sixteen, including two in the tenth inning. But it was getting late, and Birdie probably was tired. So he lifted Sam and brought in Bob Tiefenauer (who lost the game in the eleventh).

The second-guessing of Tebbetts aside, the point was that it was not uncommon for McDowell to pitch a lot of innings. For example, he went ten innings again in 1965, this time beating Detroit, 2–1, as he fanned fifteen. He even appeared in seven games as a reliever in 1965. The other members of that 1965 starting rotation for the Indians were Sonny Siebert, Luis Tiant, and Ralph Terry. In the broadcasting booth was Herb Score—thirty-two-year-old Herb Score. Suppose Herb had not been hurt and suppose he had been anchoring this pitching staff. Nah, all that does is make Tribe fans reach for sharp objects.

As it was, those 1965 Indians were a good team, a team with an 87–75 record, a team with Rocky Colavito back in the lineup. They still finished in fifth place, fifteen games behind pennant-winning Minnesota, but you had to like the 1965 Indians—especially considering that they haven't won as many as eighty-seven games since.

But who knew that at the end of the 1965 season? After watching McDowell, the assumption was that this guy would be cranking out twenty-win seasons as if he were the new Walter Johnson. "He's bigger than Score, faster than Feller, and not yet twenty-four," wrote the *Akron Beacon Journal*.

Meanwhile, McDowell was still complaining about Tebbetts calling all his pitches, saying he would be even better if he were left on his own.

And 1966 started so well for McDowell. He pitched consecutive one-hitters. The first against Kansas City, the second against Chicago when he lost his bid for a no-hitter on a bloop double off the end of the bat of Don Buford that landed on the right-field line, about 120 feet from home plate. That game was the Indians' tenth consecutive victory; they were 10–0 to open the season.

"We played great, but what I remember was that Baltimore was right behind us at 9–1," said shortstop Larry Brown.

After twenty-two games, those Indians were 17–5. Sonny Siebert had thrown a no-hitter against Washington.

After that 17–5 start, the Tribe went 64–76, to wind up even at 81–81. Birdie Tebbetts had a heart attack in July, and George Strickland took over as manager. McDowell began to suffer a sore shoulder; maybe it had something to do with throwing 273 innings at the age of twenty-three, though some reporters criticized Tebbetts for not pitching him even more!

Anyway, McDowell finished the season at 9–8 but still led the league in strikeouts with 225 despite pitching only 194 innings. The 81–81 Indians ended up in sixth place, sixteen games behind the first-place Orioles.

In 1967, McDowell was a disappointing 13–15, his ERA a very high 3.85. The Indians finished 75–87 under Joe Adcock, perhaps the most hated Cleveland manager, at least by the players, since Oscar Vitt in 1940.

In 1968, Gabe Paul hired Alvin Dark, and Dark would play a crucial role in the careers of both McDowell and Paul.

"I'll tell you the guy who made me a pitcher," said McDowell. "It was Alvin Dark. The first time I met him was at a winter banquet. He took me aside, and we talked for an hour. He said that he knew about everybody calling my pitches. He said he wasn't going to do that. He said he wanted to teach me to pitch, and to do that he knew that I had to get my nose bloodied. Alvin showed more confidence in me than I ever had in myself."

All of that sounds interesting, and some of it may even be true. Certainly McDowell was never a better pitcher than he was under Alvin Dark.

But McDowell's agent, Ed Keating, tells this story: "By 1970 I was representing Sam, and his drinking was starting to become a problem. But he also was pitching great. At that point Alvin had moved Gabe Paul out of the general manager's chair and was negotiating the contracts. We were at a winter banquet. Alvin and Sam were both there, and Sam was drinking too much and saying all the wrong things. Meanwhile, Dark was catching this act and getting worried.

"Dark pulled me aside and said, 'What are we going to do with Sam?'

"I said, 'Look, he throws hard, he's a great pitcher, and you know it.'

"Dark asked me how much we wanted to sign, and I said $75,000.

"Dark said, 'But there is one thing I want in his contract.'

"I asked what it was. He said, 'I want it in writing that Sam can't throw a breaking pitch unless I authorize it during a game.'

"I asked, 'How are you going to make him do that?'

"Dark said, 'I'll give the signs to the catcher, the catcher will give them to Sam, and Sam can't shake him off.'

"I knew exactly what Alvin was thinking. Sam would have a no-hitter for six innings, blowing guys away with 12 strikeouts, and then get bored and start throwing his junk up to home plate. Anyway, I told Alvin I'd get back to him. I went to Sam, had a few drinks with him, and told him what Dark wanted. Sam kept saying, 'Goddamn it, I have a great curveball. You just don't understand my curveball.' I tried to tell him that Dark wanted it in his contract that he couldn't throw a breaking pitch without permission. As it turned out, we got the $75,000 we wanted. Dark was not allowed to put that clause in the contract itself, but we did have a side agreement in writing, although no one paid attention to it."

Hearing that story, McDowell stuck to his version.

"I don't remember that," he said. "Alvin was the one manager who let me pitch."

Of course, McDowell was drinking at the time. But then again, his agent also was known to stay until last call. Both men have since stopped drinking entirely.

Maybe a third party can settle it.

"What I remember is that I'd get a sore neck from looking into the dugout as Alvin was calling the pitches," said Ray Fosse. "But most of the time Sam just shook me off and threw what he wanted."

McDowell also loved Dark for the manager's creativeness.

"Because of Alvin, I'm the answer to a trivia question that I once saw on the back of Cory Snyder's baseball card," said McDowell. "I'm the last left-handed second baseman in the history of the majors with a 1.000 fielding percentage."

The cause of that was Dark's fear of Washington slugger Frank Howard, which bordered on the pathological. Dark would intentionally walk Howard *even with no one on base.* He feared that Howard would hit a homer, and he also thought the lumbering six-foot-seven-inch giant was a liability on the bases. Besides, he'd rather pitch to Mike Epstein, who batted behind Howard, even with the bases loaded, than to Howard under any circumstances.

But sometimes the bases were already loaded. Dark was not about to intentionally walk in a run, so he had to pitch to Howard. That happened once when McDowell was on the mound. Dark did not want the left-handed McDowell facing right-handed Howard, but rather than remove McDowell from the game, Dark put him at second base. Yes, a left-handed pitcher playing second.

"Frank Howard owned me," said McDowell. "He hit me no matter what I threw him. Alvin had a rule: In the last three innings of a game when Howard came up, I went to second base for a batter, and Alvin brought in a right-handed reliever to pitch to Howard. After Howard, I'd go back to the mound and finish the game. I even had a couple of balls hit to me and fielded them cleanly."

Well, whatever happened under Dark, McDowell's records were 15–14 with a 1.81 ERA in 1968, 18–14 with a 2.94 ERA in 1969, and 20–12 with a 2.94 ERA in 1970, and he was an All-Star in all three of those seasons. He took the ball every fourth day, and sober or hung over, he was truly a bullpen saver, completing 45 percent of his starts.

And during that three-year span, a week never went by when McDowell didn't tell someone, "I'm a pitcher, not a thrower anymore." McDowell would talk about starts where he was told to throw nothing but fastballs. "I was 6–0 under Birdie Tebbetts, 0–3 under Mel McGaha, and 0–7 under Joe Adcock when they made me do that."

Of course, in the spring of 1970, he also predicted he would win thirty games, although his only twenty-victory season was yet to come. He said he was "the world's greatest drag bunter." He said he was "the second-best hitter on this team." He said he wanted to make more money than anyone in Indians history. According to a *Sports Illustrated* story, McDowell "told interviewers that strikeouts mean nothing to him, that his biggest thrill was his 1,500th strikeout; that he never loses his temper; that he once got so angry at an umpire that he threw the ball into the upper deck; that records mean nothing to him; and that he wants to break all of Bob Feller's records . . . and in his spare time he collects and builds guns, constructs model boats inside bottles, trains German shepherds, and shoots pocket billiards."

His teammates would hear some of those comments and just shake their heads.

"But that was just Sudden Sam," said Larry Brown. "He was a good guy, and you learned to take him on his own terms, even if he did drive you crazy."

Drive them crazy he did. His teammates were thunderstruck by his talents and couldn't understand why he never figured out how to better utilize them. It wasn't a case of having the tools but not learning how to think; what McDowell never learned was the value of *not* thinking, particularly when you can throw as hard as he could. He had the gift to be an annihilator, but he wanted to be an artist.

Larry Brown: "Dick Tracewski has only 4 homers for his career [actually 8], and I know he has at least two off Sam to win games. I remember a game against Detroit where Sam had 13 strikeouts after five innings. They had all those great hitters—Al Kaline, Norm Cash, Bill Freehan—and Sam was just blowing them away with his fastball. But here came Tracewski. The only way he could hit a home run off Sam was to pull the ball directly down the line. Tracewski wasn't strong enough to hit it out any other way. Nor was he about to pull one of Sam's fastballs. But Sam got into one of his things where he thought he could trick a .150 hitter. So he threw Tracewski slow curves and change-ups, and the guy owned him."

Vern Fuller: "There was another game against Detroit. Sam had something like 15 strikeouts after six innings. I was playing second, Larry Brown was at short. I recall saying to Brown that they had no chance against Sam. Larry said, 'He won't strike out another guy.' I don't know if Sam did strike out anyone else or not, but the point is that he started throwing his off-speed stuff, trying to trick Dick Tracewski. In this game we lost it when Sam threw a change-up to Ray Oyler. Think about that—Ray 'Cotton Pickin' Oyler. He may have been the only guy who was a worse hitter than Tracewski. Ray Oyler couldn't hit Sam if Sam ran the ball across home plate, but Sam had to throw him slow stuff."

Larry Brown: "In Boston, Lee Stange was batting. Lee was a pitcher. All Sam had to do was throw Lee three straight fastballs and Stange was gone. But Sam turned to Max Alvis at third and said, 'Stay alive. I'm going to make him pull the ball.' I'm thinking, 'The pitcher is batting, and Sam wants to make the guy pull the ball.' Sam threw him a slow curve, and Stange hit a soft liner over my head into left field for a single. I thought, 'Well, Sam, you made him pull it.' "

Vern Fuller: "Sam loved to change his pitches in the middle of a delivery. The catcher would put down one finger to signal a fastball. Then Sam would brush the front of his uniform once to make it a curve, twice for a slider, three times for a change-up. Sam was forever adding or subtracting from the original signal. Poor Joe Azcue. There were games when he had no idea what Sam was going to throw, and Azcue was the catcher. All he could do was hold up the glove and hope for the best."

Larry Brown: "Not only did Sam have the best fastball in the league, but he had the best curve and slider. But he just didn't take advantage of his ability. I just think that Sam didn't take the game as seriously as a lot of us did. He was just a big, friendly kid playing ball. But there were times when it seemed to us that he was goofing around out there while we were bust-ing our tails just trying to survive and make a living in baseball."

Vern Fuller: "Personally, I liked Sam, and I like him even better since he has quit drinking and straightened out his life. I admire him for what he has accomplished since baseball. But he obviously had a fear of succeed-ing as a pitcher. I also find it ironic that he is a sports psychologist today because back when he played he certainly could have used one."

Fuller and Brown speak for the majority of McDowell's teammates.

Listen to Ray Fosse: "I caught for Sam when he won twenty games in 1970. Alvin Dark was calling the game through me, but Sam was shaking me off and throwing what he wanted. I think he had a tendency to second-guess himself right in the middle of his windup. It was just the opposite of when I was in Oakland and I caught for Catfish Hunter. I'm telling you, Catfish never shook me off. I asked him about that, and he said, 'It's your job to know the hitters. Tell me what to throw and where to throw it, and I'll do it.' "

Today, we would know exactly what was wrong with a young Sam Mc-Dowell and exactly what to do with him. If we were smart, we would send young Sam to talk to the Sam McDowell of the 1990s, the Sam McDowell who is a sports psychologist and who works in the area of rehabilitation with a Pittsburgh-based company called Triumphs Unlimited.

But there really were no sports psychologists in the 1960s or early 1970s. As for baseball players with drinking problems, what else was new? Wasn't Babe Ruth a boozer? Didn't Mickey Mantle get so blind drunk after games that he saw two baseballs the next day when he was at the plate? Baseball players were supposed to drink after games. In McDowell's case, it began because he wanted to be one of the boys.

"You were idolized if you stayed out all night after a game, then went 4-for-4 the next day when you could hardly stand up," said McDowell. "The other guys were in awe of it, talked about it. The newspapermen knew about it, too, but no one said anything publicly."

But there were times when McDowell's problems became newspaper headlines. In 1969 he was arrested for driving while intoxicated in Tucson during spring training. He also was in a few car wrecks that made news.

"Sam was a very likable guy," said Hank Peters, "but he had such demons inside him. We called him the Terror of Speedway, which was a street with a lot of bars in Tucson. He usually went out alone, and by the end of the night he would be cut up and bruised. He usually had some cockadoodle story about how it happened, but he really was in a fight. Sometimes he'd end up in jail, and we'd quietly bail him out."

"I called him Canvasback," said his agent, Ed Keating. "That's because he never won a fight, despite how big he was. He'd go out, get loaded, and then get the crap kicked out of him."

One of McDowell's roommates was Mike Paul, a rookie pitcher with the Indians in 1968. "I was excited when I was assigned to room with Sam," he said. "I told all my friends about it. He was a great left-handed pitcher, and I was a left-handed pitcher. Little did I know that every rookie would room with Sam, and then he'd switch to someone else when a new guy came to the team—and the new guy would draw Sam. Anyway, 90 percent of the time I loved being Sam's roommate. He was kind to me. He talked to me. He listened. He would buy my meals because he knew that I didn't make much money. But when he was drunk, he was very belligerent. It was impossible to be around him."

Now McDowell knows what happened.

"I had very low self-esteem," he said. "Part of it comes from the environment where I grew up, but the other part is that I continually heard about all the God-given talent I had. If I pitched well and won, it was because of my natural talent. If I lost, it was because I did something wrong. The success was never due to something I did, only the failures. I wasn't strong enough to say, 'Damn it, I am working hard. I am doing something good.' But when it came to drinking, it wasn't because of my environment. I drank because I wanted to and because I was addicted. There are some alcohol problems in my family, and I have the chemical changes in my brain and the genetic problems that lead to alcoholism."

Neither the Indians nor McDowell knew how to cope.

"When Sam got drunk, he would make these terrible deals for himself," said Keating. "First, he lived at Stouffer's Hotel instead of in an apartment, which would have been cheaper. One night Sam called me, and he was drunk. He told me that he met a guy in a bar, and the guy had a deal on a Cadillac.

"I said, 'Sam, you already have a free car [from a local dealership]. What do you need a Cadillac for?' Sam said, 'I've leased it.' I said, 'Why do that?'

Sam said, 'The payments are $530 a month.' I said, 'Sam, you can rent two apartments for $530.'

"But it was too late. Sam had signed the lease, and the guy was having Sam make a year's worth of payments in six months. It was just a bad situation. Sam had a great wife and three super kids. He was a good guy, but he just had to drink. Another time Sam got drunk on the plane to Tucson for spring training. By the time he got off, the cops were waiting for him, and he was arrested. We had to bail him out before camp even began."

Pete Franklin liked McDowell—most of the time.

But Franklin was also one of McDowell's major critics. Like most fans, he was frustrated by McDowell's inability to be truly great. McDowell also made for a great talk show subject as fans loved to call in and say how many games they would win if they had Sam's stuff.

"Once I was doing a talk show from Swingo's, which was a nightclub in downtown Cleveland," said Franklin. "I was in a glass booth, and I could see Sam was there, drinking with Duke Sims. Sam was fine until he got two drinks in him. Then he came over to me and pounded on the glass booth, screaming, 'I'll beat the shit out of you.'

"I came out of the booth and said, 'Sam, what's bothering you?'

"Sam said, 'You said something a few years ago that really pissed me off.'

"I laughed. 'A few years ago?' I said.

"Meanwhile, Duke Sims was screaming, 'Sam, kill the bastard.'

"There were all these people watching. Then the bouncer showed up and led Sam away. The next day I went to the Stadium and right into the dressing room. I figured if Sam had anything else he wanted to say to me, I was ready. But he came up to me, apologized, and then he gave me this beautiful piece of jewelry that was inscribed SAM MCDOWELL, STRIKEOUT KING.

"I said, 'Sam, I can't take this.' But he insisted. He said he wanted me to have it. He felt bad about what had happened the night before. So I took it."

While Alcoholics Anonymous existed in the 1960s, it was perceived by athletes as an organization for derelicts, not ballplayers.

"I talked to Sam a lot about his drinking," said Gabe Paul. "I know that he had some really bad moments at home with his wife and kids. I'd talk to her, and she'd say, 'It's a sickness. We have to treat it as a sickness.' I did get him some help, but Sam just went out and got drunk again."

McDowell said that Paul sent him to a psychiatrist. "It was in 1967," he said. "Ironically, I had quit drinking right before that just to show everyone that I wasn't an alcoholic. We know now that in most cases psychiatry isn't going to help. The reason I drank wasn't that my mother didn't treat me right or that I had some trauma as a child. I had a disease, and I had to straighten up and start being responsible for treating that disease. Well, that second approach wasn't discussed back in 1967.

"The thing was that I hardly drank in 1967, and I was 13–15, one of my worst seasons. Then I started to drink and had a good year in 1968, so no one said anything. There was a feeling in baseball that if the guy was winning games or hitting well, he couldn't be an alcoholic. He was just a guy who liked to drink. I was able to stay clean the day before I pitched. But I started after the game, and you could kiss my ass good-bye. I'd drink all night long. The next day, I'd try to sweat it out, but that night I'd get bombed out of my mind again. But I'd be good for the next two nights and not drink. Then I'd tell myself that I couldn't have a problem because I didn't drink the last two nights. In fact, the alcohol meant so much to me that I was going to perform as well as I could on the field so no one would take it away from me. For a while an addiction can motivate an athlete because you want to make sure you're being successful so that no one will force you to address your drinking problems."

McDowell won twenty games in 1970 but got into a major contract snit with Alvin Dark.

"He didn't want to give me a raise because he said the team was losing and drawing poorly," said McDowell. "I said that wasn't my fault. I deserved a raise."

McDowell missed most of the 1971 spring training because of a holdout. Then he was fat when he arrived in camp—later in his career he had a tendency to put on weight. He started opening day and had arm troubles. By the end of the 1971 season, McDowell was 13–17 with a respectable 3.39 ERA. But Gabe Paul was concerned about his drinking and his unwillingness to stay in shape. McDowell had been fined $1,000 during the 1971 season for "disorderly conduct on the team bus."

Paul believed that even though McDowell was not yet thirty, he was past his prime. He called around, looking for the best offer he could get for McDowell, and that came from San Francisco in the form of Gaylord Perry.

"I had a lot of good reasons for wanting to trade Sam," said Gabe Paul. "I never understood why the Giants were willing to give up Perry. Usually I don't believe in trading a starting pitcher for a starting pitcher. That is just making a trade to make a trade. But in my mind Gaylord was a much better pitcher than Sam."

The record backed Paul—even before the deal.

From 1966 to 1971, Perry never won fewer than fifteen games, and he was a twenty-game winner twice. In 1971 he was 16–12 with a 2.76 ERA and fourteen complete games. Giants manager Charley Fox went from a four-man to a five-man rotation, which Perry didn't like. Also, the National League umpires had been trying to crack down on Perry's spitter. None of that was reason enough to trade him for McDowell. At least, not on a rational level.

However, some baseball men—namely, Fox—were convinced that with a change of scenery McDowell would indeed be great. They said that Perry had won more games, but McDowell had pitched for worse teams. Put McDowell on the Giants, and he'd become a twenty-game winner. The Giants also heard the drinking stories and said, "So what? A lot of guys drink."

"One of these days, the lights will go on for the big guy," Fox told San Francisco reporters, then added that the Giants were desperate for a left-handed pitcher.

But as Pete Franklin said, "On this deal you've got to give Gabe credit. He had the wisdom of Solomon. There aren't many times when Gabe was right, but this was one."

"What the Giants told the writers was that Gaylord was thirty-three and Sam was twenty-nine, so they were getting a younger pitcher," said Paul. "What I said was that Gaylord would still be pitching long after Sam had retired. Perry had a much younger body than Sam, and I told the writers that, but most of them didn't believe me."

This was a scary commentary on McDowell's conduct at this point in his life. Paul was an executive who never worried much about a player's off-field behavior; in fact, he believed that being a son of a bitch helped a player become a star—or at the very least it never hurt guys like Ty Cobb. When he was informed of the trade, McDowell told Cleveland writers, "The Giants gave up too much for me. A pitcher like Gaylord Perry, I'd much rather be playing with him. He's done it all. He's a fantastic pitcher and a fantastic competitor."

This wasn't just for newspaper consumption. McDowell believed it, as was demonstrated years later when he talked about his lack of self-esteem. Perry was the kind of pitcher McDowell wanted to be, capable of throwing any pitch, anywhere, at any point in the count.

McDowell tried to take a positive view of the trade, but he was shaken. He never believed the Indians would deal him, regardless of what he did.

"There were no rumors about a deal, and it caught me completely by surprise," said McDowell. "I became very angry. I wanted to blame someone, but I didn't know if it was Gabe's fault or [General Manager] Phil Seghi's. I knew that the Indians also got [shortstop] Frank Duffy in the deal, and Seghi always liked him. I had made some noise about wanting $100,000 after I won twenty games in 1970, and the front office didn't like that. But this was 1971, and I was making only about $70,000. I felt hurt and abandoned. I was their best pitcher. How could they trade me? Then I acted very juvenile. I ripped Cleveland and the Indians every chance I got. I was at the height of my alcoholism. I was probably the biggest drunk in baseball."

In his usual fashion McDowell reported to the Giants' spring training camp in Phoenix and was immediately arrested for being drunk and disorderly.

"So what else is new?" Fox told San Francisco writers. "It happened every year with Cleveland, too. If he keeps stepping out of line, he'll be a pauper. We already have our fines set up. We call it the Sam McDowell Fund."

While Perry won sixty-four games in the next three years for the Indians, McDowell slid deeper into the abyss of an alcoholic haze. He would win only nineteen more games in his career. In his own words, "I didn't retire. I got kicked out of baseball because of my drinking."

He was trying to hang on with the Pittsburgh Pirates in 1975 when the team had an off-day in Los Angeles.

"I promised I wouldn't drink anymore, but I went out and got drunk," he said. "I was sick for three days and couldn't go to the park. By now I was a binge drinker. But I found a doctor who said I had the flu. [Pittsburgh general manager] Joe Brown came to my room and went through my suitcases, my closet, the drawers, everywhere, looking for bottles of booze. He couldn't find anything, but he said, 'I know you've been drinking. One more time, and you're done.'

"A month later I pitched a good game against the Mets, and we won.

Then I went out to celebrate, got drunk, and the next morning I was still drunk when I showed up at the park. They let me go and brought up Kent Tekulve from the minors. Even though my whole career was at stake, I couldn't stop drinking."

McDowell continued to drink until 1979.

"Over the five years I was out of baseball, I often contemplated suicide," he said. "I was in the last stage of alcoholism when the depression really hits. I even took a pistol, cleaned it, loaded it, and sat there holding it in my hand, watching TV and waiting for a chance to shoot myself. But I passed out instead."

The remarkable aspect of this story is McDowell's redemption. He signed as a seventeen-year-old out of high school but went to college for twelve years part-time during his baseball days and after to earn postgraduate degrees in psychology. Now he works with Ph.D. candidates in applied sports psychology at the University of San Diego in addition to running his own sports psychology business.

"I took the psychology courses to help myself," he said. "Today I work with three big-league teams and athletes from other sports. I just wish there had been a program like this for me back when I played."

The man whom sportswriters called Sudden Sam deserves more credit than he will ever receive in Cleveland.

Despite his idiosyncrasies, he and Gaylord Perry remain the Indians' two premier pitchers since 1960, and McDowell was used in a trade to bring Perry to the Tribe.

"People always complained when I got beat on an off-speed pitch," said McDowell. "But they kept pitching charts on me, and I kept track of every time I got beat with a fastball. I lost far more games on my fastball than I did on my breaking pitches or change-ups. But people would get so pissed off at me for throwing anything but a fastball, they couldn't rationally look at the situation. The assumption was that I threw so hard that I could throw it by anyone, and that wasn't right."

It must be pointed out that McDowell was one of the most popular members of the team. He was kind to rookies, never forgetting the cold-shoulder treatment he had received. During the Vietnam War he visited veterans hospitalized in Guam, Japan, and the Philippines.

Perhaps no other player in Indians history was required to explain himself as much as McDowell.

"I just got so tired of hearing people say, 'Sam was really good, but he could have been better,' " he said. "I would hear that after I lost a game 1–0. I pitched a great game, just got beat by one pitch. Really, I just wasn't perfect. I say, look at my record, compare it to other guys, then judge me. They talk about Bob Feller being a great strikeout pitcher. He averaged about five a game. I averaged nine per game. I led the league in strikeouts five times. I won a lot of games for some very bad teams, and that should count for something."

And then after it had all slipped away from him, he confronted his demons and overcame them. That should count for a lot.

6

Rocky Comes Back

If trading away Rocky Colavito the first time was the biggest mistake in the history of the Indians franchise, then trading *for* Colavito might be viewed as the second biggest. But how was anyone to know that in 1965?

"When I took over the Indians [in 1961], one of my goals was to get Rocky back," said Gabe Paul. "I must have made over a hundred offers to Detroit for him."

The Tigers weren't interested. Maybe it had something to do with Colavito's averaging 33 homers and 105 RBI in his four years with Detroit.

But in 1964, Colavito was traded to Kansas City, where he hit 34 homers and drove in 102 runs. The A's lost 105 games and finished last, and owner Charlie Finley was looking to deal anyone.

Paul was more than president, he was the team's owner and treasurer by 1965. He was counting the pennies and watching the dollars from the gate shrink. In Colavito's last season in Cleveland (1959), the Indians drew nearly 1.5 million fans. By 1964 they were at 653,293 for a team with an 81-81 record.

"We were in a real financial bind," said Paul. "We had opportunities to move the club, and we knew if we didn't draw more people, we were going to have to move. It seemed like a lot of the fans just lost interest after Rocky was traded."

At the 1964 winter meetings, Paul approached the A's about Colavito. But Charlie Finley didn't like any of the players Paul had to offer. Knowing that Finley loved money, Paul offered $300,000 for Colavito, although he had no idea where he'd get the cash. He must have been relieved when Finley turned him down.

Meanwhile, the Chicago White Sox wanted to deal for Indians catcher John Romano. Paul told the White Sox to get Colavito, and he would deliver Romano. Chicago traded outfielders Jim Landis, Mike Hershberger, and pitcher Fred Talbot to the A's for Rocky. Then the White Sox came knocking on Paul's door.

"I kind of liked Romano, but [Manager] Birdie Tebbetts wasn't particularly fond of how Romano caught a game," said Paul. "The White Sox wanted two prospects in the trade, and they knew they had a strong bargaining position because Rocky was so important to our franchise. First, they asked for Tommie Agee. We liked Agee, and I knew he was a helluva prospect because he could run. But he also had been up with us a few times and hadn't shown that much. I had to give up something, so I included Agee. Then they also wanted a young pitcher."

Here is one of those decisions that can change the course of a franchise. According to Herb Score, the White Sox wanted either Tom Kelly or Tommy John, both terrific pitching prospects in the Tribe farm system.

"One day I was sitting with Al Lopez in the Chicago dugout," said Score. "It was well before a game. Kelly had pitched for the Indians the night before and was great against the White Sox. But Lopez told me, 'You know, that Kelly kid has a good arm, but there is something about him I just don't like. I think he'll end up with arm trouble, the way he throws.' Since Al was managing the White Sox during the deal for Rocky, I'm sure he had some input in wanting Tommy John."

Whether it was the opinion of Lopez or the fact that Kelly was a right-hander and John was a lefty, and baseball men always love lefties—for whatever reason, the White Sox insisted on John. He was twenty-one at the time. In 1964 he was 2–9 with Cleveland and then was sent back to Class AAA Portland where he was 6–6.

"Tommy was a great fellow on a ball club," said Paul, "but I didn't know if he was tough enough to be a great pitcher. I fought like hell to keep him out of the deal, but Chicago insisted on him. I looked at Tommy and thought, well, he really doesn't throw that hard. Maybe he'll be a good pitcher, and maybe he'll just be average. I knew what I was getting in Colavito. I knew he had two, three good years left and that there would be immediate excitement if we got him back. I had to make the trade. If I'd known how good Agee and John would become, I'd never have made the deal. But how was I supposed to know that back then?"

In this case it was a legitimate question. The irony was that John was a .500 pitcher before he hurt his arm in 1972. He had radical and (for the time) experimental elbow surgery and came back with a sinker that made him a twenty-game winner.

If you're an Indians fan, you're probably asking yourself, "Why do things like this always happen to my team?"

Only the Indians can trade a guy, have him be a .500 pitcher after the deal, blow out his elbow, then have him come back from the surgery as a Hall of Famer. If he was with the Indians, he probably would have been like Wayne Garland—worthless after the injury. Instead, Tommy John won 286 games after he left Cleveland. And then there was Agee, a superb outfielder for ten years after the deal.

Nonetheless, it is hard to bury Gabe Paul on this one. It is one of those cases where You Had to Be There. If you were in Cleveland on January 20, 1965, when you heard that the Indians were bringing Rocky back, you wouldn't have cared who they traded or worried about the fact that he was thirty-one.

He was still Rocky Colavito. He had hit 34 homers the year before, which was more than any Indian had hit since Colavito was traded in 1959. Besides, he was Rocky Colavito and he belonged in Cleveland, and why would you let two minor leaguers stand in the way of Rocky coming home?

As Russell Schneider wrote in the *Sporting News*: "They weren't exactly dancing in the streets. There was too much snow in Cleveland that day. But don't bet the fans wouldn't have done just that had the weather been better. . . . Immediately after the trade was announced, the Indians switchboard was flooded with calls. The switchboard of the *Plain Dealer* reported better than 8 to 1 of callers favoring the swap."

For the White Sox, the key to the deal was supposed to be Romano, who had hit 19 homers in 106 games while batting .241.

"We've needed a power-hitting catcher for some time," said Al Lopez. "In Agee we got a young, fast outfielder who can back up Ken Berry. We have good reports on Tommy John."

Think about that for a moment. Agee was supposed to be a backup outfielder. John, well, the reports are good, which is baseball-speak for saying, "Hey, I don't know about this guy."

Lopez was wrong on nearly every count, and it demonstrates just how hard it is to project trades.

Romano did hit 33 homers in two years for Chicago, but his defensive liabilities meant he was not the definite answer behind the plate, and he was traded away two years later. Of the three players, he turned out to be the least important.

It took another year, but forget being Ken Berry's caddy. Agee became Chicago's center fielder by 1966. As for John, he was 14–7 in his first season with the White Sox. But none of that mattered to the Indians because Colavito came as advertised.

"I never wanted to leave Cleveland," Colavito told writers after the deal was announced. "I've never looked forward to a season more than this one. I won't have to face Cleveland's tough pitching. . . . Look, this is my baseball home. I'm not the same guy who left here. I have some gray hairs. But I also believe that I am a better player now than I was when Frank Lane traded me."

Those words were a public relations dream and immediately inspired activity at the box office. Realizing that the team might move, then adding the fact that Colavito gave them an attraction, several civic groups helped the Indians market themselves. Before the 1965 season opened, the Indians had sold more than $900,000 worth of tickets than the year before.

Gabe Paul could not have asked for more, but he tried to pay Colavito less.

"It took me a while to find out, but Gabe did a lot of lying to me," said Colavito. "After the Indians traded for me, we talked contract. I said that I'd had a good year, 34 homers and 102 RBI. I was making $55,000, and I asked for a $20,000 raise. I also knew that they would get all the money back and a lot more because the crowds would be better.

"Gabe said he couldn't pay that much, that the team was nearly bankrupt. He begged. I mean he actually begged as he said, 'Rocky, all I can give you is a $6,000 raise. You have to believe me. We don't have the money. But I'll make it up to you next year.'

"I said, 'What if I don't have a good year?'

"Gabe said, 'Well, that is different.'

"I said, 'I've already had a lot of good years.'

"Gabe said, 'Rocky, just do this for me.'

"I said, 'Gabe, I'm going to take you at your word. But I'm also going to hold you to your word.' So I signed for the $6,000 raise."

Then Colavito went out and hit 26 homers, led the American League with 108 RBI, and batted .287. He played in all 162 games and didn't even make one error in right field.

"Rocky was such a gracious person," said Max Alvis. "He hustled all the time. The guys on the team loved him. He brought so much class to our team, and it was a real emotional thing for him to come back."

The 1965 Indians had a nice season with an 87–75 record. It was a fun team to watch because Colavito not only added his power but helped the rest of the lineup. First baseman Fred Whitfield had a career year with 26 homers and 90 RBI. Leon Wagner had 28 homers and 78 RBI.

Wagner and Whitfield were left-handed hitters. Colavito batted from the right side, and by putting Rocky between those guys in the number four spot in the order, it created a lineup that frightened most pitchers.

Whitfield was known as Wingy because he had such a terrible arm that he needed to send the ball by cab to get it from his first-base position to third base. Wagner was a popular player in left field.

"Wags had high cheekbones, deep-set eyes, and one of those open, smiling faces," said Nev Chandler. "Most hitters would stride into a pitch, but Wags would wiggle his hips and then swing, nearly falling down on his follow-through. He loved to pull home runs down the right-field line."

Wagner was a bizarre left-fielder, catching everything one-handed when that was considered a baseball sacrilege. He would say things like, "Rocky has all the Italian and Polish fans sitting behind him in right field. I have all the blacks and liberals with me in left."

What it came down to was this: Colavito's return made baseball fun again. The team improved eight games in the standings and drew nearly 300,000 more fans. It also quieted the rumors of the Indians moving—at least for a while.

The Rocky Colavito story should have ended after the 1965 season. He came back, he conquered, and the fans loved it.

"People didn't realize what a great season Rocky had in 1965," said Herb Score. "For him to hit .287 at the age of thirty-one, it's like most guys hitting .320. Rocky never got an infield hit. He ran hard, but he just never got anywhere. Later in his career he became an excellent breaking ball hitter. For all his power, he didn't strike out that much."

Or as Vern Fuller said, "The great thing about Rocky was that while he was a star, he pulled for everyone on the team, even the twenty-fifth man. He was really sincere. Everybody on the team looked up to him."

But it seems that there are never happy endings for the Indians, that this team is destined to break the hearts of its fans and even some of its best players. So it was with Rocky after the 1965 season.

"I went to see Gabe after the season," he said. "I had made the All-Star team, had led the league in RBI, and had been voted the Indians' Man of the Year. I had signed cheap before, taking the $6,000 raise. So I talked to Gabe and what did he do? He offered me another $6,000 raise. What did he think I was, an idiot? We drew nearly 300,000 more fans and he was still pleading poverty. We went around and around and finally settled for a $15,000 raise, which was still much less than I deserved. But I never felt the same about Gabe after that. The man lied to me."

Colavito also had mixed feelings about the Indians.

"I loved the fans, the team, and the ballpark, but I had doubts about the organization," he said.

In 1966, Colavito hit 30 homers, but it was his worst year since coming to the big leagues in 1956. He batted only .238; he hit 13 doubles and had 72 RBI. At last he had become what Frank Lane claimed he was in 1959: a guy who either hit a home run or did nothing. The Indians were an 81–81 team but started the year 10–0 and died late in the season. Birdie Tebbetts had a major heart attack. He survived, but would never manage again.

Then Gabe Paul pulled the kind of boner that made the fans wonder if Frank Lane was back in town. He named Joe Adcock manager. Adcock had never been a manager or a coach on any level before he was hired by Paul. In 1966 he was a part-time first baseman for California. A power hitter in the late 1950s and early 1960s, he spent the 1963 season with the Tribe, and Paul reportedly liked Adcock because he was supposed to be one smart son of a bitch.

Well, he got the son-of-a-bitch part right.

"Adcock was great to me because he played me every day," said Vern Fuller. "But he could be a tough guy. I remember that he loved Gus Gil. Don't ask me why. He played the guy, and Gil couldn't hit a lick. I mean, not at all. [Gil was 11-for-96, .115.] He also had no range in the field. The guy was l-for-40 at one point. Adcock was the kind of guy who would tell George Culver, 'I want you to go out there, throw at Jim Fregosi, and hit him in the leg. If you get him, I'll buy you a new suit.' Culver did try to hit Fregosi but missed, and Adcock really chewed out Culver at the end of the inning."

Colavito and Adcock had major problems.

"Rocky and Adcock just never got along," said Herb Score. "Adcock had been a home run hitter like Rocky. Right from the start they seemed to have problems."

Adcock decided to platoon Colavito and Wagner in left field, something new to both players. Neither liked it. They didn't have their best seasons in 1966, but they still combined for 53 homers. Adcock used Chuck Hinton in Colavito's old spot in right field, but Hinton batted only .245 with 10 homers. Colavito and Wagner looked at Hinton and thought, "Okay, Hinton is younger than us and he's a better glove man, but we'll be able to outhit this guy when we're fifty."

"I remember a game in Fenway Park. When Rocky was coming to bat, Boston changed pitchers, and then Adcock sent up Leon Wagner to bat for Rocky," said Larry Brown. "How could you pinch-hit for Rocky Colavito in Fenway Park with that short left-field wall? Rocky went nuts when Adcock took him out, and none of the players blamed him."

"Without question Adcock was the worst manager I ever played for," said Colavito. "He had a sour disposition. He was vindictive. He started platooning Wagner and me, and we both had good springs in 1967. I'll tell you, he ruined both of our careers."

On July 30, 1967, Colavito was traded to the White Sox for Jimmy King and $50,000. Colavito had been demanding that Adcock play him or trade him. He even challenged Adcock to step outside and settle their differences, but Adcock refused. He never spoke to Adcock again after the deal.

You may be wondering just who was Jimmy King. At the time of the deal, King was a thirty-four-year-old outfielder at the end of his career, but hardly anyone noticed because he was a lifetime .240 hitter. But even that modest level was beyond his capabilities at this point.

The headline in the *Akron Beacon Journal* was: ROCKY TRADED FOR .188 HITTER. In part, the story said, "Colavito, of course, is over the hill and on the downgrade that leads only to retirement. Any bitterness arising from his second departure from the organization comes from the fact that he goes in exchange for an old-timer who never made it to the top. But such is life, and life will go on as usual in the lakefront stadium, what little life there is left in the Indians."

Adcock was fired at the end of 1967.

"He was the biggest mistake I ever made when it came to hiring a manager," said Gabe Paul, and that took in some real territory because Gabe Paul hired a lot of dubious managers.

Meanwhile, Colavito played in 1967 and 1968, hitting 8 homers each season. He moved from the Indians to the White Sox to the Dodgers to the Yankees. In his last season with New York, he won a game as a reliever, pitching 2⅔ scoreless innings. That gave him an 0.00 ERA in 5⅔ innings for his career.

Colavito retired with 374 homers in fourteen years and a .266 batting average.

Periodically in the 1970s, Colavito returned to the Indians, first as a coach, then as a broadcaster. One year he was both. How's that for getting a double bang for a buck? Before the game he worked with the hitters. If the game was televised, he'd change out of his uniform and go into the broadcast booth. Perhaps his most notable pupil was Frank Duffy, a lifetime .232 hitter who had his best season of .269 while being tutored by Colavito in 1973.

"I thought Rocky was a very good color analyst," said Nev Chandler. "He wasn't polished, but he was Rocky Colavito. He spoke his mind, and Tribe fans cared about what he had to say. If someone stunk, Rocky wasn't afraid to say it."

Today, Colavito has a mushroom farm outside Reading, Pennsylvania.

"I think Rocky now has some resentment toward the Indians organization," said Rich Rollins. "He probably would have welcomed a chance to manage the team. He was the kind of guy who could command instant respect, and he knew the game. He may have been a good manager, but no one ever asked."

"I was a coach and I thought about managing," said Colavito. "I think I suffered from the theory that good players don't make good managers, which is garbage. I mean, how do you think a guy becomes a good player? You have to know the game. Some people said that because I was a star, I couldn't understand it when a player struggled. Well, I could relate to that because I had to work for everything I got, and I had my share of struggles.

"Yes, I wanted to manage. I was offered Class AAA jobs but never the Indians job. I would have liked to at least talk about the job."

The way Colavito saw it, no matter what, he couldn't have been worse than Joe Adcock.

7

Great Arms in 1968

If Joe Adcock was the worst manager ever hired by Gabe Paul, then Alvin Dark could have been the best—if only he hadn't eventually decided he wanted Paul's job, too.

No one knew this in 1968. Not the players, not the fans, not Paul, and not even Dark himself. All Gabe Paul knew was that he needed an experienced manager, and Dark knew he needed a job. Maybe it was a deal with the devil, but for one year this shotgun marriage worked.

Dark came to the Tribe from Kansas City where his A's finished dead last in 1967. The main reason for that was something out of Dark's control, namely, owner Charlie Finley. Paul knew this, and he knew that Dark had managed San Francisco for four years, winning a pennant and twice finishing in third place.

Yes, although he denied them, there were rumors that Dark had politically incorrect attitudes (namely, he hated Latin players and wasn't thrilled with blacks). Or as Pete Franklin said, "I had some very weird conversations with Alvin. He was from Lake Charles, Louisiana, and had been a star quarterback at LSU. This guy was a real southerner with real southern attitudes from the 1940s. So he came from that redneck background and ended up playing with and managing some of the greatest black stars in baseball history. I am sure that there were things about him that were racist, but because of where he came from, he honestly didn't know it was racist. It was hard for him not to consider minorities inferior. But Alvin was never hateful or spiteful about it. He would just say strange things, like certain players couldn't play for reasons that had nothing to do with baseball. He would say something like a Latin guy played better during the week than on weekends. I don't know why. Sometimes Alvin made sense; other times I didn't know what the hell he was talking about. He had a very cold personality. But when it came to baseball, he knew his stuff."

That was all Paul cared about. He pointed out that the Giants had a lot of black stars, such as Willie Mays and Willie McCovey, and Dark got along with them well enough to have averaged ninety-two victories in his four seasons in San Francisco. Meanwhile, Dark was pleased to get a chance to manage a decent team, one that was a terrible underachiever in 1967 under Adcock.

He took a look at the roster and saw pitching, great pitching. The Indians actually had another Big Four in Sam McDowell, Luis Tiant, Sonny Siebert, and Steve Hargan. As a fifth starter and reliever, veteran Stan Williams had come back from arm troubles and was throwing the ball nearly ninety miles per hour. With pitching, Alvin Dark knew he could win.

"Guys hated to come to Cleveland, but not because of the city," said Larry Brown. "They would look at our staff and think, 'Well, that's 0-for-16.' We had the best arms in baseball."

The 1968 Indians were perfect for Dark. He was the opposite of Earl Weaver. He believed that any manager who waited for the three-run homer was a man who would stand on the corner waiting for a bus that would never come.

"If you couldn't bunt or couldn't hit to right field behind the runner, you didn't play for Alvin Dark," said Rich Rollins. "All managers say they stress fundamentals, but Dark really did. He believed in moving the runners up, and he liked to run."

With Rocky Colavito and Leon Wagner both gone, the Indians' only power hitter was Tony Horton, and he had only 14 homers.

The team in the field was underwhelming: Duke Sims and Joe Azcue, catchers; Tony Horton, first baseman; Vern Fuller, second baseman; Larry Brown, shortstop; Max Alvis, third baseman; Lee Maye, Jose Cardenal, Lou Johnson, and Russ Snyder, outfielders.

As Fuller and Brown pointed out, the Indians were average at best when it came to position players, but this team had something so few Cleveland teams have had ever since: chemistry and a sense of togetherness.

"I recall Dark telling me that he didn't care what I hit," said Brown. "He just wanted good defense and smart baseball out of me. I'm suspicious when a manager says he doesn't care what you hit, because they all do. But he made his point. In the end I didn't like Alvin much and not many other people did. But that first year, he was such a positive change from Adcock. Alvin gave you the impression that he really knew what he was doing, and that gave us a lot of confidence."

Or as Ray Fosse said, "Along with Dick Williams, I considered Dark one of the best managers I played for. Alvin was always thinking two innings ahead. He had a plan, a way he wanted his team to play. In 1968 that was pitching and defense. I was on the injured list most of that year and never played much, but I saw Alvin, and he really impressed me."

In 1968 no one in the American League hit for power or hit much of anything, period. Boston's Carl Yastrzemski was the league's only .300 hitter, and he was at .301. Number two in the batting race was Kansas City's Danny Cater, and he batted only .290. The A's led the league with a .240 batting average, and the average American Leaguer hit .230. The Indians batted only .234. They had the second fewest homers in the league, but they also were second in stolen bases and in the middle of the pack in runs scored.

What Alvin Dark did was manufacture runs. A guy would walk. He'd steal second. He'd be bunted to third base. Then he'd score on a sacrifice fly. That was the typical Indians rally.

But it also was in perfect tune with the times. Only three guys hit at least 30 homers—Frank Howard (44), Willie Horton (36), and Ken Harrelson (35)—so it made no sense to play the power game.

Then there was the pitching. The ERA for the entire league was 2.98, but the stingiest staff was found on the shores of Lake Erie: The Indians were at 2.66 and led the league with twenty-three shutouts.

"This was the most fun I ever had in baseball," said McDowell. "There was so much competition among the pitchers. One guy would throw a shutout, then you'd want to do it. If Tiant threw a four-hitter, then I wanted to throw a three-hitter. If Siebert struck out fourteen, I was going for sixteen. All of our key pitchers threw hard. We could knock the bats right out of people's hands."

You already know what kind of pitcher the Indians had in McDowell. But Siebert was also special. Good fastball. Good curve. Decent change-up. Exceptional control. Mentally tough. That was how many of his Indian teammates recall Siebert.

"He didn't throw as hard as Sam, but no one did," said Vern Fuller. "But Sonny was a dedicated, well-conditioned athlete. In terms of changing speeds and throwing to spots, he was the best of the four pitchers."

In five seasons with the Tribe, Siebert had an ERA of 2.75. His record of 61–47 was a bit deceiving because he seemed to lose more than his share of low-scoring games. He also had more than his share of injuries.

"He would have all these strange injuries," said Pete Franklin. "If there was one little hole in the outfield, Sonny would find it and trip when he was out running sprints. He'd wake up in the morning, stretch, and pull a muscle. It was as if this gray cloud was following him around. But this guy was a helluva pitcher when he was healthy."

Or as Mike Paul said, "Sonny did throw a no-hitter [in 1966], and there were nights when he sure looked unhittable."

Then there was Tiant. Yes, that Luis Tiant. It's hard for Indians fans to imagine today, but the Tribe dug up this guy when he was pitching for the Mexico City Reds in the early 1960s. Of all the Tribe pitchers who had tremendous years in 1968, he was the best at 21–9 with a 1.60 ERA. In 258 innings, he struck out 264.

Most baseball fans remember Tiant in the final stages of his career, when he was using that herky-jerky, no-look windup and lobbing up slop to home plate for Boston or New York. But with the Indians, Tiant had finesse and a fastball, too.

The fourth starter was Hargan, a guy with an above-average fastball and a wicked slider. He threw a "heavy ball," meaning that when batters made contact with a Hargan pitch, it felt as if their bat was hitting a rock.

"Gabe used to give guys a suit of clothes when they pitched a shutout," said Hank Peters. "In 1968 we had the best-dressed pitching staff in the league."

Tiant had nine shutouts, Siebert had four, McDowell three, and Hargan two. Another guy who had a monster year was Stan Williams, who was thirty-one and had been a fine starter for the Dodgers in the early 1960s. But Williams hurt his arm and was in the minors from 1965 to 1967 before his arm came back. In 1968, Williams was 13–11 and had a team-leading seven saves and a 2.51 ERA. He started twenty-four games and completed six of them.

The 1968 Indians were 86–75, finishing in third place. But Detroit won 103 games and won the pennant by twelve games over Baltimore, then beat St. Louis in the World Series.

Detroit was a great team, but the 1968 Indians were very good. In fact, the Indians haven't won eighty-six games or finished as high as third place since.

The next year this same team would lose ninety-nine games, with a rain-out on the final day of the season saving them from a one-hundred-loss season. Tribe fans asked themselves, "How the hell did that happen?"

"That's easy," said Pete Franklin. "Alvin Dark started playing cards and hanging around with Vernon Stouffer."

Tragic Tribe

When I heard that Tribe pitchers Tim Crews and Steve Olin were killed in a boating accident and that Bobby Ojeda was lucky to survive the crash in March 1993, I wasn't shocked. Nor was I stunned when pitcher Cliff Young died in an auto accident in November 1993. Surprised, sure. You never imagine anyone that young dying for any reason. But when you grow up an Indians fan from my generation, you expect terrible things to happen to your team. Other teams have sore arms, bad knees, and the usual baseball injuries. Indians are haunted by tragedy.

When I was coming of age as a Cleveland baseball fan in the 1960s, we had Walter Bond and his leukemia, Max Alvis and his spinal meningitis, Tony Horton's mental breakdown, and Ray Fosse's terrible collision.

As a kid you're pretty resilient; you have far more of a feeling of optimism than a sense of history. But after a while you begin to get the idea about the Indians, the idea that your team is not like other teams. Your team is cursed, and if you're going to be a fan of theirs, you'd better prepare for the worst.

At least that was how I felt. I found that I sighed more than cried when something horrible happened to the Indians. Yes, I ached for my team, but I just figured, well, these things always happen to the Indians, and asking why is pointless.

When it came to the Indians, there were far more calamities than answers. How could anyone explain the things that happened to some of the team's best players?

✧　　✧　　✧

Walter Bond had a chance to be a terrific player. He looked like Dave Winfield, an athletic six feet seven, 235 pounds. He was only twenty-two when he broke camp with the Indians in 1960. He was the man who was supposed to help take the place of Rocky Colavito.

In spring training he batted .391 with 6 homers and 29 RBI in thirty games. Stories from Tucson told of Bond's 450-foot home run to dead center field at Hi Corbett Field. The only other hitter ever to clear that wall was Ted Williams. Later in the same game he was decked by a pitch at his head. He dusted himself off and hit another titanic home run on the next pitch.

Bond was selected by the *Sporting News* as the player most likely to win American League Rookie of the Year honors for 1960, even though he was jumping from Class A Reading to Cleveland. The *Sporting News* mentioned that this was a huge step, but it said the last player to do it successfully was Hank Aaron, and Bond had the same type of promise as the man who would become the majors' all-time home-run king.

Manager Joe Gordon said that Bond "gives the fans as much a thrill beating out an infield single as he does hitting a homer. His stride is so big, he doesn't seem to be moving. He covers twice the ground of a normal player."

One *Sporting News* report stated, "As popular as any of the veterans with the autograph seekers was king-sized Walter Bond, an easy figure to pick out in a crowd. The rookie outfielder wore a gray overcoat, a dark blue hat, and puffed on a fat cigar."

Yankee manager Casey Stengel said, "That fella is a tree hitter. Everything he hits is in the trees."

But Bond wasn't ready in 1960; he batted only .221 in forty games in Cleveland before going back to the minors. He came up again in 1961 and 1962 but never stayed with the Tribe. In 1964, Bond hit 20 homers and had 85 RBI for Houston.

"If you saw Walter in spring training, you would be convinced that he'd become a great player," said Mudcat Grant. "None of us knew it at the time, but Walter was battling leukemia. I'm not sure when Walter found out, but I don't think it was until his last season [1967]. We were together that year in Minnesota. It was spring training, and we were playing cards. Then I walked over to him and gave him a friendly slap on the back. I nearly knocked him over. This huge man had had all of his strength sapped right out of him. As that year went on, he began shrinking physically. Sometime that year they determined he had leukemia, and Walter was dead before the end of the baseball season."

Bond passed away on September 14, 1967. It was three weeks before his thirtieth birthday.

"Talk about a beautiful person," said Grant. "He was hospitalized in Houston. I was visiting him, and Walter told me that he had just bought some jewelry on an installment plan. Here he was in a hospital bed, dying, and he told me, 'Mudcat, I don't know if I am going to make it, but that is the one debt I have and I want you to take care of it for me.' I went to see the jeweler, but he wouldn't take any money. That always stayed with me, how Walter wanted to pay off his debts before he died."

While leukemia killed Walter Bond, it was spinal meningitis that nearly ended the life of Max Alvis. Alvis was one of the stars of the Cleveland farm system in the early 1960s. He had been a football player at the University of Texas and was a solid six feet and 190 pounds.

"I always kidded Max about playing in Selma in 1959," said Larry Brown. "We were the left side of the infield. I played short, he was at third, and we combined for 87 errors that year, yet we made the [Class D] Florida-Alabama League All-Star team. I made 43 errors, Max had 44. At third, Max had a real gun. He'd fire that ball across the infield and scatter the people sitting in the stands behind first base. But you could tell Max was going to be a good player."

And he was. By 1963, Alvis had taken the third-base job from Bubba Phillips, and he batted .274 with 22 homers as a rookie.

"Max was the kind of young player who, if you just put him out there and left him alone for ten years, the position would be his," said Sam McDowell. "He was the best-conditioned, most disciplined athlete on our team. If he was supposed to run fifty laps, Max would do sixty. He almost never drank, which made him the exception back then. He was probably the most decent human being I met in baseball. It's just a shame he got sick."

Alvis was off to a good start in 1964, but he began having severe headaches at mid-season.

"They got really bad on a flight from Minnesota to Boston," said Alvis.

"By the time we landed they took me to the hospital, ran some tests, and said I had spinal meningitis. I'd never heard of it. They started telling me about possible brain damage, paralysis, and said I could even die from it. They told me that they had no idea if I could ever play again. I stayed in the hospital for two weeks. They gave me a combination of three different drugs, and I beat it."

Six weeks after being diagnosed with the potentially fatal disease, Alvis was back at third base.

"I played, but I wasn't the same player," he said. "I just wasn't as strong physically. It had been a real shock to my system."

His teammates noticed the difference.

"Max used to be the strongest guy on the team," said Vern Fuller. "Later, his skin color was different, more pale. He lost some of his muscle tone. He got tired much faster. He should have sat out the rest of that season."

Alvis played with the Indians from 1962 to 1969. He even made All-Star teams in 1965 and 1967, seasons when he hit 21 homers. But he was known primarily as a .250 hitter with some power and a reliable glove.

"I guess in the end I was sort of a good, average player," said Alvis.

Larry Brown played next to Alvis on the left side of the Tribe infield from 1963 to 1969. Like Alvis, he was not known as a spectacular defensive player, but he was reliable. He was a .237 hitter and a smart player. But no one remembers any of that.

"When people meet me for the first time, they ask about the collision," he said. "That was probably the most famous thing that ever happened to me."

The date was May 4, 1966. The Indians were playing at Yankee Stadium. Roger Maris lifted a fly ball into left field. Brown ran out for it, and Leon Wagner came running in.

"Wags was not a good outfielder, so I figured that I'd better catch the ball if I could get to it," said Brown. "I thought the ball might end up a foul ball in the stands, but the wind blew it back into play. Wags may have called for it, but I doubt it. He never called for many balls, and I never heard anything. I didn't call for the ball because I didn't know if I could reach it."

In the *Cleveland Press,* Bob Sudyk wrote, "There was a sickening crack of heads heard all over the park. They bounced ten yards apart and lay motionless on the ground. A doctor jumped out of the stands to aid Brown, who was in convulsions and bleeding from the ears, nose, and mouth."

"We literally hit head-on, banging skulls," said Brown. "I swallowed my tongue. [Trainer] Wally Bock saved my life when he got it loose. I was in the hospital in intensive care and unconscious for three days."

Brown was carried off the field with a fractured nose, fractured cheek-bones, and a "frontal and basal fracture of the skull." Wagner received a broken nose and a slight concussion.

"When I came to, my wife was at my bedside," said Brown. "I asked her, 'Where were you?' She said she had been waiting there for three days. She told me that when she first came into the intensive care area, she couldn't find me. My face was such a mess that she didn't recognize me.

"After ten days they still wouldn't let me walk. I was transferred from one hospital to another, and they carried me on a stretcher. I was in the hospital for eighteen days and lost 10 pounds, which was a lot because I only weighed about 160."

The Indians originally said that Brown would be out for the rest of the season. He missed only forty-three days.

"Chico Salmon had taken over for me at shortstop, and he was hitting," said Brown. "Like everyone else, I had a one-year contract, no security. So I wanted to get back out there and reclaim my job."

After hitting .253 as a healthy player in 1965, Brown's average fell to .229 after the collision.

"For busting my butt to come back so soon, Gabe Paul offered me a $500 raise because I didn't hit much," said Brown. "That was how they did business back then."

Brown was grateful to be alive. His brother Dick, Herb Score's high school catcher who played in the majors with four American League teams, died in 1970 at the age of thirty-five because of a brain tumor.

"When I was in the hospital in 1966, Dick was already having the severe headaches that would become the tumor," said Brown. "They would do surgery on him twice, but the brain tumor kept coming back. There was nothing the doctors could do."

❋　　❋　　❋

Larry Brown's dramatic collision was only the second most memorable one involving the Indians when I was a kid. The most famous one featured a player I also remember being in some terrible television commercials for a soft drink called Big Red.

Ray Fosse appeared in these ads wearing traditional Native American clothing, including a huge headdress, and saying something like: "Me, Ray Fosse. Me, dodging the posse. Me like wampum and me like Big Red."

Then he held up a can of this wonderful firewater.

Put that on the air today, and ten thousand Native Americans led by Russell Means would have every right to picket TV stations and boycott the product.

The commercial ran in 1970 B.C.—that's Before Collision. Fosse was on the verge of becoming an All-Star catcher, maybe the best catcher in the history of this franchise. That's not just my opinion. Herb Score thought so, too.

"Ray had everything," said Score. "He was a tremendous defensive catcher and handler of pitchers. He was a leader. He threw pretty well, and not only could he hit but he hit with power. I know this: He was the best catching prospect I've ever seen with the Indians."

The irony is that Fosse nearly didn't become an Indian.

"I was heavily scouted in high school [in Marion, Illinois], and it seemed as if I talked to scouts from nearly every team except the Indians before the 1965 draft," said Fosse. "Houston showed the most interest, and I figured they would draft me. But when I heard that Cleveland took me, I was stunned. I couldn't understand why. Then I heard that they belonged to a scouting co-op with several other teams. The Indians wanted a catcher, and they looked at the co-op reports and saw I was the highest-rated catcher when it came their turn to pick. So they drafted me on someone else's report."

For once the Indians got lucky. Or maybe, considering the way their scouting staff was being slashed, drafting a player based on other people's reports wasn't such a bad idea after all.

"My parents were divorced, and my mother raised us three boys," said Fosse. "My mother had no idea what to do when it came to my signing with the Indians. Cleveland sent a scout named Walter Shannon to sign me. My high school coach was very close to me, and we asked him to handle the negotiations. Anyway, Walter Shannon was talking to my coach, and they couldn't agree on anything. Then Walter walked out, and I ran out on the porch after him. I was telling my high school coach, 'Get him. Don't let him leave. I'll sign. I don't care about the contract.' I was panicking. I was worried that he would not offer me another contract, and I'd never be able to play pro ball. I was so naive. I was the number one pick. Of course they would try to negotiate with me. But I didn't know that, and I didn't have an agent or anyone to tell me. Anyway, I signed for exactly $28,000, which was cheap even back then for a first-round draft choice."

By 1968, Fosse was hitting .301 at Class AAA Portland. The Indians had a catching platoon of Joe Azcue and Duke Sims, but they knew that was only temporary. A real catcher was on the way.

"I remember my first game in Class AAA," said Mike Paul. "I walked the bases loaded but got out of the jam. I went into the dugout and sat down. Ray sat next to me. I said I wasn't throwing well. Ray said, 'Now listen to me. You can pitch in this league. I know—I'm your catcher.' It was the perfect thing to say to me. The pitchers loved Ray Fosse. We called him 'Mule' because he was strong and could carry us. The thing about Ray was not only could he hit and catch, but as a young player he could really run, which was unique for a catcher."

Fosse made the Indians in 1969 but batted .172 and played in only thirty-seven games because he broke his right index finger. Then came 1970. Ray Fosse would never be better than he was in 1970 when he was only twenty-three years old.

By the All-Star break he was hitting .313 with 16 homers and 45 RBI. But even before the collision with Pete Rose, Fosse had a close call. The Indians were playing in New York on June 24, and fans were throwing cherry bombs onto the field.

"I had a sixteen-game hitting streak and caught the first game of a doubleheader," said Fosse. "I was supposed to rest in the second game, but I was feeling strong and playing well, so I caught the second game. Mike Paul started for us. There was a runner on first base, and it was a bunt situation. The batter missed the first pitch, and I stood up and threw the ball back to Mike Paul. Normally, I would have squatted back down, but I stayed standing for a few extra seconds because Mike was taking a lot of time between pitches. All of a sudden there was this explosion at my feet.

It was a cherry bomb that had been thrown from the mezzanine. The thing exploded about four feet from the ground, then it hit the dirt at my instep. I was wearing kangaroo leather spikes, and it burned a hole through them and through my two pairs of socks. It felt like a torch burning into the bottom of my foot."

According to Bob Sudyk's story in the *Cleveland Press,* trainer Wally Bock feared Fosse had been shot. Fosse was on the ground in a fetal position, and Bock was trying to find a tear in his uniform to see where he had been injured. Finally, Bock discovered it was Fosse's left foot and took off his shoes and socks. Fosse was treated for ten minutes, then insisted on returning to the game and continued catching.

"I was so fortunate," he said. "I could have been blinded. I could have had my foot blown off. I told Mike Paul, 'Lucky you took some extra time or I'd have been squatting, and who knows what would have been blown off.' "

But at the All-Star Game in Cincinnati three weeks later, Fosse's luck would run out.

Pete Rose took Sam McDowell and Fosse out to dinner the night before the game, and then they went to Rose's home. The next day, McDowell pitched three scoreless innings for the American League, leaving after the sixth. Detroit's Bill Freehan was the starting catcher, then Fosse took over. After nine innings the game was 4–4. It stayed that way until the bottom of the twelfth. With two outs, Rose banged out a base hit and moved to second on a single by Billy Grabarkewitz. Clyde Wright was pitching for the American League, and he gave up another single, this one to Jim Hickman.

The moment the ball was hit, Rose was thinking about scoring the winning run. Amos Otis fielded the ball in center field, knowing he had to make a good throw to home plate, where Fosse was waiting.

"I was a few feet up the third base line," said Fosse, "not that I was intentionally trying to block home plate, but that was where the throw was going. I saw Rose out of the corner of my eye, and I figured he was going to try to slide headfirst. That is what he usually did."

Not this time.

"I was reaching out for the ball, and he hit me," said Fosse. "I wasn't dug in at the plate, waiting for him. I didn't have the ball. Then Pete hit me."

Rose was like a linebacker blindsiding a quarterback. Fosse was flattened. The ball and Rose appeared to arrive at the same time, the ball tipping off Fosse's glove as Rose slammed into the Tribe catcher. Fosse could not hang on to the ball, and Rose scored the winning run.

"I always thought that Pete could have used a hook slide to get around me," said Fosse. "Pete has his version, and I have mine. Pete says he was just trying to score, he didn't want to hit me. If he did it on purpose or not, only Pete can answer that."

Rose said that the last thing he wanted to do was hurt Fosse. He mentioned that Fosse was at Rose's home until 3:30 A.M. the night before the game and he considered Fosse a friend, so why would he try to cheapshot a buddy? Rose also insisted that he wanted to use a standard slide, but Fosse had done such a great job of blocking the plate, a slide wouldn't work. So he decided to go through Fosse because he had no other options.

Rose missed three games because of a bruised knee.

As for Fosse, he missed out on a great career. He would play eight more years, but he would never be the same.

"After the All-Star Game, my left shoulder really hurt," said Fosse. "They took several X rays but said they couldn't find anything. The next morning I flew back to Cleveland with Sam McDowell. I went to the park. I couldn't lift my left arm over my head. The doctor checked me, but he couldn't find anything wrong. At this point they figured it was a very bad bruise. The All-Star Game was Tuesday in Cincinnati. I was examined Wednesday in Cleveland. On Thursday we flew to Kansas City to open a series. I went to the park figuring I'd get the night off, but I was in the lineup, catching and batting fourth. In batting practice I could hardly swing, and I was lucky to hit the ball out of the cage."

It became a test of wills. Fosse was waiting for Manager Alvin Dark to see that he was injured and scratch him from the lineup. Dark was waiting for Fosse to tell him that he was hurt and couldn't play. After his first year with the Indians, this was the typical state of communications between Dark and his players. Anyway, no one said anything. The game began, and Fosse found himself catching for Sam McDowell. Remember that McDowell threw the ball as hard as any Indians pitcher ever. And remember that Fosse caught the ball with his left hand, meaning that every pitch into his glove put pressure on his shoulder.

"I couldn't reach out or up to catch anything," said Fosse. "If the pitch was high, I had to stand up and sort of get my torso in front of the ball. At the plate I had no bat speed whatsoever. I just wasn't the same guy."

But Fosse also was the Mule. He was stubborn and he kept pushing on because there was supposed to be honor in playing through pain.

"I had a twenty-three-game hitting streak snapped right before the All-Star break," said Fosse. "Man, I was tearing the cover off the ball. But after the injury, my left arm just hung there. I developed a lot of bad habits trying to compensate for the arm when I swung the bat. I obviously was hurt, but I figured unless the bone was sticking out of the skin, you played. But no one came to me and said, 'Ray, are you hurt? What's wrong? Why don't you take some days off?' They had to see something was wrong. But I played through July and August, then I broke my right index finger in early September and my season was over."

Swinging with one good arm, Fosse still batted .297 after the All-Star break. But he had only 2 homers and 16 RBI.

"The following April I was being examined for some back pains," said Fosse. "The doctors took X rays and discovered I'd had a fracture and a separation in that shoulder. They said that from the impact of the collision, the inflammation and swelling was such that the fracture just didn't show up on the X rays right after the game. The amazing thing was that I hit 2 home runs with a broken shoulder. I played for eight more years, and I was on pennant winners in Oakland [1973–74]. But I never had the same power or the same swing."

Fosse retired as a .255 hitter. He had 16 homers in the first half of the 1970 season but only 39 more over the next seven and a half seasons.

"Ray was just such a tough guy. Maybe if he had sat out a month or two after the collision, he would have been all right," said Herb Score. "He played in such pain, but it messed up his swing for the rest of his career. Then he started having other injuries."

Fosse broke his right index finger three consecutive seasons—1968, 1969, and 1970—each time on a foul tip.

"I caught one-handed, so that was not supposed to happen," said Fosse. "Sometimes it's just rotten luck. What are the odds of breaking the exact same finger in the same place the same way three years in a row?"

Breaking the index finger led to an annoying habit for Fosse. Before throwing the ball back to the pitcher, he often would pump two, three, even four times before letting the ball go. He had no problems throwing the ball to second base, just to the pitcher.

"Some people said I developed a mental block about throwing the ball back to the mound," said Fosse. "But that wasn't it. With my broken finger, I had trouble getting a good grip on the ball, and I wanted to make sure that I had control of it before I threw it."

After the collision, it was one injury after another for Fosse. He broke every finger on his right hand. He broke up a fight between Billy North and Reggie Jackson. "For being a peacemaker," said Fosse, "I shattered seven vertebrae in my neck."

He even had major surgery on both knees.

"I never asked 'Why me?' " said Fosse. "I guess I considered the injuries part of the game. I'd get hurt, have surgery, wait until the cast came off, and then rehabilitate like crazy so I could get back and play again. I really don't have any regrets. It seems like it all started downhill after the collision, but being a part of the World Champions in Oakland means as much as anything in my career. I didn't talk to Pete Rose for ten years after the collision. He never called me to see how I was doing or anything after the collision, and since we were in different leagues, we didn't see each other by accident. Then I saw him in 1980. Pete said he planned to slide headfirst, then saw me in his way and tried to avoid me when the collision occurred. I'm sure he didn't want to hurt me, and he said he didn't do it on purpose. I believe him. Besides, you can't change history."

To me, the most tragic Indian was Tony Horton.

In April 1970 there was a story in the *Akron Beacon Journal* under this headline: HEY GIRLS: YOUR DREAMBOAT'S WAITING! There was a picture of Horton with what was considered to be the relevant data for the female readers:

Salary: $45,000.
Height: 6-foot-3
Weight: 210
Eyes: Sky blue
Disposition: Dreamy

The lead-in to the story was: "Tony Horton has the kind of clear, sky-blue eyes that a girl can get lost in. Yet the tall, blond, and disarmingly handsome first baseman says he has trouble finding a date."

In the story Horton talked about his idea of a good date: "A movie, dinner, quiet conversation."

He talked about liking "intelligent girls, not that a girl has to have a college degree. But she has to be smart." He said at twenty-five he considered himself "a little too young to get married. I would have to get more established before I took on that responsibility."

Obviously, they don't write stories like these anymore—and for good reason. But the article by Janis Froelich does serve as a reminder to Tribe fans that Horton was supposed to be the next heartthrob . . . and, yes, another Rocky Colavito.

He came to the Indians from Boston for Gary Bell in 1967, after hitting 26 homers and batting .297 at Class AAA Toronto.

"Tony and I both grew up in southern California, and I played Little League against him," said Vern Fuller. "He was a great athlete, especially in high school. And not just in baseball: He was an All-City basketball player in Los Angeles. I saw Tony play, and he was a lights-out shooter. Boston signed him for a pretty big bonus. They figured he'd be a star."

The problem was that while Horton may have been a great high school athlete, he was a hitter first and a first baseman next. And he wasn't a very good first baseman. Remember, this was before the designated hitter. Boston already had a young first baseman in George Scott, so there was no room for Horton; and, as usual, the Red Sox needed pitching. When they wanted live arms in the 1960s and 1970s, they usually went to the Indians and Gabe Paul. Boston fans still thank the Tribe for sending them Dennis Eckersley and Sonny Siebert.

Early in the 1967 season, the Indians dealt Bell for Horton. Bell moved into Boston's starting rotation, went 12–8, and helped the Red Sox to the World Series. But there were no complaints from Indians fans about Horton.

"He was a terrific prospect as a hitter," said Pete Franklin. "We are talking about a kid who was big and strong, and I mean very strong. He had a great swing. He was more of a line-drive hitter than a power hitter, but he was so strong he hit line drives out of the park. He also didn't strike out that much. But he had a strange personality. He was one of the most intense people I've ever met. At the plate he would squeeze the bat and squeeze it as if he were going to turn it to sawdust right in his hands."

Horton's best season was 1969 when he batted .278 with 27 homers and 93 RBI, and his real power was to right-center, unusual for a right-handed hitter. He was only twenty-four years old and making $25,000. That winter he became locked in a contract dispute with Alvin Dark. Horton knew the Indians were paying Ken Harrelson more than $100,000. He asked Dark for $60,000, hoping to get $50,000. Dark offered $40,000. The manager worked the press well, making Horton appear to be a greedy ingrate who was trying to cash in on one good year. Agents were representing some players, but Horton didn't have one. His father was his adviser.

"Tony went his own way when it came to business," said Larry Brown. "He didn't have a bubble gum card contract or a bat contract like the rest of us because he refused to join the Major League Players Association. I don't know whose idea it was, but it was not smart."

It would have helped if Horton had an agent, if for no other reason than to handle the media. When a player tries to make his own case for a better contract, it usually sounds as if the guy is bragging or whining.

"Tony and I were roommates, and he is a good person," said Mike Paul. "He seldom drank. He had some dates but didn't really chase women. Being young and single, it would have been easy for him to be out on the town every night, but Tony had excellent personal habits. He had tunnel vision about baseball. He was obsessed with success and thought he should hit 65 homers and drive in 200 runs every year. He took it as a personal failure each time he made an out. That's why the pressure of the holdout was tough on him. He just wasn't comfortable being in that kind of spotlight. I know that Dark finally gave in to the point where they were $5,000 apart. Then Tony said, 'Keep the extra $5,000. Just make sure that anytime I want early batting practice, you get someone to throw to me.' This was back when $5,000 was a lot of money."

Horton signed for $45,000 after sitting out the first three weeks of spring training, and Dark hardly made him welcome. This was another example of why a manager should never negotiate contracts. As Bob August wrote in the *Cleveland Press*: "Dark can display all the personality of a mollusk. He can be remote and chillingly uncommunicative, a strange, secretive man. . . . It was observed that a manager who lives in such close quarters with his players is asking for trouble on a grand scale when he undertakes to talk money with the men he must lead."

Horton was already tightly wound; the holdout must have made his head feel as if it were in a vise. Every day he was tighter than the last.

"Because of the holdout, the fans booed Horton early in the season when Tony got off to a slow start," said Larry Brown. "He wanted so much to prove he was worth the money he got, he just made everything worse."

The Indians had a promotion called Banner Night, where fans made signs and banners, and the best ones received prizes. Today they screen those signs, but in 1970 anyone with a sign that wasn't obscene could parade around the diamond with it before the game. One of the fans brought a huge piece of plywood on which he had crudely spray-painted HORTON STINKS! As he carried it around the stands, fans cheered. Horton just stared at the sign, wondering why anyone would do such a thing. Couldn't the fans see that he was trying?

"Tony even went so far as to do eye exercises," said Mike Paul. "He wore a patch over one eye, then read a chart on the wall. Then he did the same with the other eye covered. He thought this would strengthen his eyes and make him a better hitter."

Horton's efforts to cope with stress only put more pressure on him.

"If I have one memory of Horton, it is that he never smiled, even after he hit a home run," said Rich Rollins. "In 1970 the Indians picked me up. It was the end of my career. I was more of a coach than a player because they had Graig Nettles at third. I was the guy who usually threw batting practice to Tony. We would meet at the Stadium at 2:00 P.M. before a night game, and I'd throw to him by the hour. This wasn't a fifteen- or twenty-minute thing. I mean, it went on at least an hour every time. I had heard about guys taking batting practice until their hands bled, but I never saw it until Tony. He hit ball after ball into the left-field stands. I'd say, 'Tony, you've got a game tonight.' He'd say, 'I know. Just a few more.' And I'd throw to him for another half hour."

"Occasionally, Tony would go nuts in the dugout," said Pete Franklin. "Once, he made an out with the bases loaded. He took a bat and started whacking everything he could at one end of the dugout. He was frightening, and guys just got out of his way. You couldn't talk to him when he was like that."

On June 24, 1970, the Indians played a doubleheader in New York. Exactly one month earlier, Horton had hit 3 homers in a game at Yankee Stadium. But this time there would be something else for him to remember. It was the same afternoon that a fan threw a cherry bomb at Ray Fosse. In the opener, Horton faced Yankee lefty Steve Hamilton, who was throwing his "Folly Floater." It was a blooper pitch, something you'd expect to see in a softball game. Hamilton only used it once in a while. Prior to the game, Horton had asked Hamilton to throw one of his lobs if they faced each other. In the ninth inning Hamilton entered the game and Horton led off. His first pitch was a floater, and Horton fouled it off. He called time out and dared Hamilton to throw him another. The pitcher did, and Horton swung mightily and hit a lame pop-up to the catcher.

"Horton looked like a guy trying to hit a fly with a sledgehammer," wrote Bob Sudyk in the *Cleveland Press*.

Horton crawled back to the dugout on his knees, as if he were begging for mercy. Players on both teams were laughing.

"It seemed pretty funny at the time, but that was a very scary sign," said Rich Rollins. "It was obvious that Tony needed help. At that point probably the only person he was listening to was his father. His parents would occasionally fly in from California and stay at the same hotels where the team stayed."

"As the season went on, Tony wore down," said Vern Fuller. "Even after good games he couldn't relax. I don't think he felt anything but relief when he played well, and then he was so anxious about the next at bat or the next game. He would not allow himself to enjoy anything. A few times he told me, 'No matter what I do, I just can't sleep.' At the end I thought sleep deprivation was getting to him. He looked like he never slept at all, he was just dragging himself. But he still had those piercing eyes and a constant frown. It's a facial expression I'll never forget."

Those who knew Horton also believe that he went through periods of asking himself, "What kind of person should I be?" Many players lived like hedonists on the road, and that life-style was not only accepted but often praised.

"Tony was single, and women were something he thought a lot about," said Larry Brown. "He could be very shy, but I also saw him once eating breakfast. He saw a pretty girl walk by on the sidewalk and left his food at the table. He went out of the restaurant to track down the girl. I know that he was trying to find religion and come to terms with himself as a person. He had a lot of things going on in his head."

Pete Franklin has a similar memory.

"I was a judge at a beauty contest at Jim Swingo's nightclub in Cleveland," said Franklin. "Tony was there, and he saw this beautiful girl named Kathy. He was almost foaming at the mouth, wanting me to introduce him to her. I did. She gave me a phone number to give to Tony because he had sort of disappeared before he got around to asking for it. But I later saw the girl, and she said that she never heard from Tony. That was hard for me to believe because Tony had acted as if the only thing he wanted in the world was to meet that girl. But Tony was like that. He could change radically from day to day. One day I'd see him in the dressing room and we were old friends; the next day he'd look at me, and I could tell he couldn't remember who I was."

Tony Horton's baseball career ended on August 28, 1970. At the time he was batting .269 with 17 homers and 59 RBI. If he had finished the season, he could have hit something like 23 homers with 75 RBI. Nice numbers but not nearly good enough for Horton, whose personal demons haunted him each day.

"The last game Tony played, I was on the bench," said Larry Brown. "Tony was playing first. His hands were on his knees, and he looked as if he was in a trance. I said to Alvin, 'I think you might want to get Tony out of there.' Alvin asked me why. I told Alvin to take a close look at him. At the end of the inning he came into the dugout, and he was talking real loud and swearing, which was out of character for him. He did manage to finish that game. He left the park, and when I saw him at the Stadium the next day he was wearing the same clothes he'd had on the night before. It was obvious that he hadn't slept or changed from the night before."

The Indians were playing a doubleheader against California on August 28.

"I was pitching, and usually I never talked to anyone on the day I pitched," said Sam McDowell. "The players and writers respected that and stayed out of my way. But Alvin came up to me and said, 'Something is wrong with Tony, and he told me that he wanted to talk to you.' Tony and I were not good friends, but I don't know if he had any good friends because he didn't let much of anyone in his world. But at the time I also knew he was in trouble, so I told Alvin I'd talk to him."

McDowell said that Horton was wearing a T-shirt, underwear, and a pair of shower shoes.

"Tony said, 'Do you know what is wrong with me?' " said McDowell. "Tony was talking about his hitting. I told him that I was a pitcher; he should talk to our batting coach. Tony said, 'You're a pitcher. You know how to handle hitters. How would you pitch to me?'

"I told Tony how I'd pitch to him, hoping that would satisfy him. But I was right in the middle of a sentence when he said, 'What do you think of me as a person?'

"I was honest. I said, 'Tony, I don't consider you a friend. You're a teammate and I respect you for that, but I really don't like you that much.' I looked at him and there were tears in his eyes.

"Then he said to me, 'Sam, I appreciate that. You're the only one who has been straight with me.'

"Now I was feeling really bad for him. I said, 'Tony, it's not personal. I just don't understand you. I really don't understand anything about you.'

"Tony stayed with me for the rest of my pre-game routine, following me into the trainer's room for a rubdown, to my locker when I put on my uniform, and into the dugout where I sat and watched batting practice. Then I went to the bullpen to warm up for the game. When I came back to start the game, Tony was already gone from the park."

After McDowell left Horton in the dugout, Horton returned to the clubhouse, still wearing his T-shirt, underwear, and shower slippers.

"He went to every player's locker, looked up at the name plate, and talked about whether that player 'was a man or not,' " said Larry Brown. "He also had been talking to me about what it meant to be a man and if he was acting like a man. Things like that."

Vern Fuller said that he had the same kind of conversation with Horton. "He wanted to know what I thought about him as a person," said Fuller. "I think he was going to every player he could find, asking that same question."

Sometime during that Sunday afternoon, Horton left the park. He reportedly spent a few weeks hospitalized in Cleveland, then flew home to Santa Monica, California, where he also was hospitalized.

"We tried to contact Tony in the mental hospital," said McDowell, "but his parents said that they didn't want anyone from baseball to talk to him."

In January 1971, the Indians announced that Horton was still hospitalized in California. They said he'd miss spring training and probably all of the season.

"I went to see Tony about a year after his breakdown," said Gabe Paul. "Physically, he was in good health, but the meeting didn't go very well. You could tell that he'd never play baseball again. This was one of the saddest things I've ever seen in baseball."

The Horton family blamed the pressures of the major leagues for bringing Horton to the mental brink. They believed that the best way for him to recover was to distance himself as far as possible from baseball, and that is what he has done.

In 1973 the *Plain Dealer*'s Russell Schneider had a phone interview with Horton. The former first baseman said, "I never think about playing baseball again. I have an entirely new life, and baseball is not a part of it. I play a little golf, but the game I like best is handball. It's fascinating, and I play it a lot. I started my life over, and baseball is not a part of it."

Mike Paul said that he exchanged Christmas cards with Horton for several years but has lost touch. "I last heard he was working in a bank in the L.A. area, but I don't know for sure," said Paul.

Recent attempts to reach Horton were unsuccessful.

Now a sports psychologist, McDowell believes he has an idea of what happened to the Tribe's promising slugger.

"Tony was a perfectionist in a negative sense," said McDowell. "Because of his low self-esteem, he was continually trying to prove he was a failure by setting unrealistic goals, such as perfection. If you make your standard perfection, then you don't have to accept yourself as you are, flaws and all. I've seen other guys as tightly wound as Tony, but none would take failure as hard as he did. When he was 0-for-4, it was like the world caved in. I've never seen a player so despondent after a game. Back then there was no such thing as a sports psychologist. The guys on the team did what they could to help him, but none of us had the training we needed. It's really sad. Tony had good numbers for a young player, but they were nothing to him. He had set himself up to fail no matter how well he played."

Tony Horton was only twenty-five when he played his last game for the Indians.

Gaylord the Great

In 1973, Gabe Paul resigned from the Indians to go to the New York Yankees. At least Cleveland had Gaylord Perry.

The McDowell-Perry deal may have been the best ever for Paul, or at any rate for Paul with the Tribe. His presence alone ensured that the Indians would not lose a hundred games, as they did in 1971.

Perry had a presence about him. The team could stink the other three days when someone else started, but when he was on the mound, the guys had better make the plays. He planned to pitch well, and he expected them to do the same with the bat and the glove. If they didn't, they heard about it.

"Jack Brohamer used to tell me, 'I can make a thousand errors as long as all thousand of them come when someone else is pitching,'" said broadcaster Joe Tait. "Brohamer was still a young second baseman. He'd tell me, 'When you made an error behind Gaylord, he would just stand on the mound and *stare* at you. I mean, you wanted to just shrivel up right on the spot.' Gaylord came to the team with instant credibility. He was a twenty-game winner. At six feet four and two hundred-some pounds, he was physically a big man, and he could intimidate you simply by how he looked at you. He'd see me in a hotel lobby in the morning and say, 'Cab goes at eleven. We need a fourth for gin.' I went. I never thought of anything else. Gaylord could impose his own will on you, and it just seemed like the best thing to do was go along with him. If Gaylord Perry wanted you to play cards, you played cards."

Duane Kuiper came to the Indians at the end of the 1974 season.

"Rookies were treated differently then than they are now," said Kuiper. "Gaylord would say, 'Kid, go get me a cup of coffee.' I'd get him a cup of coffee. Then he'd taste it and say, 'Not enough sugar,' and he'd pour it on the floor. This would go on two, three times until he decided that you had paid your dues. It wasn't just Gaylord, it was most veterans.

"When I joined the team, one of the captains was John Ellis. I was starting at second base in place of Brohamer. Ellis said to me, 'Jack Brohamer is a friend of mine. Until you prove to me that you can play, I'm not going to talk to you.' That was it. Then my first big-league start was with Gaylord pitching. I believe he was going for his twentieth win. As I was getting ready to step out of the dugout for the first inning, Gaylord leaned over to me and said, 'You make any errors, and you'll never play behind me when I'm pitching again.' I remember running out to my position and thinking that major league baseball was not a whole lot of fun."

But Kuiper didn't make any errors. And Perry did win. And eventually Ellis did talk to him—but that took a while.

"There was a game right at the end of his career with the Indians where Gaylord had a 2–1 lead in New York in the ninth inning," said Joe Tait. "Bobby Mercer hit a high fly ball to center field. There were a couple of Yankees on base. George Hendrick went back for the ball—he was really nonchalanting it. The ball dropped over his head, and two guys scored. Game, set, match. After the game Gaylord went over to Hendrick's locker, stood in front of him, and said, 'I never want this son of a bitch in center when I pitch again.' Then he walked away, and Hendrick never said a word. No one did."

Perry was much like Michael Jordan with the champion Chicago Bulls. He viewed the other players as "his supporting cast," although it was Jordan, not Perry, who actually used that phrase. But the idea was that in order to receive excellence, you have to demand it. Perry would say up front that he planned to pitch a great game. Now, were you man enough to play a great game behind him? And if you didn't, it was known in the Cleveland clubhouse that Perry had enough clout with young manager Ken Aspromonte that he could make sure you sat when he pitched.

Charlie Spikes was one of the players Perry hated to have in the field when he was on the mound, and the quiet but sometimes slothful Spikes seldom was in the same lineup as Gaylord Perry.

Perry got his way because Gaylord was great. Perry was 24–16 with a 1.92 ERA in 1972, his first season with the Tribe. He started forty games, completed twenty-nine. He was a Cy Young Award winner, the Indians' last. He also was an All-Star, and his twenty-four victories were the most by an Indians pitcher since Bob Feller won twenty-six in 1946.

Perry was 19–19 in 1973, then 21–13 in 1974, the last twenty-game season by any Cleveland pitcher.

But more than numbers, Perry was fun. Teams were convinced that he threw the greaseball, the Vaseline ball, the spitball, nearly any kind of ball that you weren't allowed to throw. And Perry did, but not as much as hitters believed.

"I wanted them to spend most of their time thinking about me throwing it rather than worrying about how to hit me," Perry often said. So he had a routine where he put his fingers to his mouth, to the bill of his cap, to the back of his head, and to his sideburns. Rules were changed, aimed at stopping Perry. First, a pitcher could not put his fingers to his mouth unless he wiped them on his uniform afterward. When hitters insisted that Perry was wiping, but not the correct fingers, the next rule was that pitchers could not put a hand to their mouths unless they were on the infield grass.

Then hitters said maybe he didn't throw a spitter; he was hiding grease somewhere and putting that on the ball. So TV cameras zeroed in on Perry, trying to discover where he hid the "foreign substance." When that didn't work, hitters asked the umpires to go to the mound and check Perry for signs of grease, perhaps shake down the pitcher. So umpires would wander out there, and Perry would hold out his glove and his bare hand. He might hand them his cap, which the fans loved because Perry was as bald as an egg on top. Through it all, he smiled. This was exactly what he wanted. To Gaylord Jackson Perry, pitching was more than a physical act, it was psychological warfare, and he was winning every time a batter worried more about what he was about to throw than about how to hit the ball.

The umpires never found anything on Perry.

The Indians were 72–84 in 1972 under rookie manager Ken Aspromonte, a man wise enough to know exactly what he had in Perry. By 1974, Aspromonte had developed a system that he hoped might squeeze something extra out of the team.

"He turned control of the clubhouse over to Gaylord and John Ellis," said Tait. "Gaylord was allowed to do anything he wanted. If he wanted to run, fine. If he wanted to go home to his North Carolina farm for three days between starts, that was fine, too. In New York, Gaylord never took the team bus. He had his own personal cab driver, a guy named Jerry from New Jersey. He took care of Gaylord. He also had his own schedule, and if anyone questioned Aspromonte about it, he simply said that when you have accomplished as much as Gaylord has, then you can have his privileges, too. But in return, Gaylord backed Aspromonte when it came to team policy. And if the players in question didn't listen to Aspro or Gaylord, John Ellis was there to supply the muscle. Ellis was a throwback, the kind of guy who loved a good brawl. He would stick his arm out and get hit by a pitch if he thought that was what was needed to win a game. In one game when Lenny Randle was with Texas and Milt Wilcox was pitching for the Indians, Randle bunted down the first-base line. Wilcox fielded the ball, and Randle intentionally ran over Wilcox. But as Randle ran to first base, John Ellis was there. Ellis was like a machine. He hit Randle three times—one, two, three—and Randle dropped before he ever got to the bag."

So that was Ellis and Gaylord, and the 1974 Indians were their team.

Making it more fascinating was that GM Phil Seghi brought Jim Perry back to Cleveland in a three-way deal. The Indians sent spare outfielder Walt Williams to the Yankees and obtained Jim Perry from Detroit.

At the start of the 1974 season, Jim Perry was thirty-seven and Gaylord was thirty-five. The two brothers combined for a 38–25 record and shared the team's Man of the Year Award. Jim Perry had been the Indians' Man of the Year back in 1960.

While Jim was on his way to a 17–12 season, Gaylord had a fifteen-game winning streak. It ended in Oakland in the tenth inning when a nineteen-year-old rookie named Claudell Washington drove in the winning run with a pinch single just three days after coming to the big leagues. Perry ended the season with a 21–13 record. Their thirty-eight victories accounted for just about half of the team's total of seventy-seven.

The 1974 Indians were a .500 team and within six games of first place on Labor Day, but that wasn't good enough for GM Phil Seghi. He didn't like how Aspromonte was handling the team.

"Phil was second-guessing Aspro," said Tait. "Later, we found out that Phil would second-guess every manager. But I knew that something was up at the start of the 1974 season. We had a pre-game radio show called 'View from the Top.' That had been a pre-game interview with the manager, but in 1974, Seghi took the show from Aspromonte. That led to a lot of speculation that Aspro would be lucky to last the season, but the team got hot and really, they were winning with mirrors. I recall Aspro telling me, 'I'd just like to finish in the top three, and then we'll see if Phil has guts enough to fire the Manager of the Year.' But the team fell apart in September."

On September 12, Seghi claimed Frank Robinson on waivers from California. The future Hall of Famer was thirty-nine years old and at the end of his career. Seghi said he brought Robinson to Cleveland to help in the pennant drive.

On the day of the deal, the Indians were 71–70. They finished at 77–85, meaning they went 6–15 after Robinson joined them. Part of the reason was that no one believed Robinson was coming to Cleveland just to play, especially not Aspromonte.

"As far as I knew, I was brought to Cleveland as a player, period," Robinson said in 1993. "On my first day I went to Aspromonte and told him that I was happy to be there and wanted to help the team any way I could. He seemed fine. Then the next thing I knew, Gaylord went off in the papers and Aspromonte quit. It was as if the Bronx Zoo had moved to Cleveland."

Perry also felt threatened by Robinson's appearance in the clubhouse.

"It started with a newspaper story," said Kuiper. "Gaylord found out that Frank was making more money than he was. The story said that Gaylord wanted 'one more dollar' than Frank. Well, Frank saw the paper and didn't like it.

"Frank went over to Gaylord, who was sitting on a stool in front of his locker. Frank said, 'Keep me out of your negotiations and out of the paper. What you do is your business, but keep me out of it. If you don't, then I want you to stand up. And if you stand up, then I'm going to knock you on your ass.'

"Gaylord just sat there. You could tell that he was thinking of standing up, but he also knew that he didn't stand a chance against Frank. So he just sat there.

"Then Aspromonte came out of his office and said, 'Guys, would you mind keeping it down? I have an announcement to make. They are not going to hire me for next season, so I guess I've been fired.' "

According to Robinson, he took the newspaper to Perry and said, "Did you say this?"

Perry said he did.

"I told Gaylord that I didn't appreciate my salary being dragged through the papers," said Robinson. "I was making more money than Gaylord, but the Indians picked me up for only the last few weeks of the season. They weren't going to pay me for the whole year. Gaylord couldn't understand that, and we started screaming at each other before some other guys stepped in and broke it up. People said we came to blows, but we didn't get close. It was just a screaming match, then Aspromonte came out of his office and quit. It was the damnedest thing."

According to Tait, Aspromonte handed Herb Score his letter of resignation and asked Score (who said he didn't recall the incident) to give to it Phil Seghi when Score interviewed Seghi for the pre-game show.

"Seghi came into the booth," said Tait. "Herb said, 'Well, Phil, I guess the first business we have tonight is for you to comment on this letter.' Phil took the letter. It was only a couple of lines, with Aspromonte saying that he resigned effective the end of the season. Phil never said a word. He just got up and left with the letter. Then Herb explained to the fans what had happened. At the end, Aspro and Phil hated each other, and Aspro did it this way to embarrass Phil."

Ken Aspromonte would never manage again. He went into the beer business with his brother Bob, a former big-league infielder.

"They ran a Coors distributorship in Houston," said Mike Paul. "I think after his experience with the Indians, Kenny just figured that he didn't need baseball anymore."

Meanwhile, the Indians were preparing to make Robinson the first black manager in baseball history.

Breaking the Color Line

The man who decided that it was time baseball had a black manager was Ted Bonda. He was a business partner of Howard Metzenbaum, the liberal Democratic senator from Ohio. Bonda made his money in rental cars and parking lots. In August 1973 he was asked by his good friend and team owner Nick Mileti to run the Indians, and he had some ideas that no other Tribe executive had considered.

"I always wondered why we didn't have more minority fans," he said. "Cleveland broke the color line in the American League with Larry Doby. We had a number of black stars, yet the number of our black fans was well under 10 percent. When Phil Seghi claimed Frank Robinson on waivers, Phil was simply looking at Robinson as a player. I immediately thought of him in terms of being our next manager. There was nothing really wrong with Ken Aspromonte, though I thought he could be more aggressive. But we needed a drawing card, someone who would bring attention to the franchise. Aspromonte was not about to do that. Frank would. He had charisma."

Robinson was vocal about his ambition to be a big-league manager. He had managed in Puerto Rico for the previous six winters.

"Sooner or later someone was going to hire Frank," said Bonda. "I also felt very strongly about civil rights. Teams were just reluctant to be the first to hire a black manager. Someone had to go ahead and take the step, and to me it was a privilege to do it. Phil Seghi went along with the idea. He agreed that Frank had the talent to manage, but I don't believe Phil thought the timing was right. I believed that it was as good a time as any, and that it was terrible that baseball had to wait until 1975 to have a black manager."

After Aspromonte resigned in the middle of September, it was clear that Robinson would be the next manager. Only no one had told Robinson.

During the last week of the 1974 season, Robinson's agent, Frank Keating, received a call from Seghi.

"Phil told me that they liked the fact that Frank was a big name and that they wanted him to be a player/manager," said Keating. "They thought that Frank would help attendance, especially in the minority community. Phil and I met in the far corner of the Stadium, away from everyone. We sat there right during a game and banged out an agreement. After the game I met Frank at the Theatrical Restaurant, and they took us to the booth where Aspromonte usually sat, which was kind of ironic. That was when I told Frank that he was going to be the next manager of the Indians. I didn't say the first black manager. As we were talking, Aspromonte came in, and they led him to the table right next to us. That wasn't real comfortable, so we went to the bar."

The next day they met with Bonda and Seghi.

"We had a three-game trip to Boston to end the season," said Robinson. "The Indians wanted me to agree to manage before the trip but not to say anything until the season was over. Even when I was sitting in Seghi's office, I wasn't sure I wanted the manager's job. I still thought of myself as a player. I was in my nineteenth season, and I wanted to play twenty years in the majors. Then they said they wanted me to be the player/manager.

"I said, 'Wait a minute. Managing is tough enough, let alone playing.'

"They said, 'We want you as a player/manager.' What they were thinking was that I had another year on my contract (at $180,000), and they figured they could get two things for the price of one.

"I said, 'How much will you pay me just to manage?'

"They said, 'twenty thousand.'

"I said, 'Hold on. You'll pay me $180,000 to play, but only another $20,000 to manage?'

"They said that was the offer, a total of $200,000.

"I said it wasn't enough.

"They said, 'Take it or leave it.'

"I was ready to tell them to forget it when Keating asked to meet me in the hallway. So we left the office, and Ed asked me, 'Do you want to manage in the majors?' I said I did. Ed said, 'Well, this is your chance. If you don't take it, you'll never know when you'll get another opportunity—if ever.'

"I thought about it, and Ed was right. I realized that there had never been an opportunity for a minority to manage before, and if I turned it down, they could say, 'Hey, we offered the job to a black person, but he didn't want it.' They would use that as an excuse to keep the door closed to blacks as managers. I went back inside and told them, 'I'm not happy with the salary arrangement, but I'll take the job.' "

The announcement was made on October 3, 1974.

"It was the biggest press conference in the history of the city," said Pete Franklin. "The mayor was there. Media from all over the country. It was huge, huge news. You have to give Bonda credit for it. He was the world's greatest liberal, and he had a chance to make a statement for equality, and that was great. As for Seghi, he just wanted to get rid of Aspromonte, and he took a lot of heat when Aspro quit. Well, this announcement let Seghi right off the hook."

An interesting sidelight was that Larry Doby was on the Tribe coaching staff. Not only was he passed over for the managerial job, but Robinson did not rehire him as a coach. He replaced him with Rocky Colavito.

"When I joined the Indians, I saw that Aspromonte, the white coaches, and the white players sat at one end of the dugout," said Robinson. "Doby and the black players were at the other end of the dugout. I sat in the middle. When it came time to name my coaches, I wanted coaches who backed the manager, and I didn't see Doby do that with Aspromonte."

Robinson says that he and Doby still don't speak because of his decision.

"Phil Seghi took credit for hiring me, but it was Ted Bonda's idea," said Robinson. "The thing I disagreed with Bonda about was his thinking that a black manager would bring more fans to the game. Fans don't come to the games just to see a manager. They come because of the players."

Actually, the Tribe's attendance went *down* every year that Robinson managed. In 1974, when the Tribe flirted with the pennant race in August, the team drew 1.1 million. In Robinson's first year, it was 977,039. Then it dropped to 948,776 and 900,365 in his next two seasons.

✿   ✿   ✿

The Indians thought they were getting two for one in Robinson. They knew he was thirty-nine years old, but they also knew that he hit 22 homers and had 68 RBI in 1974, mostly with the Angels. The front office saw that 22 homers would have tied Charlie Spikes for the team lead in 1974, so they thought Robinson would manage and bat cleanup.

"They wanted Frank to be another Lou Boudreau," said Keating. "They wanted a player/manager who played a lot. But age was starting to catch up with Frank, and he also had a very bad shoulder. All he could do was DH, and even swinging the bat was very painful."

But Robinson did put himself in the lineup for the opener in 1975. A crowd of 56,715 was at Cleveland Stadium on the very brisk afternoon of April 8.

"Before the game, the last words I heard from Phil Seghi were, 'Hit a home run,'" said Robinson. "I batted myself second as the DH. I hadn't hit much in spring training because I found that managing took up so much of my time. I thought maybe I could handle the bat well enough to move the runners along, get a hit to right field. I also thought I could set the tone of the kind of aggressive baseball I wanted to play. The last thing I intended to do was swing for the fences."

As Robinson came to the plate in the bottom of the first inning, he received a huge ovation. Doc Medich was pitching for the Yankees.

"He threw me a couple of sidearm pitches, and suddenly the count was 0-and-2," said Robinson. "Then I barely fouled a ball off. I stepped out of the box. I was sort of numb, and then I realized that this guy was trying to embarrass me. He had 2 strikes on me, and he didn't even bother to waste a pitch. He was trying to embarrass me on my day."

Nothing ever motivated Robinson as much as anger. He often played the game in a rage over real or imagined slights. On this day he knew that every eye in baseball was on him. All he had to do was look around in the on-deck circle. As he knelt there awaiting his turn at bat, he was surrounded by at least twenty photographers and TV cameramen. Reporters from across the country jammed the press box, and Commissioner Bowie Kuhn was there to make a pre-game address about the significance of the day. This wasn't just Robinson's moment, it was baseball history, and Robinson knew it.

"I fouled off a couple of pitches and ran the count to 2-and-2," he said. "Then I hit an inside fastball out. I floated around the bases, and it wasn't until I got to third base that I realized the full impact of what I had done. Dave Garcia was coaching third, and he was jumping up and down like a little kid. As I came home, there were a ton of photographers and cameramen waiting on the field. I had to step around a couple of them to touch home plate."

The first player out of the dugout to greet Robinson was none other than Gaylord Perry, the starting pitcher that day.

"When Frank hit that home run, the place went insane," said Joe Tait. "It was one of the most dramatic moments in sports that I've broadcast because we all knew how much pressure was on Frank."

The Indians beat the Yankees, 5–3, Perry picking up the victory.

Robinson said, "This wasn't my most memorable moment in baseball—nothing can mean more to me than going into the Hall of Fame—but it was pretty amazing what happened that afternoon. Then, after that, every day, often every day, I had to sit down with writers and do the First Black Manager Story. I knew that it was important and that everyone wanted to have their own angle, so I did it. But it did get old. I kept wishing that I could get through the first trip around the league and just be considered another manager."

A winter did nothing to cool the heat between Gaylord Perry and Robinson. During the first week of spring training, Robinson wanted his pitchers to run fifteen laps from one outfield foul line to the other.

Perry wasn't interested. He'd always had his own training program with the Indians, and he was not about to let a rookie manager tell him what to do, "especially some superstar who'd never pitched a game in his life," Perry told reporters. Perry wanted to take ground balls in the field as he always had. Robinson didn't like his pitchers to do that, fearing a bad hop would break a finger on their pitching hand.

Robinson wanted Perry to be the leader of the pitching staff by leading the running and other conditioning drills. Perry had other ideas.

"That first spring training was a long time ago," said Robinson. "But I didn't ask Gaylord and Jim Perry to do anything out of the ordinary. Gaylord kept saying he had his own program. I said, 'We are a team, and we do things together, not as individuals. If you want to do anything on your own, you do it before or after the workout.' Gaylord wanted to go home between starts. No way. I felt I had to put a stop to that. You can't have one guy doing his own thing and everyone doing something else."

This situation seemed doomed from the start. They were two talented, proud, stubborn men, and neither was about to bend.

"Right from spring training you could see that it was just a matter of time before Gaylord would have to be traded," said Duane Kuiper. "Gaylord and Frank were a lot alike in terms of how competitive they were. They simply butted heads."

Or as Joe Tait said, "They were like two stallions who wanted to be the head of the herd. They just argued about everything and truly hated each other."

There also was a racial element.

"Gaylord was as close to a southern gentleman as I ever met in my life," said Tait. "He was very patrician. He felt that there were stations in life, and you belonged to your particular station. He had a lot of attitudes common in the South back then. But he also was very close with a blind black woman named Matty Coltrain. She lived in a cabin on his farm from the time Gaylord was born, and she had taken care of him when he was growing up. Gaylord always wanted me to make sure that I said hello to Matty on the radio for him. We had a fifty-thousand-watt signal, and she listened whenever Gaylord pitched. Gaylord was genuinely concerned about her and her health."

But Robinson also was the kind of aggressive man who made him nervous, just as Perry was the kind of man who worried Robinson.

But it also must be mentioned that doing it Perry's way made Gaylord one of the premier pitchers in baseball. Gaylord believed that Robinson was trying to assert his authority by controlling him.

John Ellis, the other team leader from the pre-Robinson era and Perry's sometimes catcher, complained to writers that Robinson was "second-guessing the hell" out of their pitch selection. "Gaylord has been winning twenty games for years. How can you second-guess that?"

Jim Perry also wasn't thrilled with the new manager, but he usually kept quiet. Jim was thirty-eight years old, and his pitching tank was empty. After winning seventeen games in 1974, he was 1–6 with a 6.69 ERA under Robinson before being sold to Oakland for $15,000.

"I'm next," Gaylord told reporters.

When Gaylord was taken out of a game by Robinson, reporters smelled trouble and surrounded his locker. He would do nothing to neutralize the situation, saying things like "Don't ask me. I just work here."

Gaylord was having a difficult time, and Seghi began to wish he had been allowed to make the trade he wanted with Boston in 1974—a deal Bonda vetoed. Seghi wanted to deal Perry for three young pitchers—John Curtis, Lynn McGlothen, and Marty Pattin.

As the June 15 trading deadline approached, newspaper speculation had Gaylord headed to nearly every American League team. Anywhere was fine with him as long as Robinson wasn't the manager. Early in June, Perry told reporters, "Nobody is happy around here. There is no communication. Losing has a lot to do with it, but so does the man. . . . Look at the newspapers. The guy never makes a mistake."

Perry knew that Robinson would hate reading those comments, and he hoped they would fuel his trip elsewhere.

As for Robinson, he implied to reporters that Perry had a sore arm but was hiding it.

In the middle of their May and June feud, Robinson was suspended for a clash with umpire Jerry Neudecker. He also tangled with umpire Ron Luciano. And he had a terrible game on June 9 when the Minnesota Twins had two of their hitters batting out of order but Robinson never noticed and lost a chance to protest it. Instead, the Twins won 11–10 in eleven innings. Robinson also admitted that he gave a squeeze bunt sign to third base coach Dave Garcia but didn't mean to. He called the entire evening "My Most Embarrassing Moment as a Manager."

Just a whole lot of fun in the wigwam.

Finally, the Indians traded Perry to Texas for Jim Bibby, Jackie Brown, Rick Waits, and $150,000. Seghi actually had the gall to say that the $150,000 had nothing to do with the deal. He pointed out that the three pitchers won thirty-two games for Texas in 1974, compared to the twenty-one Perry won for the Indians, so the Tribe came out ahead.

Perry's record was 6–9 with a 3.55 ERA at the time of the deal. In his last nine starts for the Tribe, he was 2–7 with a 4.22 ERA. In a diary of his rookie season as the Tribe manager, called *The First Year*, Robinson said, "Gaylord will be thirty-seven in September, and at that age I don't think he's going to come around. He'll win some games for the Rangers, but he'll never be Gaylord The Great again. . . . I was disappointed that Gaylord never tried to make my job any easier. . . . He never asked if there was anything he could do to help me as a rookie manager. I never went to him, either."

Well, Perry did win a lot of games for Texas. He finished that 1975 season with a 12–8 record, making his overall mark 18–17. And he kept pitching until he was forty-four years old, and he even won twenty games again and another Cy Young Award after leaving Cleveland. Gaylord won 110 of his 314 career victories after the trade to Texas.

Being the first black manager meant hate mail and death threats. One guy phoned Bonda and threatened to shoot Robinson unless he was fired immediately. Another stopped by the Tribe office, said he wanted to tell Robinson something "very important," and it would be "disastrous" if Robinson didn't hear what he had to say. Then he left before the police could be called.

"I was having lunch with Ted Bonda when I got a call at the restaurant," said Ed Keating. "It was my wife. She said people were calling the house and saying, 'We know that you are responsible for having that nigger manage the Indians. We know where your kids go to school. We know what time they leave the house and what bus they take. You'd better watch out because we'll get your kids.' We called the police, and they rode the bus with my kids to school for a month. My kids were seven, six, and five. Frank was getting racist mail, and so was I. Luckily, nothing ever happened to us or our families, but I kept thinking that this was the middle 1970s. I thought we were beyond all that. Given what Frank had to go through, he had a great first season."

The Indians had a poor first half, hanging about ten games under .500. Robinson was questioned in the media about his outbursts with umpires and his feuds with Gaylord Perry and John Ellis. But at mid-season he persuaded Phil Seghi to promote Duane Kuiper, Jim Kern, Rick Manning, and Eric Raich from the minors. They joined Buddy Bell and Dennis Eckersley to form the core group of what appeared to be an exciting young team. Robinson finished with a 79–80 record, and the Tribe was 27–15 in the final six weeks of the season.

"People had the wrong idea about Frank as a manager," said Kuiper.

"They thought he was screaming at us all the time, which was not true. The only time Frank really chewed out a guy was when he made a mental mistake. He didn't harp on physical errors. He wasn't challenging people to fights. He could call a clubhouse meeting and yell for fifteen minutes, using every four-letter word you've ever heard and a few more he made up. He'd threaten to send us all to Triple-A if we didn't start hustling. He had the kind of body language that could frighten the entire team. But he didn't do that very often. I liked playing for Frank Robinson. So did Manning, Eck (Dennis Eckersley), Buddy Bell, all of the young guys. If you tried to break up double plays and hustled down the first-base line, he left you alone. The thing was that if you got the bunt sign from Frank and put down a great bunt that moved the runner to second base, when you got back to the dugout, you probably would not get a compliment from Frank. That was what you were supposed to do, and he wasn't going to pat you on the back for doing your job. Some guys had a tough time with that, but most of us understood Frank and appreciated how much he knew about the game."

The Indians were 81–78 in Robinson's second season, as he continued to develop young players such as Kuiper, Manning, and Eckersley. He also played very little because of a sore shoulder.

Nonetheless, Robinson had problems with some veterans, especially Rico Carty. Carty had come to the Indians from the Mexican League in 1974. He called himself the "Big Mon," and he was a .320 hitter in his first three years as the Tribe's DH. His only position was batting because his knees were shot, and he was never interested in doing anything with a baseball but hitting it.

"Rico did his own thing," said Chandler. "He was from the Dominican Republic. He played winter ball there and figured he didn't need much spring training, so he was always late. He also was a general in the Dominican Army Reserve, and he used that as an excuse to be late. He'd always tell the Indians, 'Doan worry about the Big Mon, he will heet. He always heet. I be here sooner, but I had to be in a big army parade in Santo Domingo because I'm the general.'

"Stuff like that didn't thrill Frank. But then Rico would grab a bat that was as big as a telephone pole and he'd hit pea after pea off the wall. He hit line drives so hard that they'd start out eight feet off the ground and stay there until they hit the wall. The fans loved Rico."

Joe Tait called Carty a bigger-than-life personality; he was a hulking man, about six feet four, with a baritone voice. Tait said that Carty liked to be a father figure to the young Latin players. When Alfredo Griffin came to Cleveland, Tait wanted to interview the rookie Dominican shortstop.

"Rico was my translator," said Tait. "I'd ask a question. Griffin would say one word, '*Si.*' Then Rico would say into my tape recorder, 'Alfredo say that he is happy to be here. Playing in the big leagues is a goal he had all his life. He say he like Cleveland. . . .' It was pretty funny."

"Rico always played with his wallet in his back pocket," said Kuiper. "He didn't trust the valuables box in the dressing room, so he kept his wallet with him on the field, and you could see the bulge. Besides, he never slid, so it wasn't like something would happen to him on the field and his money would fall out."

While the fans were amused by Carty, he and Robinson had no sense of humor when it came to each other.

"Rico thought I was there to take playing time away from him because he was a DH," said Robinson. "But my shoulder was killing me. I couldn't play that much. When I did, I had to DH, and I used Rico at first base, but he was a liability there. Ted Bonda and Phil Seghi were always on me to play more, but I said that my shoulder was so bad I couldn't play in the field. I had Rico as the DH and he was a .300 hitter, so why should I bench him? Phil thought I was cheating the organization because I didn't play more. Rico thought I wanted his job on those rare days when I did play. It got personal, and Rico thought I just didn't like him, which wasn't the case."

Well, at least not at first, but that changed.

"There was a game in Oakland where Rico was out with a hamstring injury," said Robinson. "He was second-guessing every move I made. I'd signal for a bunt, and I'd hear Rico say, 'Why is he bunting here?' That went on and on for several innings. Finally I threw him out of the dugout and sent him to the clubhouse. The next day I had Phil Seghi send him back from Oakland to Cleveland, supposedly to get treatment on his leg, but I just wanted him out of there for a few days."

Carty went on the Pete Franklin show and pleaded his case, saying he was fined $1,000 and didn't deserve it. The fans sent him money to pay the fine, which really gnawed at Robinson. Then Carty made a nice grandstand play by donating the fans' money to charity and paying the fine himself.

Carty befriended an infielder named Larvell Blanks. Blanks thought he was a better player than Frank Duffy and should have been the regular shortstop. Blanks was half right: He hit more than Duffy, but his glove gave back the runs he produced. When Blanks wanted a sympathetic ear, he found one in Carty.

"I believe that Rico poisoned his mind," said Robinson. "One day I walked in the clubhouse, and Blanks had thrown his uniform, his glove, his bats, everything in the trash because I didn't start him. I fined him. Then he was on the bench wearing a piece of tape over his mouth. After my first year, Carty and Blanks were the only players I had trouble with."

But his clash with Carty became very destructive.

"We were at the Wahoo Club for an afternoon luncheon for the media and fans," said Robinson. "Rico was being honored as the 1976 Man of the Year, and he received the Golden Tomahawk Award. He accepted it and said, 'They talk about leadership on our team. They say this player or that player. Who is the best leader of the team? It's the manager. I say this with all my heart. Frank, we need leadership from you. Frank, we aren't getting it. Frank, we need you.' I was stunned. This guy was taking a tomahawk to me. He was out to get my scalp. This was my last season in Cleveland, and the whole time Rico was talking, Phil Seghi just sat there puffing on his pipe. Afterward, all Phil said was that Rico had the right to his opinion. He didn't come to my defense at all. That was when I started to wonder if Seghi wrote that speech for Rico, and I knew I was in big trouble."

The Indians gave Robinson one-year contracts to manage. In his first two seasons he earned $200,000 because he was a player/manager. But he batted only 185 times in those two years—hitting .234 with 12 homers—because of his shoulder problems. So in 1977 he received an $80,000 contract just to manage, which he saw as a $120,000 cut, hardly a rousing vote of confidence because it was a one-year deal.

"I said, 'Wait a minute. I've heard all this stuff from you guys about how I should play more, but now you don't want me as a player/manager?'" recalled Robinson. "I told them to trade Rico Carty, and I'd get in shape and be the DH. I said, 'I may not hit for as high an average as Rico, but I'll drive in more runs and hit more homers.' But they weren't interested. They said they just wanted me to manage, and I didn't have a very good feeling about that."

The front office saw Robinson's proposal as a ploy to keep his higher salary. They didn't believe his body could stay healthy enough to be the everyday designated hitter. Also, the Indians were forever looking to save a few bucks, and in Robinson's case it was $120,000.

Robinson also did things to hurt himself.

In 1976 the Indians had an exhibition game in Toledo, the home of their Class AAA team. The Toledo management did not believe that seeing the enormous Boog Powell in the Tribe's all-red uniform was enough to draw fans. "I look like the world's biggest Bloody Mary," said Powell. The Mud Hens' front office announced that Tribe batting coach Rocky Colavito and Robinson would come to the plate during the game.

In the fifth inning Colavito batted against Bob Reynolds and lined a single. Not bad for a forty-two-year-old. Then Robinson stepped to the plate. Reynolds, who was known as "Bullet Bob," had been a teammate of Robinson's in Baltimore in the early 1970s. But Robinson had cut him during the 1976 spring training. Robinson was under the impression that Seghi would tell Reynolds that he had been sent to the minors. But Seghi thought Robinson would do it. Instead, a sportswriter did, and that made Bullet Bob very mad. Three months later he was still seething when he faced Robinson. His first pitch sailed well behind Robinson's head.

"You're gutless," Robinson yelled at Reynolds. "If you're gonna throw at somebody, at least come close enough to knock him down."

Not exactly a mature attitude on the part of Robinson. The rest of the at bat was uneventful, and Robinson flied out. As he was leaving the field, he passed Reynolds and said, "You're really gutless, throwing at someone in a game like this."

"At least you're talking to me now," said Reynolds. "I should just take care of you."

And Robinson decked him with a right-left combination. Two quick punches, and one pitcher was knocked flat.

"What a game that was," recalled Bob Quinn. "I had heard that Reynolds was telling guys in the bullpen that if he had a chance to pitch to Frank, he was going to knock him down. I mean, before Reynolds could even get his glove off, Frank had landed his punch. Reynolds hit the ground like a sack of potatoes. It was really scary. Then Frank went into the dugout where he saw a rookie pitcher named Tom McGuff. He told McGuff, 'If you don't pitch well, the same thing is going to happen to you!' The poor kid just turned white. It was a very ugly incident. Frank just lost his temper."

Robinson had to apologize to the Toledo Mud Hens and their fans. Reynolds was all right, but the real damage was to Robinson's reputation. He looked as if he was losing control of both himself and his team.

That was the opinion of Joe Tait, the Tribe radio broadcaster at the time. Tait filled in one night for Pete Franklin on his "Sportsline Show."

"A caller asked me if I were the general manager of the Indians, what I would do with Frank Robinson," said Tait. "This was Frank's third year, 1977. I said, 'If I were the GM, Frank would not have been back this year because I don't think he's good for a young team. But now that the die is cast, I don't think changing managers at this point is going to mean anything, so he may as well continue.' The newspapers got hold of that, and it came out, 'Tait: Robby Must Go.' That wasn't what I said, and when you read the stories with my quotes, I didn't say he should be fired. But this came in the middle of Frank's troubles with Rico Carty. The team was losing. It was a real mess."

"Joe Tait's comments were probably the last straw," said Robinson. "It blindsided me and really pushed me over the edge. I didn't care if the station was paying his salary, he was working for the club. The team had to okay him to do the games. I didn't think it was right for him to take a cheap shot at me on the air. I really believe that the front office coerced him into doing it."

"That's not the truth," said Tait. "I meant what I said. I know Frank thinks Phil Seghi told me to say it, but he's wrong. I thought that Frank was a terrible example for a young team off the diamond because of his social behavior. He could be very crude. There was a lot of drinking on that team, period, and Frank did nothing to help the situation."

The Indians set up a mend-the-fences meeting between Tait and Robinson.

"Ted Bonda, Phil Seghi, and I were there," said Tait. "Phil was sitting directly across the table from me. Frank was to my left. We sat down, and Frank whipped out the *Plain Dealer* with the story. He held it right up to my face, as close as he could, to intimidate me.

"He said, 'Joe, how could you do this to me?'

"I said, 'Well, Frank, quite honestly, I think you're a lousy manager.'

"He went bozo. It seemed like for the next hour and a half he called me every name in the book. It went on only a few minutes, but he was ripping me a new one. He was stringing words together that I never knew could go together. I just sat there and took it. I wasn't going to stand up and challenge him because he'd kill me.

"But out of the corner of my eye I spotted Phil Seghi. Phil was lighting his pipe. He caught my eye and winked at me. Then I looked at Ted Bonda, and it was as if he was nodding off. He could care less what Frank said. Then it hit me. I thought, 'Frank, you poor S.O.B. You're dead meat. The GM is winking at me, and the team president is falling asleep.'

"Later, I learned from Seghi that they had planned to fire Frank the day my story hit the papers, but they had to hold off for a few weeks because they didn't want to make it look as if I had something to do with it."

Franklin also had become a Robinson critic.

"Actually, I cut Frank more slack than I would a normal manager because he had a fantastic personality and because he was a black man and I wanted him to succeed," said Franklin. "For about a year I backed off from tearing into him, even though I could see that perhaps Frank did not behave like a man in a leadership position should. After that first year, we really got into it, and it became a horrible, horrible feud. We haven't spoken to each other since. Later on, he improved a lot as a manager and as a person. He communicated with people better, and he didn't act like such a hotshot. There was too much pressure on him in Cleveland. He felt the whole world was watching him, but Frank's way of dealing with it was to be very arrogant and unreasonable. Actually, he can also be a very charming guy, and I think that part of his personality came out more after he left Cleveland and managed elsewhere. The guy is very bright, and he really knows baseball. But he was abrasive as hell, and that wasn't good for young players."

Yet most of Robinson's troubles were with veterans—Gaylord Perry, Rico Carty, John Ellis, and Larvell Blanks.

"As he matured as a manager, Frank developed communication skills," said Andre Thornton. "But when I came to the Indians in 1977, Frank was a perfectionist. I think he still was adjusting to the fact that he was no longer a player. He went off the pedestal of being a superstar to being a modern manager, who often feels like a servant of the players. Frank would eventually resolve these issues, but in Cleveland he dealt with it through intimidation. Some people intimidate because they are afraid to communicate or because they don't know how else to communicate. Frank could get the best out of Frank, but he couldn't get the best out of a Charlie Spikes or a Larvell Blanks."

It probably would not have made much difference, but Robinson received little help from his general manager. It wasn't long before Phil Seghi began to distance himself from his inexperienced manager, making it obvious that Robinson wasn't so much his choice as he was the pick of Ted Bonda.

"Phil constantly second-guessed me," said Robinson. "From the dugout I could see where he sat in the press box. He would stand up and pound his fist on his desk when he saw things happen on the field that he didn't like. In my third year there was a day when I stopped in Phil's office before the game and asked if there was anything we could do to improve the team. He said, 'No, nothing.' I sat there for about five minutes, then left.

"About ten minutes later he and Ted Bonda showed up in my office in the dressing room. Phil asked, 'Where are the coaches?' They were on the field working with some players who wanted early hitting. I went to get them, and we were all in my office. Then Phil started yelling at my coaches: Why aren't we doing this? Why is that player doing that? Why don't we bunt better? Why don't we get a better lead off first? 'I sit up in the press box, and I see guys at first base . . .'

"On and on it went. Phil never looked at me, but he was talking to me through the coaches. He was all over Rocky Colavito about guys not getting a better lead off first base. I said, 'Phil, this is my job we are talking about. If the players don't do something, it comes back to me.'

"Phil never looked at me, but he said, 'Well, someone ought to do something. When I was managing . . .'

"When he said that, I slammed the desk with my bare hand. *Bam!* I yelled, 'Damn it, you are not the manager of this team. If you want to say something to me, you tell me alone, not in front of my coaches. These guys are busting their asses. They don't deserve to hear this. If you want to manage this ball club, here's the lineup card. I'll quit.'

"Then Bonda said, 'Hey, guys, let's settle down and talk this out.' We cooled off for a while.

"That was the biggest confrontation I had with Phil. I wished we had talked more. Instead, he second-guessed the hell out of me to other people and to the press, and that would get back to me. I knew I was on borrowed time."

Seghi had won two pennants in his seven seasons as a minor league manager, mostly in the Indians' system in the early 1950s. As the years passed, Seghi's ability as a manager grew in his own memory to the point where he probably saw himself as Casey Stengel.

"For a while Phil wanted to fire Frank," said Bonda. "They weren't getting along. I was there the day they almost had a fistfight in Frank's office. I kept resisting Phil's desire to get rid of Frank. But in the middle of the 1977 season, I had an eye operation. I was weak, and the team wasn't playing well. I finally let Phil do it, and I've regretted it ever since. I might have let Frank go at the end of the season, but there was no reason to embarrass him and fire him in the middle of the year like that. Our team wasn't going anywhere."

Robinson was in his office when he received a call from Seghi on a Saturday evening. The team had a 26–31 record and had won its last two games. In Robinson's defense, other Tribe managers have been far worse.

"Phil wanted to meet with me at eight o'clock Sunday morning," said Robinson. "When I hung up the phone, I knew I was fired. Phil was never in the office at 8:00 A.M., and certainly never on Sunday. I went home that night and told my family that I had managed my last game in Cleveland. I said that no one gets a vote of confidence in the general manager's office at eight o'clock Sunday morning."

Seghi should have dropped the axe right after the Saturday afternoon game instead of letting Robinson agonize all night. Seghi knew that Robinson was aware of what was coming, so why wait? But Seghi didn't like conflict. He preferred to snipe around the fringe rather than aim straight at the target. For six weeks there had been newspaper speculation that Robinson would be replaced by Jeff Torborg, one of his coaches.

"Ted Bonda would not tell Frank that he was fired," said Bruce Fine. "He left that to Phil to do alone."

"When I went into his office, Phil said they had to make a change," said Robinson. "I asked him who was the new manager. He said they were going to promote Jeff Torborg. I told Phil that Jeff was a good man, and I thanked him for the opportunity. Phil wanted me to go to the press conference, but I told him that was a bad idea. The press conference was Jeff's day. But I said I'd be in my office in the clubhouse if anyone wanted to talk to me."

Out of loyalty, Torborg was reluctant to take the job. "I told Jeff that if he ever wanted to manage in the majors, and I knew he did, this was his opportunity," said Robinson. "I said I'd feel better if he got the job than if it went to someone else."

Robinson exited with dignity and certainly handled the situation with more grace than the front office.

"But inside, Frank was shattered," said Ed Keating. "We talked all that night. I tried to tell him that even the great managers are fired, but here was this superstar, a man who had succeeded in baseball, and he felt he'd failed when he was fired. It was the only time I've ever seen Frank emotionally broken down and showing how much he was hurting. His style was always to keep things in. What made me mad was at the press conference, Phil Seghi was just gloating about Frank being fired because Phil got his way. It would have been easy for Frank to rip Phil, but he didn't. He said all the right things to the reporters."

Robinson called the next two weeks the worst period of his life. He was forty-one years old. He had spent his life in baseball, and he felt as if baseball had rejected him.

"When you're fired, it means you failed," he said. "I kept going over and over my years in Cleveland, thinking about what I did and what I could have done differently. After a while I realized that what I did at that moment was what I felt was right. If I had another chance, I might do something else. Looking back, I would not have had the shouting matches with Rico Carty, and I would have talked to him more behind closed doors. Maybe I could have handled some of the other players differently. But this was my first managerial job, and I was learning, too."

It would have been more productive if Robinson had been able to come to terms with Gaylord Perry because the two men really could have led the team. But when Robinson challenged Perry in the dressing room late in the 1974 season, their relationship was doomed. Perhaps the white southerner was not used to a black man talking to him like that, and he never forgot it. It seemed as if the racial tension was always there, especially with older players. Maybe that is why Robinson was more successful with the kids such as Eckersley, Kuiper, and Manning. They didn't worry about the color of the skin of the manager. To them, Frank Robinson was a man they wanted to impress. But Robinson had a tendency to come off as if he knew not only all the answers but even the questions before he was asked. That part of his personality softened after the Cleveland experience.

"Cleveland was not the ideal place for Frank to break in as a manager," said Andre Thornton. "Being a black person in a blue-collar town such as Cleveland could not have been easy for Frank. I also think that Phil Seghi and Frank were both going through periods of adjustment. Phil still saw himself as a manager and Frank saw himself as a player because neither was that far removed from it. This was Phil's first GM job, and it was Frank's first managerial job. Later you could see how much Frank had grown as a manager and a person."

Robinson managed Class AAA Rochester in 1978. In 1979 he worked for Earl Weaver in Baltimore as the Oriole's outfield coach, and it was apparent that Robinson had both matured and mellowed. When the Orioles won the 1979 pennant, that helped revive Robinson's career, and he was hired to manage in San Francisco. He also managed the Orioles later and had some very successful seasons. He is now a vice president with the Orioles.

"It's funny. I tell people that I liked Cleveland, and they look at me like I'm crazy," he said. "But I did like the town, and I thought overall I did a pretty good job. Just check the record."

Robinson was 186–189 with the Tribe. The only manager with a better record since is Dave Garcia (247–244 in 1979–82).

"I ran into Rico Carty in 1990 at an old-timers' game," said Tait. "Rico hugged me and said, 'Hey, my friend Joe, we got rid of that son of a bitch, Robinson, didn't we?' This was thirteen years later, and Rico still hadn't forgotten. Those two guys were probably never going to get along."

"A few years after Frank was fired, I had a conversation with Ted Bonda," said Keating. "Ted told me, 'The one thing I regret when I ran the Indians was that I fired the wrong guy. I should have gotten rid of Phil Seghi.' "

Manning and Eckersley

They were the two guys who were going to make a difference: Rick Manning and Dennis Eckersley.

In 1972 the Indians made Manning their number one selection in the free-agent draft. Eckersley went in the third round. The Indians talked them up. Why not? After a 60–102 record in 1971, they had to talk about something, and it sure couldn't be the guys who already were in Cleveland. So the Tribe talked about the kids. Not just Manning and Eckersley but Duane Kuiper, Jim Kern, and Buddy Bell—Bell being the only one in the big leagues in 1972.

Manning was a high school shortstop from Niagara Falls. He batted .614 and never struck out—not once during his senior season. He also was a nineteen-point scorer as a six-foot-one guard in basketball, a good enough athlete to be offered a scholarship by Frank Layden to play at Niagara University. The Indians had the number two pick in that draft, and they never hesitated: Manning was their man.

"I was seventeen years old, and I got a $65,000 bonus," said Manning. "I thought I had died and gone to heaven. One day, no one knew who I was. The day the Indians made me their number one pick, I had TV stations and reporters wanting to talk to me. I was one of six kids. We never had a lot of money in my family. The whole thing was pretty amazing."

Eckersley was a star at Washington High School in Fremont, California, which is just outside Oakland.

"It was just like in the movies," Denise Jancinto (the future Mrs. Eckersley) told writer Hal Lebovitz. "He was the high school hero, and I was the head cheerleader. We knew each other from our freshman year, and we lived only a mile apart. Dennis never wanted anything but to play baseball. From day one that was all he wanted. Not a job. Not college. Nothing else."

Denise could understand that mind-set. She was the daughter of a minor league infielder who once played for a manager by the name of Paul "Daffy" Dean, the younger pitching brother of Dizzy Dean. When Dennis Eckersley pitched for the high school team, Denise served as the team's official scorer.

"We were Dennis and Denise, which our friends thought was cute," Denise told Lebovitz.

The Indians signed Eckersley for $32,000 and sent him to Class A Reno, where he roomed with the team's number one selection in that draft—Manning.

"Reno was in the California League, and we had been playing for about six weeks when I got a call from [General Manager] Phil Seghi," said Duane Kuiper. "Phil knew that I had an apartment in Reno, and he wanted Manning to room with me. The idea was that I was twenty-two, and Manning was seventeen. He was their hottest prospect, and they thought I'd be a mature influence. I already had a roommate. I also had my jaw wired shut from a collision at second base the week before. Actually, I had about eight guys staying in my two-bedroom apartment some nights, guys sleeping anywhere they could. But Phil Seghi stressed to me that he wanted me to look out for Manning. We all knew that he was the number one pick and had hit .750 or something like that in high school."

Manning immediately became the starting shortstop.

"I don't think the Indians saw me as an infielder," he said. "They knew I could run and thought I'd end up in the outfield. But I wanted to try shortstop because that was my position in high school. I was so naive. I didn't even know about how to get a cup into your jock. In my first game I saw guys with a protective cup, and I wondered what was that?"

The Indians were right, Manning was not a shortstop.

"I made 17 errors in fourteen games," he said. "I know guys were looking down at me and wondering how the Indians ever could have given me all that money."

"I was a roving minor league instructor, and I saw Rick break in at Reno," said Rich Rollins. "He had a game in Visalia where he made 5 errors. By the end of the night, he was begging us to put him in center."

A few weeks after Manning came to Reno, the Indians sent Eckersley to stay in Kuiper's apartment.

"Like Rick, Eck was seventeen," said Kuiper. "I was from a farm in Racine, Wisconsin, Rick was from outside of Buffalo, and Eck was from the Oakland area. In a lot of ways they knew more about the world than I did. I didn't have to entertain them at all. Actually, it would have been very easy to get into a lot of trouble in Reno. The casinos are open all night. They would cash ballplayers' checks because they knew some guys would gamble and give it all back. Some of those places, they would take your personal check for $15 but pay you only $10. The other $5 was a service charge. But Rick and Eck weren't gamblers. They were the two youngest guys on the team, and they seemed to be inseparable."

Kuiper was amazed by Eckersley's ego.

"His first pro start was in Visalia," said Kuiper. "I think he won, 4–2. A lot of balls were hit hard off Eck but right at guys. At one point in the game I went to the mound to calm him down, and Eck said, 'You know, I must be throwing the ball awful damn hard for those guys to hit it off me like that.' He was serious, and he turned a negative into a positive."

Of the three players, Kuiper had the best year at Reno: He hit .300 and was the All-Star second baseman. Manning batted only .241 with 66 strike-outs in 214 at bats. Eckersley was 5–5 with a 4.80 ERA.

"I was always amazed that Dennis became a great pitcher," said Rollins. "During his first year at Reno, I'd warm him up in the bullpen. He threw sidearm. He had this flat curve, and he didn't throw hard at all. I thought one of our scouts had made a mistake on this guy."

Nothing much mattered to Dennis and Rick. They both were convinced they were big-league bound and that it wouldn't take long.

"I'm sure the older guys thought we were young cocky jerks," said Manning. "Dennis was really arrogant. Even at seventeen he thought he was the greatest pitcher ever."

In 1973, Rick Manning and Dennis Eckersley were sent back to Reno. Dennis had married Denise in the spring, and the three of them were close friends.

Denise told Lebovitz that their first night after the wedding was in a Ramada Inn in Bakersfield, and the second night of their marriage was spent at the Visalia Inn. Manager Lou Klimchock had lifted his ban on wives staying with their husbands on the road so Dennis and Denise could have some sort of a honeymoon.

This time Reno worked well for both players. Manning hit .280, and Eckersley was 12–8 with 218 strikeouts in 202 innings. They were both eighteen.

Eckersley got to the majors first. The year was 1975. Frank Robinson had just been named manager, and the first time he saw Eckersley fling the ball up to the plate with such passion, he wanted the twenty-year-old on his team.

He was known as The Kid. He drove fast cars and had long black hair that flowed out from under his baseball cap. When he struck out a hitter, he sometimes would point his index finger at the batter as if it were the barrel of a gun; then he would shoot it and blow away the smoke. Or else he'd yell to the batter on deck, "Okay, you're next." He didn't take the mound, he stood on it as if he owned it; and he dared anyone to try to knock him off.

"In high school I threw a bunch of no-hitters, and in my first pro start at Reno I threw a shutout," said Eckersley. "I thought I was going to the big leagues in another month. I got racked a couple of times after that. But then I settled down and got my confidence. I tried to throw so hard. I had so much energy. I was so intense. I know other guys don't like me because I'm so emotional, but I don't care. That's me. I get excited. I love to pitch. It's a release to me."

Eckersley's motion made him unique. He came from the side, whipping the ball to home plate. To a right-handed hitter, the ball had to look as if it were about to take off his left ear. Eckersley not only had a 90-mile-per-hour fastball, he had a wicked curve. The bottom line was that he actually scared some hitters, and their left knees buckled a bit as they went to swing at his pitches.

Nearly everything Eckersley threw was a strike. "Phil Seghi wanted to send Eck back to the minors for another year," said Robinson. "Dennis had never pitched in Class AAA. But every time I used him in spring training, he got people out. I mean, every time. He didn't have one bad game. They were worried about his confidence if he got hit a couple of times in the majors, but Dennis had tremendous confidence. Finally, I said, 'Look, let me keep him. I'll work him out of the bullpen, break him in gradually, and keep the pressure off.' That is the only reason Dennis opened that season as a reliever. I wanted to start him, but the front office wouldn't let me. I figured that having Dennis in the bullpen was better than not having Dennis at all."

For the first two months of the season, Eckersley bailed out starters such as Eric Raich, Roric Harrison, and Fritz Peterson. He came out of the bullpen ten times and didn't allow a single earned run. His first major league victory came on May 2, 1975, when he threw 2⅓ innings of scoreless relief and the Indians beat Baltimore, 4–3.

"I'll never forget that game," Eckersley said. "I came out of the bullpen, and Marty Springstead was behind the plate. I was throwing cockshots, and he was calling them balls. After three or four in a row—I mean these pitches were splitting the plate in half—I got into it with Springstead. I could tell that he didn't like my act. I had long hair, and he probably thought I was cocky. Really, he could have thrown me out, but he knew he was wrong."

His first major league start was on May 28. He threw a shutout against Oakland.

On and on it went. Eckersley did not allow an earned run in his first 28⅔ big-league innings.

While Eckersley was astounding the Cleveland fans, Frank Robinson was watching the scouting reports early in the 1975 season. At Class AAA Oklahoma City, Rick Manning was hitting .316. Duane Kuiper was batting .244, but that didn't bother Robinson; he was a Kuiper fan and also wanted to bring him to Cleveland when the Tribe left spring training.

"Late in May, I went to Phil Seghi and told him that we weren't going anywhere with the veterans we had," said Robinson. "I said that we knew our older guys weren't going to get any better, so let's bring up the kids and go with them. I felt even if we lost a lot of games, at least the kids were hungry and they'd give me an effort."

By early June, Kuiper had taken over as the starting second baseman. Manning was in center field. Jim Kern had joined the bullpen. The Indians had Buddy Bell at third.

"It was something to build on," said Robinson. "Kuiper, Manning, Eckersley—these guys brought us some life. We started winning games. We played with enthusiasm and got the fans talking about us."

Manning was an instant hero.

For those who saw only a disheartened Manning after 1980 jogging to first base after hitting a grounder to the second baseman, it is hard to imagine the player he was in 1975. At the age of twenty, this kid *loved* baseball and ran everywhere.

"Rick was a little Pete Rose, a real gung-ho player," said Pete Franklin. "He was a slap-hitter who beat out a lot of infield hits and was daring on the bases. He was always a great center fielder, but early in his career he could beat you at the bat, too. I'm telling you, this kid looked like a .300 hitter who'd play the hell out of center field and steal a lot of bases."

Kuiper was just a solid second baseman, fearless turning the double play, and a singles hitter who seldom struck out. He and Manning tied for the team lead with nineteen stolen bases.

When the 1975 season was over, the Indians had a 79–80 record, their most wins since 1968. Kuiper hit .292, Manning .285, and Eckersley was 13–7 with a 2.60 ERA.

Eckersley was a lot of fun, saying things like "Give me two runs, and I'm going to win."

The fans loved it. Eckersley believed. So did Kuiper, Manning, and Buddy Bell. There was hope.

In 1976 the three rookies weren't great, but there were no Joe Charboneau belly flops. All three survived the sophomore jinx.

Manning was the best of the bunch, hitting .292 and winning a Gold Glove for his defense in center. "He was really an exciting player," said broadcaster Joe Tait. "The fans loved him."

Kuiper hit a respectable .263 and was superb at second base, leading the American League with a .987 fielding percentage.

Eckersley was 4–8 with a 4.94 ERA at the All-Star break. Robinson put him in the bullpen for two weeks to work out some mechanical problems with his motion. He did, and he returned to the starting rotation, going 9–5 and striking out 127 batters in his last 106 innings. His final record was 13–12.

Meanwhile, Denise and Dennis Eckersley often had Manning over for dinner, and the three of them went to movies and nightclubs together.

Then came 1977, their last year together, the year that would change their lives.

Going into the 1977 season, Eckersley had a 26–19 big-league record. In his second season he became only the eighth pitcher in baseball history under the age of twenty-two to strike out two hundred batters in a season.

"I was throwing so well that year that I knew I would throw a no-hitter, I just knew it," he said. "I went out every game expecting to throw a no-hitter. I didn't think anyone should get a hit off me, and I was so pissed off when someone did. At this point in my career, I was truly overpowering."

On May 25, Eckersley went all twelve innings and beat Seattle, 2–1. In the final 7⅔ innings, he did not allow a hit.

His next start was May 30 against the Angels in Cleveland.

"Eck pitched against Frank Tanana that night," said Kuiper. "That was back before Tanana's arm injury, when he was Fast Frank. Both of these guys were just throwing smoke, and they were yelling at each other as they walked off the field after each inning. They were so alike—young, cocky, and with great arms."

As the ninth inning began, Eckersley came out of the dugout. Angel right fielder Joe Rudi was running off the field, and he had the ball after catching a Ray Fosse fly for the final out of the inning.

"Joe looked right at me, kissed the ball, and threw it to me," recalled Eckersley.

It was much easier for the Angels to kiss it than to hit it. As Rudi would say after the game, "Eck had a great fastball, a great curve, a great everything."

After every inning, Eckersley would sit down in the middle of the bench, put on his jacket, and take off his cap. Then he'd get up, go to the water fountain, take a drink, and spit it out. Then he'd go back to the exact spot in the middle of the bench and put his cap back on.

When the ninth inning came, it was worth noting that Eckersley had already thrown twenty innings in five days and had not allowed a hit in the last sixteen, dating back to his May 25 start.

No problem. California's Bobby Grich, Willie Aikens, and Gil Flores went down one, two, three, with Flores fanning to end the game.

"I just punched Flores out, all fastballs," Eckersley recalled one spring afternoon in 1993. "He was taking his time coming up to the plate, trying to distract me. I yelled at him to get his ass in there, I needed one more out. Boy, I had great stuff that day and great concentration on every pitch."

When Flores was wasted, Eckersley ran off the mound and leaped into the arms of Fosse, a picture taken by former *Cleveland Press* photographer Paul Tepley that has since become a classic moment in Indians history.

In what would become his first and last no-hitter, Eckersley walked only one and struck out twelve. He beat Tanana, 1–0. Eckersley threw 114 pitches; only 35 were balls. He threw 83 fastballs, 31 breaking pitches. In his previous start, the twelve-inning game at Seattle, he threw only 5 breaking pitches all night.

Phil Seghi announced in the dressing room that Eckersley would receive a $3,500 bonus; Fosse got $1,500 for catching the no-hitter.

In his next start, Eckersley went another 5⅔ hitless innings before giving up a home run to Rupert Jones in Seattle. That gave him 22⅓ hitless innings, right behind the major league record of 23 innings set by Cy Young in 1904.

Robinson lifted Eckersley after the sixth inning. Jim Kern pitched the final three frames, and the two pitchers allowed only one hit as the Tribe won, 2–1.

Later in the season he threw a one-hitter against Milwaukee.

The reason for all these details is that many Tribe fans have forgotten what kind of pitcher they had in Eckersley. He was twenty-two and had a 40–32 record. He made an All-Star team, threw a no-hitter, and averaged nearly nine strikeouts per start.

"Frank Robinson had a lot to do with my development," said Eckersley. "There were games where I'd go crazy on the mound, screaming at everyone. It just poured out of me. Frank would scream 'Grow up' right back at me. A couple of times he dumped on me in front of all the other players. He made me small, but that was okay. I needed it at that time in my career. Frank would take Rick and me out drinking a couple of times, and we talked the game. He took great care of us. He was the best manager Rick and I could have had. We loved the guy, and we loved being with the Indians back then."

✦   ✦   ✦

The day after Eckersley and Kern combined for the one-hitter in Seattle, Rick Manning was in center field as usual for the Indians. The date was June 4, 1977.

"During the game I slid headfirst into second base," said Manning. "I felt like I did something to my back, but it didn't seem too bad. I got up and played the rest of the game. I even played the next three games, but it got harder and harder to run, and my back just felt worse. The scary part was that my legs would go numb."

Duane Kuiper said, "It was as if Rick bounced into second base off that Astroturf in the Kingdome."

Manning's back was placed in a brace for six weeks, and he was out until September.

"It took them about a month to diagnose what was wrong," said Manning. "Then they figured out that I had fractured a vertebra."

"It was hard to believe," said Kuiper. "Rick was only twenty, but he broke his back. When he came back and played, he just didn't have the same raw speed. For whatever reason, he also changed his approach to hitting. He tried to pull the ball a little more instead of slapping it to left field."

Manning agreed: "I just didn't get the infield hits that I used to, so I tried to hit with a little more power," he said. "I know that I hit .292 and .285 in my first two seasons, but those were very soft numbers because about everything I hit was a single. Later in my career I thought I was more productive hitting .250 than I was hitting .285."

While that point is highly debatable, the back injury changed his career in two ways. First, he was never the same hitter. Second, the injury made him rich.

Manning ended that injury-marred 1977 season batting only .226.

"This was just as free agency was becoming a factor," said Manning's agent, Ed Keating. "The Indians sent Rick a contract that cut his salary by 25 percent. I looked at it, did the math, and it kept coming out to a 25 percent cut. Then I checked the rule book, and it was exactly as I thought: You were not allowed to cut a player more than 20 percent, or he became a free agent. I called the Players Association to check, and they said I was right. If a player was cut more than 20 percent, he automatically became a free agent."

Keating called Seghi and told him that there was a problem with Manning's contract. Seghi pulled Manning's contract out of the file. Keating heard Seghi pounding away on an adding machine.

"That's just a little mistake," said Seghi.

"No, that's an illegal contract," said Keating. "He's a free agent."

"What do you mean, he's a free agent?" asked Seghi.

"We don't have a contract," said Keating. "We are free to negotiate with any team, or we can negotiate with you."

Seghi told Keating he would call back; he wanted to do some checking. An hour later Seghi was on the phone.

"Ed," he said. "You're not going to hold this mistake . . . I mean, it's just a tiny little mistake. . . ."

"Phil," said Keating. "I have a responsibility to my client. You're a friend, but I can't let this go. So what are we going to do here?"

What Keating did was pull out the negotiating pistol and place it right to Seghi's temple.

"Rick would have made maybe $75,000 tops that next season and signed a one-year contract," said Keating. "Instead, we got a five-year, $2.5 million deal. Rick was coming off a broken back, and the contract guarantee was so strong that he would have gotten the $2.5 million even if he had never played another game."

The Indians caved in because they had made a stupid blunder and were caught. They caved in because they tried to lowball an injured player instead of doing the decent thing and just sending him a contract for the same amount as he had made the year before. They caved in and made Manning one of the highest-paid players in baseball because they were embarrassed and they thought Manning would heal from his back injury and be the .290-hitting spark plug who owned center field.

"I couldn't believe it when Ed told me that I was getting all that money," said Manning. "Here I had just broken my back. Then I hit the jackpot."

This did not sit very well with the blue-collar Cleveland fans. They knew only that Manning had hit .226. They didn't care that he was hurt or that the front office messed up. It just seemed as though he was cashing in on a technicality instead of earning the money. They began to view Manning suspiciously.

On March 30, 1978, the Indians traded Dennis Eckersley. It didn't matter who they received in return. Eckersley was their pitching equivalent of a young Rocky Colavito—you just don't do it. Especially when the guys the

Indians received from Boston were Rick Wise, Mike Paxton, Bo Diaz, and Ted Cox.

"But this was different from the Colavito deal," said Gabe Paul. "We had to do something, but we traded the wrong guy."

The problem was that Denise Eckersley had become closer to Rick Manning than to her own husband. Furthermore, Dennis and Denise Eckersley had a daughter in 1976, Mandee.

"Rick was living at their house, and he ended up living with her," said Paul. "It was a bad situation, and we had to trade Rick or Dennis. We thought Manning was going to be a star."

There was one other element to this story: Eckersley's sidearm delivery.

"Some of our baseball people thought that Eck was putting too much pressure on his elbow and that he would be damaged goods," said Bob Quinn who was farm director at the time. "I don't believe that we in the front office were aware of the situation with his wife."

"The late Phil Seghi told me two things before he made the deal," said Bruce Fine. "He thought that Dennis had a slow motion to home plate and that hurt him when it came to holding runners on base. He also said that with his sidearm motion, Dennis would hurt his arm. He never said anything else."

Gabe Paul had returned to run the Indians about six weeks before the deal was announced.

"I clearly remember that we knew what was going on between Rick and Eckersley's wife," said Paul. "We had to trade someone before the whole thing blew up in our faces. Manning had the bad back, and his trade value was down. Besides, I really thought he'd be one of the great stars. Boston wanted Eckersley badly, so we made the deal. It turned out that Eckersley became the star. He always was a great performer, and he never let his troubles affect his pitching."

Ed Keating was the agent for both Manning and Eckersley.

"It was funny, but I wasn't aware of the situation," he said. "Rick, Dennis, and Denise had always been so close, going back to the minors, that it was hard to see the signs. Now that I know what was happening, I can look back and see all kinds of clues. But I just never suspected, and neither did Dennis. Even when the deal was announced, I thought they did it because of Eck's motion. They talked about that all the time, how he would hurt his arm and how he seemed to strain so hard when he threw. Of course, he had been throwing that way all his life. It was natural to him. Anyway, I thought, well, maybe the deal will be good for both of them. Rick and Dennis used to run together on the road, and it might not be a bad idea to split them up."

Keating was aware that Eckersley was having some marital problems, but he didn't know what kind.

"Denise thought that Dennis had been drinking too much," said Keating. "Another factor was that Rick stayed at their house when he was recovering from his bad back, which meant he was there when Dennis was on the road with the team. That also was not a good situation when you think about it."

Keating said he had this conversation with Eckersley right after the pitcher joined the Red Sox.

"I found out who it is that Denise has been with," Eckersley said.

"Who?" asked Keating, who was expecting it to be someone from Eckersley's old neighborhood in Oakland.

"It's Rick."

"Rick?" screamed Keating. "Can you be sure?"

"I'm telling you, it's Rick," said Eckersley.

"I'm going to call him right now," said Keating.

Eckersley begged Keating not to contact Manning. For two days Keating didn't call Manning. He thought about the relationship between the two players and Denise.

"How dumb could I be?" said Keating. "Really, you could see it if you knew what you were looking for."

Then the agent confronted Manning.

"Rick told me, 'Look, I didn't start this thing. She started it, way back when we played in Reno,' " said Keating.

"I said, 'Rick, don't give me your bullshit because you're trying to get off the hook.'

"Rick said, 'That's the truth. No one is going to believe it anyhow. It was her move, not mine. I'm not proud of it, but I did it.' "

Then Keating called Eckersley and said, "Dennis, for what it is worth, she started it." Dennis said, "I don't give a shit. If you're a friend, you don't do something like that."

Certainly, Denise had a different version of this story. Manning prefers not to discuss it, so the circumstances of who started what will always remain murky. Keating found himself in the bizarre situation of representing two players, one whose wife had just left him for the other. "Both of those kids were like my sons," said Keating. He wanted to do what was best for everyone and without taking sides. In another life, Keating must have been a high-wire walker because he remained the agent for both of them throughout their careers. He also kept the two guys from killing each other.

"After the deal, I went to Boston, and Denise and Mandee stayed with Rick in Cleveland," said Eckersley. "That messed me up terribly. I never knew for sure what the situation was between Rick and Denise until the trade and my family didn't come with me. Our marriage was in the middle of breaking up, but I didn't think that Rick—I'm not even sure if they knew what they would do, but the trade kind of forced them to make a decision, too. I also was really pissed off by the deal. I wanted to stay with the Indians my entire career. Everyone was looking at me like I was supposed to be happy because I was going to a good team in Boston, but I was torn. I was losing my baseball family and my real family. Almost everybody else wanted out of Cleveland, and I wanted to stay. I broke down and cried like a baby. There had been some rumors that I might be traded. They kept talking about my motion. Pete Franklin used to say on the radio that my arm was going to fall off. Probably the first time you see me throw, you think that because my delivery is different from most players'. When I was in the minors, they tried to change my motion to throw more overhand. But I throw like I always did, a high leg kick and a little down from the side. I honestly don't know if the front office was aware of what was happening with Denise. If they knew before the deal, then they knew before I did."

Unfortunately for Eckersley, they apparently did know before he did.

"I was so lonely after the deal," said Eckersley. "But I threw myself totally into baseball. I played hard and I lived hard. But I found I loved pitching more than ever. The mound became my refuge. Sometimes, away from the park, I'd completely break down. I'd just cry and cry and not know when it would stop. Then I'd go out and party all night. It was a crazy life. I had some of my best games after I had been out all night. Baseball was my salvation because I stuck my nose into the game. On the mound I was an angry young man, and that arrogance carried me a long way."

As an Indians fan would expect, Eckersley became a great pitcher right after the deal. He was 20–8 with sixteen complete games in 1978 for Boston, then 17–10 with seventeen complete games the next season. In both years his ERA was exactly 2.99.

What about the four guys the Indians received for Eckersley?

Rick Wise was a veteran pitcher who was 24–29 in two seasons for the Tribe, then became a free agent and signed with San Diego.

Mike Paxton was 10–5 in his rookie year with Boston, then 12–11 for the Tribe. But he hurt his arm and was finished by his twenty-fifth birthday.

Bo Diaz became an All-Star—with Philadelphia. He brought the Indians Lary Sorensen, who was mediocre at best for the Tribe for two seasons.

Finally, there was Ted Cox, who had been the MVP in the International League in 1977.

"Ted Williams once said that Cox had a great swing, and everyone got excited," said Duane Kuiper. "Cox had been a good minor league player, but he never could find a spot with us."

Cox had a very slow swing, was a defensive liability, and ended up being traded for that dynamic duo of Rafael Vasquez and Rob Pietroburgo. In 272 major league games with four different teams, Cox hit .245 with 10 homers and then retired at the end of 1981. He has since played on several nationally ranked slo-pitch softball teams.

By the middle 1980s, when Eckersley was switching to the bullpen and was about to become one of the greatest relievers ever, the Indians had taken all the players they received for him and traded themselves right into oblivion.

"You look at the original trade, and the front office did its homework, at least on paper," said Kuiper. "Wise was a good pitcher. Diaz was an All-Star. Paxton and Cox were supposed to be good prospects. But you just don't trade a pitcher you developed in your own farm system, a guy who is twenty-three and you know is a good pitcher, for four guys. Dennis was crushed to be traded, and we were crushed to lose him."

For whatever reason, Manning was never the same player after his back injury—not just in terms of his performance on the field but in the perception of the fans.

When Eckersley and Manning came to the Indians, there was this image of innocence about them. They were throwbacks, two kids playing for the love of the game. Then Manning got hurt and got rich because the Indians botched his contract.

Then Eckersley was traded.

Then the story came out that Eckersley's wife had moved in with Manning, and that was why this wonderful young pitcher was traded.

Fair or not, that was how Tribe fans saw the situation. To make things worse, Eckersley was winning twenty games in Boston, and Manning was struggling to hit .250 for the Indians.

"The thing with Eck and Denise might have hurt my image, but people don't know the whole story," said Manning. "They have no clue. I know the truth, and what people think doesn't bother me at all. I don't talk about it. If anyone talks about it, it is Eck. That's the only time you'll see anything written about it because you won't get anything from me. I know what happened. That's life. You can't change history."

From 1978 to 1983, Manning was the Indians' starting center fielder. Most seasons he hit close to .250, drove in about 50 runs, and stole about 15 bases.

"When I came off the injury, I didn't feel the expectations were that high because I expected to play better myself," said Manning. "But that first year back, I still felt some pain in my back. I was afraid to go all out, to test it. Then I had Gabe Paul saying I should be a .300 hitter. Here I was coming back from an injury into all these expectations, and I had all this pressure. Some of it wore me down. I mean, I got tired of people saying, 'Well, you hit .285 and .292 in your first two seasons, you should be a .300 hitter.' But I never was a .300 hitter. As you play more, they scout you, pitchers pay more attention to you, the game gets harder. To me, rather than hitting .300, I wanted to steal a base, move the runners along, play great defense."

But Manning didn't steal that many bases; only twice in his career did he have more than 20. Nor did he learn to bunt to take advantage of his speed. Making it worse was that he grew frustrated as a hitter and wouldn't run out ground balls or pop-ups, which infuriated the fans.

They saw a young guy making five hundred grand a year, and he wouldn't even run ninety feet to first base. So they booed his butt.

In 1979, Dave Garcia became the Indians' manager, and Garcia loved both Duane Kuiper and Manning. It was as if Kuiper was the good, loyal son while Manning was the prodigal son.

As Frank Robinson said, "Kuiper always hustled and squeezed every ounce out of his ability. He was a hard-nosed son of a gun, and I always wanted him on my team."

Garcia coached third base for the Indians in 1975 and 1976, when Manning had his best seasons. He was mesmerized by Manning's defense and believed that Manning would hit, too.

"Garcia loved to talk the game, and Rick was very good at talking," said Andre Thornton. "At heart, Garcia was a scout, and he saw Manning's potential. He was blinded by that so much that he didn't understand Rick would never hit as well as he should. Duane Kuiper was a .270 hitter with much less talent than Rick had, yet Rick settled for hitting .250. I felt part of it was because of Rick's personal problems. He was never fully at peace with himself. That was a factor. Also, Rick never understood what he could do for the team at the plate. He wasn't a power hitter, yet he wasn't a contact hitter who got on base a lot. He was caught in the middle, and that didn't make him a very productive hitter. I think he believed that if he played good defense, that made up for it."

As an outfielder, he was one of the best in the American League, covering enormous territory. He played shallow to take away base hits in front of him, but he had the tremendous ability to run back on a ball and wasn't afraid to challenge fences. Only on defense did it seem that Manning enjoyed the game.

"Rick had the tools to be a very good player," said Frank Robinson. "But I don't think he really dedicated himself to keeping in shape and keeping his mind on baseball. He didn't pay the price to keep himself at the top of his game."

One of the constant discussions was Manning's weight. He was never fat, but he usually looked as if he could drop ten pounds, which is especially significant since he was a player who lived by his legs.

"When a young player like Rick puts on weight, that's a very bad sign," said Pete Franklin. "It shows he just doesn't have the commitment. Look at Brett Butler. In terms of natural ability, Rick had it way over Butler. But Butler applied himself, made a ton of money, and became a much better player than Rick."

Keating believes that most of Manning's troubles were due to the front office.

"Managers liked Rick, but Gabe Paul and Phil Seghi never did," said Keating. "One day I was in Phil's office, and he was showing me what was wrong with Rick's batting stance, how he held his hands too high. I admit that Rick usually took the first two pitches, and often the count was 0 and 2 before he swung. I also thought he could have gotten a better lead at first and stolen more bases. But I also blame the manager and coaches for not staying on his ass about those things. But the front office set their expectations way too high. Just because he hit .290 one year doesn't mean he'll hit .290 every year. It would have been better for Rick and for them if they had said, 'Look, he's going to hit .260 and catch everything in center field. Let's accept him for what he is.' But they would get down on Rick in the press, it would carry over to the fans, and soon they were booing Rick. It could be brutal. Rick is a tough kid. He came from a poor family. His brothers wore leather jackets and rode motorcycles and got in fights. He was under a lot of pressure that no one knew about."

If nothing else, this last paragraph shows why Keating is an excellent agent. He's not right, but he put up one helluva defense for his client.

The facts were that Manning often was too heavy. He underachieved at home plate. Garcia became manager and continually praised Manning, and stood up for Manning to both the front office and the fans when the bombs were falling. He would say, "Rick Manning is one of the few guys I'd pay to watch play."

Yet Manning didn't repay Garcia. Too many times Manning simply did not hustle. Too many times he jogged to first base. Too many times he just gave in at home plate instead of trying to figure out how to reach base.

"I remember Dave Garcia dressing down Rick in front of the whole team in the clubhouse, saying, 'I love you like a son, but you have to run out those ground balls,' " said Kuiper. "Rick told me later, 'I don't want to hurt Dave's feelings. Maybe I should run them out just for Dave.' But then he'd hit the ball back to the pitcher and become so disappointed, he'd forget to run it out. On defense he never gave up on anything. But at bat . . . I know there were times he wanted to apologize, but usually he didn't say anything."

Manning occasionally would offer the feeble defense that he wasn't the only Indian who jogged to first base, but he was criticized for it more than the other players. Which was true. But if Gabe Paul ripped Manning for not hustling, that story was going in the newspaper. Manning also didn't endear himself to the press when Denise, whom he married in 1980, sent notes up to the official scorer in the middle of the game, questioning why Rick wasn't awarded a hit.

"I guess when you have speed, they expect you to run all the time," said Manning. "I never made excuses. I know when I didn't run something out. But some of these home run hitters, they would pop up and they wouldn't even drag their fat asses halfway to first base, and nothing was ever said about them. Look, the team was losing. I played every day and I played hurt. I know there were times when I made myself look like an ass, but I don't care who you are, you are going to have mental lapses."

Manning signed another five-year, $2.5 million contract in 1982. That means he played ten years, earning $500,000 annually.

"I know Rick's family put a lot of pressure on him to perform, and I think he just got burned out on baseball," said Joe Tait. "Over the years I sensed he didn't enjoy the game that much. He had distractions that also figured into his life. Dave Garcia loved Rick and always backed him, yet Rick would do things on the field that would embarrass Garcia."

Manning was traded to Milwaukee in 1983 and played until 1986. After he retired in 1987, he and Denise were divorced, and in 1989, Manning was signed by Sportschannel Ohio to offer commentary on the Indians games, a job he loves.

Thornton saw the irony in Manning's new career: "I'll say this for Rick: He always talked a better game than he could play, so maybe he's in the right line of work."

While Manning was settling into an average career that would end when he was thirty-two, Eckersley was making a bid for the Hall of Fame and acting as though he planned to play forever.

His only twenty-win season was 1978. In the early 1980s, he also seemed stuck in mediocrity. He was a .500 pitcher with both Boston and the Chicago Cubs.

"What turned my career around was in 1986 when I stopped drinking," says Eckersley. "When I was younger, I could handle it. I was drinking heavily after the Indians traded me, but I also could recover quicker. But over the years it just started to take a toll. I had been thinking about quitting for some time, but it wasn't until I saw a videotape of myself drunk. . . . That was a rude awakening. That tape changed my life. I had been trying to trick people into thinking that I didn't have a drinking problem. It was hard to keep up the masquerade."

One of Eckersley's first steps toward stability was to remarry.

"But the key thing happened when his daughter [by Denise] Mandee was visiting Dennis and his new wife, Nancy," said Keating. "It was over the holidays, and some other relatives were there. Eck got drunk, and it was pretty ugly. They taped him, and the next day, after he sobered up, they made him watch it. Dennis sat there and said, 'That's not me.' He was completely humiliated. He put himself in a treatment center in Rhode Island and came out and stayed clean. Now he's a physical fitness nut. He also does a lot of charity work. He always was a good person, and now that he's stopped drinking, he's a great guy all the time."

Eckersley was traded to Oakland in 1987. He was thirty-two years old and considered a fifth starter or long reliever.

"I was the bullpen coach with the A's when we got Eck," said Mike Paul. "We told him that he was a relief pitcher, but we needed him to make a spot start. He went six innings and pitched well. Then he told the reporters that he was a starter and really wouldn't be happy out of the bullpen. [Manager] Tony LaRussa called his ass in and chewed him out. He said, 'You're our middle reliever unless we need you to start in an emergency. So just keep your mouth shut unless you want to pitch somewhere else.' Then our short reliever, Jay Howell, went down with an elbow problem at the All-Star break. We put Eck into that role, and he has become one of the greatest relievers of all time."

From 1988 to 1992 he averaged 47 saves a year. In 1992 he won the Cy Young and MVP awards with 51 saves.

"Seeing how confident he is on the mound, you'd never guess that Eck is a bundle of nerves as the game goes on," said Mike Paul. "He'll watch the first six innings on TV in the clubhouse. In the seventh he comes to the bullpen, and you can see that he's already churning inside. It is as if this is his first big-league game. Then he goes to the mound and has two quick strikes on every hitter."

"Sometimes I ask myself if I need my stomach in knots," said Eckersley. "But I found that I need that feeling. I love the nerves right before I go into a game. People see me and some of the things I do on the mound and think I'm cocky. Really, it's to cover up for the insecurity. If you act aggressive and cocky, then people think you have it all together even if you don't. I never knew how long I could pitch, but I guess I never thought I'd last this long. After I quit drinking, I went totally into physical fitness. I got hooked on it, and now I'm trying to fight the clock. Things have been so good for me, I don't want anything to mess them up. I'm remarried, and I have a good family. I don't know if I can ever be friends with Rick Manning, but we have sort of resolved our differences. What I found out is that time heals a lot of things, and it has been a long time since I first came to the big leagues with the Indians."

Calling the Action

My first memory of listening to Herb Score was in my basement. It was the March of my youth. In Cleveland there was snow outside, but I was downstairs, bouncing a rubber ball off the wall and catching it with my father's floppy first baseman's mitt.

Herb was on the radio telling me about an Indians spring training game from Tucson or Mesa or somewhere. What I remember most about those broadcasts was that Herb sounded as if he was calling the games from inside a garbage can. There was an unsettling echo, probably due to poor production from some baseball desert outpost in the late 1960s.

To me, those games meant something. They meant baseball. They meant that it wouldn't be long before I could see the Indians at the Stadium.

What I didn't learn until much later was that spring training games were tough on Herb. He can—how can this be said kindly?—become easily confused. In the spring there are different players going in and out of the game every inning. Sometimes the umpires point out the changes, sometimes they don't. Or sometimes they do, but Herb doesn't notice because he likes to sit with his back to the field between innings, working on his tan.

But I forgive Herb. Not because he was hit in the eye with a pitch; I don't remember that. I forgive Herb for all his broadcasting transgressions because he was baseball to me when I was growing up. He has made a million mistakes, and so have the Indians. The only difference is that Herb is good-natured about it all.

On the air he sounds like the nicest guy you'd ever want to meet. Then you meet Herb, and guess what? He just may be the nicest guy you've ever met.

That's the secret to Herb Score. He's a very decent human being, a good family man, a devout Catholic, and a patient listener—even if he isn't always sure what the score is or which inning it is, or even where the game is being played.

But I understand that. Herb Score has seen more Indians games than anyone, so it's no wonder he has trouble keeping things straight. Herb pitched for the Indians from 1955 to 1959. He returned to the team as a TV broadcaster in 1964, and he moved into the radio booth in 1968. That's five years playing for the Tribe and thirty more as a broadcaster.

"Herb Score has probably watched more bad baseball than anyone in the history of the game," said Joe Tait, one of his partners on radio. Maybe that's why Score's descriptions are like no others. Try some of these:

"There's a two-hopper to Kuiper who fields it on the first bounce."

"Swing and a miss, called strike three."

"There's a fly ball deep to right field. Is it fair? Is it foul? It is!"

He called pitcher Efrain Valdez, "Efrem Zimbalist, Jr."

Growing up listening to Herb, then working with him for five years, Nev Chandler is a Herb Score catalog. He not only does some of Herb's greatest bloopers, but Chandler imitates Score's nasal voice perfectly.

"One game we were playing Boston at the Stadium, and the Tribe was losing 7–4 in the bottom of the eighth," said Chandler. "The Indians had the bases loaded, two outs. Andre Thornton hit a fly ball down the left field line. It appeared to have the distance for a homer. The only question was whether it would stay in fair territory. But Boston's Jim Rice went deep into the corner, timed his leap perfectly—I saw him catch the ball and bring it back into the park. Suddenly Herb yelled, 'And that ball is gone. A grand slam home run for Andre Thornton. That is Thornton's twenty-second home run of the year and the Indians lead, 8–7.'

"As Herb was saying this, he wasn't looking at the field. He was marking his scorebook. I saw Rice running in with the baseball. Herb was still talking about the home run. I snapped my fingers, and Herb looked up to see the Red Sox leaving the field.

"Herb said, 'I beg your pardon. Nev, what happened? Did Rice catch that ball?'

"Trying to bail Herb out, I said, 'Rice made a spectacular catch. He went up and over the wall and took the home run away. It was highway robbery.'

"Herb said, 'I thought the ball had disappeared into the seats. Well, I beg your pardon. The Indians do not take the lead. After eight innings, it is Boston 7, Cleveland 4.'

"Then we went to a commercial, and Herb acted as if nothing had happened. I would have been completely flustered. But Herb just corrects himself and keeps going."

That is why Indians fans love Herb Score. He is unpretentious, making his way through games as best he can. He makes no claims of greatness, of being a baseball oracle. He's just Herb being Herb, and being Herb Score sometimes means taking some strange verbal sidetrips. When Albert Belle hit a home run into the upper deck in left field that supposedly went 430 feet, Score asked, "How do they know it went 430 feet? Do they measure where the ball landed? Or do they estimate where the ball would have landed if the upper deck hadn't been there? And if there had been no upper deck, then how do they know how far the ball would have gone?"

Score answered none of those age-old questions of the baseball universe. He was just wondering about it one moment, and then it was forgotten by him the next.

But not by Indians fans. One of their favorite pastimes is to tell one another what Herb said the night before. One of my favorites:

CHANDLER: That base hit makes Cecil Cooper 19-for-42 against the Tribe this year."
SCORE: "I'm not good at math, but even I know that is over .500."

Well, it's not *quite* .500, but I'll give Herb the benefit of the doubt. I saw Cecil Cooper play against the Indians, and I swear he must have hit .700.

In July 1993, I received a call from a friend who said, "Poor Herb. He kept calling [rookie pitcher] Jerry DiPoto by the name of Frank DiPino in a dugout interview with [Manager] Mike Hargrove. But Hargrove never flinched. He just pretended that Herb said DiPoto."

Another friend said, "Those expansion teams are killing Herb. He keeps calling the Florida Marlins, the Florida Mariners."

But what Tribe fans enjoy the most is when Herb isn't sure where he is—what city he's in.

"The most extreme example was a Sunday afternoon game in Milwau- kee," said Chandler. "We had a night game Saturday that went something like fourteen innings. Then Herb met some friends for a late dinner after the game. I went into the broadcast booth about noon. It was a hot, humid day. As I walked in, Herb had the windows closed and the air-conditioning going. He was catching a nap. I did the first two innings like usual, then I turned it over to Herb in the top of the third. The Indians were losing 3–1 to the Brewers. The Tribe went down a quick one, two, three, and Herbie said, 'Well, that's it for the Indians in the top of the third. They go down in order, nothing across. After two and a half innings, it is Kansas City . . . no . . . I beg your pardon, we are not in Kansas City. . . . It is Boston 3 . . . no, we are not in Boston. . . . Nev, where are we?'

"I said, 'We're in Milwaukee today.'

"Herb said, 'That is right. We came from Kansas City, and we are going to Boston. It's Milwaukee 3, Cleveland 1.'

"When we got back from that trip, I saw Gabe Paul in the airport, and he said, 'Does your partner know what town he's in yet?' Then we both laughed."

Score's most embarrassing moment came when Cal Ripken made the last out of an inning, and Score thought he was off the air.

"They're just jamming the shit out of him," said Score, who not only said it to the people in the booth but to everyone listening on the radio. The broadcast finally did cut to a commercial, and when they returned to the game, nothing was said.

"But that one did shake up Herb," said Chandler, "especially since he hardly ever swears even in the most casual conversation."

Score turned sixty in June 1993, and to most baseball fans he is the best of the Indians—a bit bumbling but lovable.

"No member of the Indians organization has done more public speak- ing or charity things than Herb," said Rich Rollins, a former Indians player and former member of the front office. "He has a great base of support because people really do know him personally. Most fans think his broadcasts are entertaining. He'll say that somebody grounded into a double play and end up with four outs in an inning. That will be one of the things people talk about at work the next day. It gives him character."

Or as Jim Ingram of the *Lake County News Herald* said, "Herb is like

Ronald Reagan. It doesn't matter what he says. Everyone just chalks it up
to 'Well, that's Herb being Herb.' "

And what does Score say about this subject?

"When I misspeak, I know it right away, and I correct it," he said. "Once
it is out of my mouth, it is gone. You can't change it. Just don't try to cover
up your mistakes. You're on the air for three hours a night and saying who
knows how many words. You're human. You'll make mistakes."

Some broadcasters listen to tapes of themselves.

"I know Joe Tait does, but I don't," said Score. "I heard it the first time.
I don't need to hear it again."

Score had a more colorful explanation, according to Nev Chandler.

"Herb told me, 'I hear that shit going out. I don't need to hear it coming
back in again,' " said Chandler.

Herb Score is the line of demarcation for Indians fans. Those who remember him as a player also remember the Indians as winners.

"But most fans don't even know that I played," said Score. "They grew
up with me as a broadcaster. That's okay with me. Even some of the players don't know. A rookie will come up to me and say, 'You used to play,
didn't you?' Usually he has heard or read something about it. Me, I like it
that way. I want to be known as a broadcaster."

On the air, Score has an engaging, easygoing personality. He talks *to*
you, not at you or down to you. He comes across as a man who would make
friends quickly, a master of small talk about such things as the weather—
and the weather is one of Score's favorite subjects.

He usually opens his broadcasts with the weather, and he'll talk for a
solid minute about the sun, the clouds, the wind, and the chance of rain. A
minute may not sound like much unless you happen to hear it. Then you
know that Herb has left nothing out when it comes to meteorological details. And during the game he gives the fans updates—very detailed updates.

"Herb once soloed through a two-hour rain delay," said Nev Chandler.
"It was during the 1981 baseball strike, and we were doing the Class AAA
Charleston Charlies games. I'd work a week, then go home. Then Herb
would work a week. Once, there was a game in Charleston, West Virginia,
and Herb was talking about the weather, which was miserable. Then he

talked about the mountains out beyond the center field wall. He kept saying they were 'plush green.' He talked about the river that went through town and the railroad tracks that went by the park. I was driving around in my car, listening to all this. I was mesmerized. Herb never threw it back to the network (to play music until a decision was made on the game), he just kept going, sounding like the Charleston Chamber of Commerce. Then he saw that the grounds crew was out there trying to take off the tarp, and there was another cloudburst. That got to the lefthander. He said, 'This is it. This game is over. I am telling you, there is no way they will ever play today. I don't care what the umpires say, I say that it's over.' With that he did throw the broadcast back to the network, and a few minutes later the umpires agreed with Herb. They called the game."

The weather remains a favorite subject even when the Indians play in a dome. Score will tell you the temperature inside, then describe the weather outside the dome when he got off the team bus. This much is very true of Herb Score: He can talk for a long time about nothing much and do it in detail.

"People who know me now don't believe it, but I was very shy, so shy in high school that I hated having to give a talk in front of the class," he said. "I would stay up all night worrying about it before I had to give a speech. I couldn't put three words together. I was president of the Letterman's Club, but I made the vice president give all the talks. When I played for the Indians, the front office convinced me to go out on some public appearances, and I got used to being in front of people after a while."

But broadcasting?

"I never even thought about it until the Indians called me," he said. That was at the end of the 1963 season. Score was still pitching, with Class AAA Indianapolis, a Chicago White Sox farm club.

"September was coming and [White Sox GM] Ed Short said he was going to bring me up when they expanded the roster after September 1," said Score. "But he also said that he had gotten a call from Gabe Paul, and Gabe was wondering if I'd be interested in doing some TV work for the Indians. I was living in Cleveland in the off-season since 1956, and I knew I was coming to the end of the line as a player. So I asked if I could pursue the Cleveland job."

The opening was created on television where veteran Ken Coleman had left the Indians to do the Browns games, so Bob Neal needed another partner. Paul always like Score personally, so why not?

"Gabe called me into his office to say that there were three games left on that season's TV schedule," said Score. "I did the games, and they asked me back for 1964. I know some people didn't like Bob Neal, but he was great to me. He was a professional broadcaster. The first thing he told me was that because I was a broadcaster now, not an athlete, I had to develop a new identity. Bob Neal was the difference in my career. If the professional broadcaster doesn't like the ex-athlete, he can make you look bad, and you have no chance. It happens a lot in this business. But Bob Neal never showed any resentment toward me. Instead, he worked with me. He gave me the best advice. He said, 'You're a broadcaster now. Don't live on what you did as a player. No one cares about when you pitched. Make your reputation as a good broadcaster.' That is what I have tried to do. I just try to do a good job, get along with people. I want them to enjoy the game as much as I do when I'm broadcasting it."

Until Score joined Bob Neal, there wasn't always a lot of love in the booth.

"In my first night at the Stadium, I sat between Jimmy Dudley and Bob Neal, who were doing the radio broadcasts in the 1960s," said Pete Franklin. "I had been introduced to them individually and had made small talk before the game. I sat between them for two innings, three innings, then four innings. They never spoke to each other. They would talk to me, and I'd talk to them. But Dudley and Neal wouldn't even look at each other. I felt a chill. These guys loathed each other, and they had been working together for thirteen years."

Dudley had been the Indians broadcaster since 1948. He had perfect timing, breaking in as the team was winning its last World Series.

"Jimmy was a radiant individual, and you could hear the smile in his voice," said Nev Chandler. "He was from the South, and he had the personality of a southern gentleman. He had style: A home run was 'going . . . going . . . gone for a home run,' which is now a classic call used by countless guys since then. His double play call was a rat-a-tat 'over to second, one away, back to first, it's a double play.' "

Dudley also was a popular pitchman. He was the spokesman for "Kahns, the wiener the world awaited," and he said it like "going, going . . . gone for a home run." Another of his commercials that most fans near forty remember was for aluminum siding, where he'd rattle off the phone number in a sing-song voice, "Garfield-one, two-three-two-three, Garfield-one, two-three-two-three." Kids on the sandlots would repeat that phone number, imitating Dudley.

Meanwhile, Neal was the Indians TV broadcaster in 1952, and then he joined Dudley in the radio booth in 1957. His tone was sarcastic and distant, a real contrast to Dudley's warm enthusiasm.

What was the source of their feud?

"Neal never accepted the fact that I was the number one broadcaster," said Dudley. "He had an exaggerated opinion of himself. He would talk down his nose at the fans, and he never understood why I was the lead broadcaster. But as I told him several times, 'It may not be fair, baby, but I'm number one and it's going to stay that way.' "

Since Neal is deceased, he is not here to answer his critics. But a lot of Tribe fans felt exactly like talk show host Greg Brinda, who said, "I loved Jimmy Dudley. I hated listening to Bob Neal, and I couldn't wait until his innings were up and Dudley came back on the air."

Nev Chandler said the story that best characterized the relationship between Neal and Dudley is this: "There was a game where Dudley had a terrible case of the stomach flu. Dudley did the first three innings, then Neal did the middle three. Dudley had left the booth and was in the men's room, very sick. The old broadcaster's code is that you don't leave the booth until your partner comes back. But after the sixth, Neal left. Come the seventh inning, Dudley was still sick. For the first couple of batters in the inning, all you heard was crowd noise, the crack of the bat, and vendors yelling, 'Peanuts, popcorn.' Finally, Dudley dragged himself into the booth and finished the game with no help from Neal."

This broadcasting shotgun marriage came to an end in 1962 when Neal went back to television.

Why was Neal so kind to Score? Neal had become friends with Gabe Paul, and Paul wanted Score to succeed as a broadcaster. Also, even if you are the biggest S.O.B. on the face of the earth, how can you not like Herb Score?

I traveled with the Indians and Score for five years, and the only time I saw him truly angry was when he was at the Dallas airport. It was 3:00 A.M., and the team plane had just arrived. He had rented a car from Avis, but the lady behind the desk could not find Score's reservation. Score said he was a member of the Avis Wizard Club. She still couldn't find the reservation.

"Ah, the wizard of dodo, that's what you people are," he said.

In Herb-speak, a dummy was a dodo bird.

"Herb hardly says anything bad about anybody," said Mike Hargrove. "When he does, you know that you'd better listen because Herb is a very decent man who listens more than he talks and just naturally gets along with everybody."

The same could not be said of Neal.

"About everyone in the media detested him," said Joe Tait. "I started doing the Cavs games in 1970. In 1972, Neal's wife died, and I was called in to substitute for him for a three-game series while he was at the funeral. I got these wonderful notices in all the papers, saying how I was a fresh voice and the greatest thing ever heard behind the microphone. It wasn't so much a reaction to my work as a chance for people to take shots at Neal."

Actually, Neal and Dudley were teamed again on the radio in 1965. After the 1967 season, Dudley left to work in Seattle. "The worst move I ever made," he said.

The common theory was that Neal had finally won the broadcasting power struggle and forced Dudley out—and he replaced him on the radio with Herb Score, beginning in the 1968 season.

Score and Neal were together from 1968 to 1972. Neal was in poor health near the end of his Tribe career, and he started saying bizarre things. One night in Oakland he was very excited because the A's were giving away halter tops. Neal's interest was piqued by the women wearing them. Score would be talking about something—probably the weather—and Neal would interject, "Well, Herb, some of these ladies sure look fine in the halter tops." It went on like that for a few innings, Score ignoring Neal's comments. Finally Neal cooled off and went back to talking about what was happening on the field.

Tait and Score were paired on the radio from the beginning of the 1973 season until 1980. In the 1970s the Indians were on WWWE, a fifty-thousand-watt station that, in the words of Pete Franklin, "could be heard in thirty-eight states and half of Canada."

Franklin never said which half of Canada, but the station's powerful signal created a lot of fans, especially because this was in the pre-cable-TV era. If fans wanted baseball—especially fans who didn't live in major league cities—the radio was their only voice, and WWWE was the loudest voice of all. Franklin was one of the pioneers of sports talk; his show was sandwiched around the Tribe games.

"Pete was the only sports talk show host in town, and there were maybe twenty games on TV a year," said Greg Brinda. "Baseball was a radio game. When the Indians made a trade, the fans immediately turned on Pete's show to hear what he thought about it. His opinion mattered. He seemed to have inside information. He was a master at keeping things stirred up. He had wonderful nostalgia shows before the opener, with interviews with guys like Bob Feller and Lou Boudreau. It sounds corny and a lot of guys do shows like that now, but Pete was the first we ever heard in Cleveland."

Franklin was famous for his "funeral shows," complete with organ music and reverent reading. Usually in July, Franklin would proclaim that the Indians were dead, and he'd bury the team on the radio.

"You always knew when that happened," said Duane Kuiper. "The fans would send us sympathy cards."

"Pete was the dominant sports personality in town," said Nev Chandler. "To many fans, his word was gospel. He set the standard for sports talk in this market, and most fans would tell you that no one has come even close to what Pete did since he left [in 1988]."

"The one constant for the last twenty-seven years on the radio has been Score.

"Herb never talked much about his career," said Chandler. "He did like to talk about Ted Williams, how great Williams was and how he could never get Williams out. The only time that Herb's feelings about pitching came through strongly was a day I said on the air that this pitcher had a 'respectable 3.55 ERA.' During the commercial break, Herb turned to me and said, 'Let me tell you something. Any pitcher with an ERA over 3.00 is not doing his job.'

"I said, 'Herb, that's a pretty harsh analysis.'

"Herb said, 'It's true. If they get more than three runs off you, you are not doing your job.'

"That's because not many people got three runs off Herb Score when he was healthy. But Herb would never say anything like that on the air."

Chandler said that Score talked with him about the broadcast for only a few minutes before they went on the air for the first time. He had two rules:

1. Never say "we." The team was "Cleveland, the Indians, the Tribe," never "we" or "us."
2. The game looks easy from the press box, but it is a hard game down on the field. Don't be quick to second-guess or judge. Sometimes there is a good reason a guy made a bad play.

Chandler waited for something else, but that was it—baseball broadcasting according to Herb.

"The thing I believe in is that the players are the stars, not the broadcasters," said Score. "I don't try to be an expert on every play. I like to think that some guy is in the car with his son, and they are listening to the game. The guy will say, 'This is a good time to bunt.' Then the player bunts. In my head I know it's a good time to bunt, but I don't have to say it all the time. Why take that away from the father?"

While it is clear that Score enjoys it when the Indians win, he is not even close to being a Harry Caray homer.

"I want to be as objective as I can," he said. "I hope you can't tell who is winning the game by the tone of my voice. If the game is exciting, I'll show it. If the other team makes a good play, that excites me, too. People tell me, 'You're not critical enough when a guy makes an error.' Wait a minute. If a guy boots one, that's obvious. I see the play. I mark down the error on my scorecard, and then I tell people it was an error. No one feels worse than the guy who dropped the ball or struck out with the bases loaded. He messed up and everyone knows it, including the fans. So why dwell on it? I want the broadcast to be even-handed and to sound like a couple of relaxed guys talking baseball. It's not the opera or the White House."

Peter Bavasi loved Score's approach to the games.

"He's Mr. Positive," said Bavasi. "He doesn't care if the team lost 161 games; he figures they will win tomorrow. He makes a lot of mistakes, but so what? I worked in San Diego where Jerry Coleman once got so excited after a grand slam that he yelled, 'And they're throwing babies down from the stands.' My other favorite Coleman line was 'There's a drive deep to right. Winfield goes back to the wall. He hits his head against the wall! And it's rolling back toward the infield!' What's the big deal about Herb's mistakes? This guy is the Cleveland Indians, and to fire him would be like the Tigers getting rid of Ernie Harwell."

While some veteran broadcasters have been considered spies in the clubhouse and on airplanes for the front office, no one has ever doubted Score's integrity.

"That is why everyone talks to Herb—the general manager, the manager, and the players," said Chandler. "They know that he will keep a confidence. He is a man you can trust. If you were to put together everything he knows, Herb probably has a better handle on what is going on with the team than anyone else."

But Score is from the old school: What is said here, stays here, be it in the dressing room, the manager's office, or the dugout.

"I talked with Herb quite a bit when I played for the Indians and now even more as manager," said Mike Hargrove. "He doesn't offer advice unless he's asked, and I'll ask for it. To me, Herb is a treasure."

"If I ran the Indians, Herb Score would be my general manager, and I'd give him carte blanche to do whatever he wanted," said Joe Tait. "He is the smartest baseball man I've ever met."

Gabe Paul agreed about Score's baseball acumen but wondered if the front office would have been a good fit.

"Herb is one of the greatest persons I have ever met," he said. "He never complains. He is always on time. If you tell him to be there at eight in the morning, he is there right before eight. He is sincere and knowledgeable. But a general manager? I think Herb is too nice to be a GM or a farm director. To do that job, you have to have a little prick in you."

Well, that's baseball according to Gabe Paul. Besides, Score insists he was never interested in the front office.

"I have the best job in the game already," he said. "I have been in the game for forty-two years and with the Indians in one capacity or another for thirty-six of those years. This is perfect for me."

And he treats it as such.

"Do you know that Herb has missed only one game in all of his years of broadcasting?" asked Chandler. "It was for his brother-in-law's funeral. Tom Hamilton [Score's current partner] told me that when Herb's son got married, Herb missed the wedding. He said that they had the baseball schedule, and they knew where he'd be and when he would be off. 'I have to work,' Herb said."

Score's philosophy of life is fairly simple: You never second-guess, you don't look back, and you never look more than one day ahead.

"You owe it to the fans and the people who pay you to deliver the same game on opening day as you do on the last day of the season," said Score. "It doesn't matter if you are feeling good or bad or if you are tired. Sure, you're human. Every game is not an Academy Award, but you are supposed to be there every day, ready to do your job."

Herb Score has done just that.

13

Gabe Paul and the Money Men

Before he ever owned the New York Yankees, George Steinbrenner should have been the Boss of the Indians. At least that's the opinion of Gabe Paul, who recruited Steinbrenner to bail out Vernon Stouffer and buy the Tribe in 1972.

Paul had been the main owner of the Indians from 1963 to 1966, holding together a group of investors; Paul had only 20 percent, but that was more than anyone else. While pinching pennies to keep the team in Cleveland, he shopped for an owner and found Stouffer in 1967.

"When Stouffer bought the franchise, he had enough money to do a lot with the team," said Paul. "He had owned Stouffer foods, Stouffer hotels, a real business empire, but he sold his company to Litton Industries. Instead of taking cash, he took stock in that company. Several members of his board of directors resigned over the move. But Vernon took the stock, which I remember was worth something like $108 a share. Within a couple of years it was down to $8 a share. By the end, we had no money because of his stock deal."

Hank Peters will tell you that the year the Indians died was 1970.

"I was farm director under Gabe, and in our first two years we increased our scouting staff and added another minor league team right after Stouffer bought the franchise," said Peters. "But at the end of the 1969 season, Mr. Stouffer informed me that my farm department budget was going to be slashed by a third. We went from a little over $1 million to $800,000, and that was a major, major cut. From that $800,000 I had to pay the salaries of the scouts, managers, players, the expenses for running the farm teams, and the bonuses for the amateur players we drafted. Mr. Stouffer said to me, 'Is this going to hurt us any?' I said, 'Can I ask you a question? Do you plan to keep the team for very long?' He kind of bristled but didn't say anything.

"I said, 'In the baseball business, there are some things that you just don't do if you want to have a successful franchise. What you do in the area of scouting and player development won't be reflected at the major league level for several years. If you are going to sell the club soon, then don't look back. But if you plan to keep the team, what you are doing is committing suicide."

By the early 1970s, Stouffer was a broken man.

"His stock deal was a real tragedy, not just for him but for the entire family," said Peters. "It also destroyed the Indians."

According to those who knew Stouffer, he began to drink.

"Stouffer was into the booze, and the only guy he was friendly with was Alvin Dark," said Pete Franklin. "One night I was supposed to have Alvin on my show later in the evening. When I went on the air, Stouffer called me four, five times [during commercial breaks] to ask when Alvin would be on. I kept telling him. The next day I saw Stouffer in the press room and asked him if he had heard Alvin on my show. Vernon looked at me like he had no idea who I was. Unfortunately, he had fallen in love with alcohol and lost touch with reality."

So Paul had a majority owner who was depressed, drinking, and nearly broke. He also was friends with some Cleveland heavies in the business world—George Steinbrenner, former Tribe third baseman Al Rosen, and Steve O'Neill. He set up a deal for their group to bail out Stouffer.

"Everything was in place," said Paul. "Jim, Stouffer's son, had gone to school with Steinbrenner. He helped structure the deal. But someone had leaked word to the media, and it was in the Cleveland papers. As we got close to an agreement, we called Vernon. He was in Scottsdale [Arizona] and he was drunk. We were all in the office, listening on the speaker phone. Vernon slurred, 'Ah . . . I . . . um, I'm not interested.' Then he hung up on us. George was going to pay [$9 million] in cash."

While this was taking place, another group headed by Nick Mileti was talking to Stouffer about the team. Mileti owned the NBA Cavaliers, the old Cleveland Arena, radio station WWWE, and a franchise in the World

Hockey Association. Mileti grew up poor in Cleveland but became a master at putting together deals with other people's money and buying things with promises of a little now, a lot more to come much later. Steinbrenner had been involved with Mileti and Bruce Fine in the group that purchased the Cavaliers franchise for Cleveland.

"George had something like $50,000 invested in the team," said Fine. "But he wanted Bill Sharman to be the first coach of the Cavs. Nick Mileti wanted Bill Fitch. Steinbrenner said if Sharman wasn't the coach, he wanted out, so we paid off George. Then Gabe Paul hooked up with George for a deal on the Indians. Gabe was always good at protecting his position, and he knew that he could continue to run the team for George. If Mileti bought it, Gabe would not be in charge."

But the other factor was that Steinbrenner was offering a better deal. The Mileti group could put up only about $1 million in cash. They were going to assume the debts (worth about $5 million) and then supposedly deliver more money later.

"The night that Vernon signed the deal with Mileti, I got a call from Mrs. Stouffer, who told me, 'The lawyers are driving Mr. Stouffer home. Unfortunately, he can't drive himself,' " said Paul. "He was loaded the night he sold the team."

What Stouffer agreed to was so shaky that the American League turned it down. Then Mileti restructured the deal to show that he had some financial legs. Stouffer received about a million up front, the rest over eight years, and he was dead before the final payment was received by his estate.

"Mileti just sweet-talked Vernon into it," said Paul. "Then George, Steve O'Neill, and their group bought the Yankees, and I went to New York to run the team for them [in 1973]. This was a huge setback for Cleveland. The team George wanted first was the Indians, because he was from Cleveland. He planned to spend lots of money to revive the franchise, just as he did in New York."

"I know there was a handshake deal between Stouffer and Steinbrenner to buy the team," said Herb Score. "Steve O'Neill told me that. He could never figure out why Stouffer backed out, and neither could anyone else."

❖   ❖   ❖

When Gabe Paul left Cleveland for New York, Mileti turned the team over to Phil Seghi. In many ways that was like having Gabe Paul still in charge.

Unlike Gabe, Phil was an athlete. He was a minor league third baseman for sixteen years and a minor league manager for nine more seasons. He hooked up with Gabe in Cincinnati, being named the team's farm director in 1958.

"The thing you have to remember about Phil Seghi was that he spent his life as a second banana," said Pete Franklin. "In Cincinnati he worked under Gabe, and Gabe always beat him up. Then Phil went to Kansas City, where Charley Finley beat him up. Then Phil came to the Indians [in 1971] as farm director, so Gabe could beat him up again. I always thought that Phil knew baseball, or at least he knew a helluva lot more about the game than Gabe did. But Phil spent his life working for some of the most miserable bastards on the face of the earth, kissing their ass, and never getting one ounce of credit. He helped build the Big Red Machine and the A's that won pennants. He was the farm director. He signed a lot of great players, but no one ever remembered it."

The thing most people do recall about Seghi is his wardrobe: He dressed like some guy who desperately wanted a part in *The Godfather* but didn't get it because he overdid it with the matching white belt and white shoes routine.

"Phil could have been in the middle of an African desert where it was 500 degrees, and he would still have on a sports jacket," said Pete Franklin. "Not only that, but his shirt would be buttoned all the way to the top, and he always wore a tie. I'm convinced he never even took his tie off when he went to bed. The thing was, if Phil wore a brown jacket, then he had to wear a brown belt, brown shoes, a brown hankie in his coat pocket, and he'd be puffing on a brown pipe. Say this much about Phil Seghi, he sure could match his colors."

Seghi wore his suit and tie, and smoked his pipe when it was 90 degrees in Tucson. Meanwhile, Gabe Paul at least had sense enough to wear a golf shirt, open at the collar, and a huge Panama hat to shade his eyes. Perhaps Seghi dressed the way he thought a general manager was supposed to look. Paul always knew he was in charge, so he could dress like a rational human being.

Seghi worked for two years under Gabe with the Tribe, then took over as general manager in 1973 when Paul joined the Yankees.

Rocky and his friend.

Harvey Kuenn: Don't blame him.

A happy threesome in 1958: catcher Jim Hegan, general manager Frank Lane, and Herb Score.

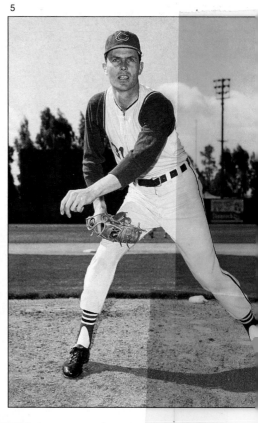

(ABOVE LEFT) Jim "Mudcat" Grant helped set the trend for Indians—traded away one year, in the World Series the next.

(ABOVE RIGHT) Jack Kralick. Who knows what makes a kid pick a favorite player? Kralick was mine.

Gary Bell, with a broad smile of someone who's just been traded to a contender.

7

Sam McDowell was wild and scary both on and off the field. If only McDowell the counselor of today had been there for McDowell the pitcher.

(ABOVE LEFT) Rocky returns, in the worst Tribe trade since Rocky left in the first place.

(ABOVE RIGHT) Tony Horton accepts a handshake from Max Alvis. Note the grim expression on Horton's face, even after a home run.

Vic Davalillo, base thief.

Alvin Dark, Gabe Paul, and Vernon Stouffer in 1970. This was not a happy threesome, as Dark was gunning for Paul's job.

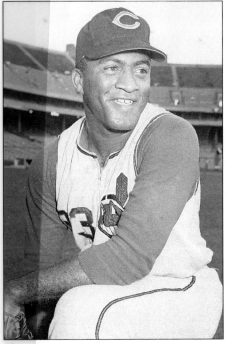

Luis Tiant, one of the great arms of 1968.

Ken "Hawk" Harrelson. Who else would lug so much luggage? Who else would wear that hair? Who else could just put his nickname on the uniform?

14

26

Gabe Paul, for better or
worse, ran the Indians
for eighteen of twenty-three
years from 1961–1984.

Len Barker—for one night
he (and Cleveland baseball)
were perfect.

27

12

Wayne Garland, in his
customary mood. He
became a target of fan
anger, but few athletes have
struggled so hard or tried to
pitch through such pain.

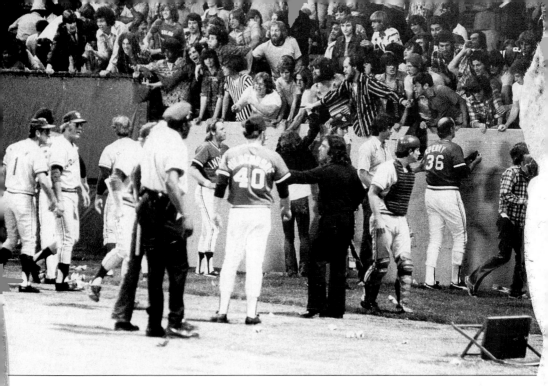

29 In the annals of Cleveland Stadium baseball fiascos, none can top Ten-Cent Beer Night, when fans who'd poured back cheap suds all night poured onto the field, causing a forfeit.

30

Herb Score, by now a broadcaster, with Rocket Man in a 1966 promotion at the Stadium.

Ray Fosse, whose career was derailed by his All-Star selection at age twenty-three.

Umpires just couldn't keep their hands off Gaylord Perry when he went out to the mound.

A swarm of cameras engulfed Frank Robinson as he awaited his first at-bat in his first game as the first black manager in major league baseball.

John Lowenstein congratulates Robinson after he homered in that first at-bat.

23 Groundskeeper Herb Bossard surveys a mountain of dirt in a futile attempt to improve the Cleveland Stadium infield in 1976.

(LEFT) Dennis Eckersley exults in Ray Fosse's arms after his 1977 no-hitter.

(BELOW) Rick Manning (in uniform) and Duane Kuiper in 1980.

24

25

Super Joe Charboneau was a symbol of wasted potential, or fan desperation, or both. But he was, and still is, immensely popular.

Mike Ferraro was manager through most of what I remember as my worst season around baseball, 1983.

Andy Thornton was a rock of class and stability through tough times for the team and tragedies in his life.

All-Star Night, 1981: What could be more symbolic than landing the midsummer classic in the year of the midseason player strike?

34

Art Modell and Peter Bavasi share a laugh after settling a generation-long battle over the stadium lease.

35

Julio Franco's hitting provided some of the few bright spots in the 1980s.

36

Survivor Bob Ojeda wipes away a tear at the funeral for teammate Tim Crews, who was killed along with Steve Olin in a tragic boating accident in the spring of 1993.

37

38

Tribe manager Mike Hargrove, on
the last weekend at Cleveland
Stadium.

(ABOVE RIGHT) Carlos Baerga, now
one of the American League's best
young stars, came to Cleveland in 1989
in what may be the trade that finally
removes the curse.

Albert Belle has rewarded the Tribe's
faith and patience with back-to-back
30-homer/100 RBI seasons—the
team's first since . . . *Rocky Colavito.*

"Phil made some truly great trades," said Franklin. "Jackie Brown for Andre Thornton—that was one of the best in the history of the franchise. Paul Dade for Mike Hargrove, a helluva deal. Jerry Dybzinski for Pat Tabler . . . Phil was at his best making minor deals."

It never was possible to accurately judge Seghi as an executive. Because he was the consummate second banana, you never knew how many of the trades were his and how many were Gabe's. As Bruce Fine said, "After Gabe returned to the Indians [in 1978], Phil was still the general manager of the team. He was also the team spokesman, unless Gabe wanted to speak."

Then Seghi would shut up as if he had slapped duct tape over his mouth. Even in the five years he ran the Indians without Paul (1973–77), the Indians were on the verge of bankruptcy. One of his priorities was to make trades that brought cash back to the Tribe, such as sending Dave LaRoche to California in 1977 for Bruce Bochte, Sid Monge, and $250,000. The one time Seghi did make a decision to throw some bucks at a free agent, that free agent was Wayne Garland, who promptly blew out his arm after signing a ten-year, $2.3 million contract.

To Seghi's credit, he never second-guessed his bosses. If a trade didn't work out, he didn't whisper, "Hey, it wasn't my idea. Gabe wanted to do it." Seghi clenched his teeth down hard on his ever-present pipe and took the heat like a man.

But Seghi also was a horrible second-guesser of his managers. It started before the first pitch, when the lineup was posted. It ended long after the last pitch, as Seghi was willing to replay the game with nearly anyone who would listen.

"You knew Phil was thinking, 'Here I've assembled this wonderful club, and my manager is screwing it up,' " said Nev Chandler.

Seghi second-guessed them all—Ken Aspromonte, Frank Robinson, Jeff Torborg, and Dave Garcia. And all the managers knew he second-guessed them, although Robinson was the only one to challenge Seghi about it. Some members of the Indians front office were convinced that Seghi's secret desire was to manage. One of the few things he would boast about was winning a couple of pennants as a minor league manager. To close friends he talked enviously about how Dallas Green came down from the Philadelphia front office to manage the Phillies to the 1980 pennant. Seghi never tried it himself, probably because he knew that Gabe wouldn't let him.

"To me, Phil Seghi was a weak person," said Joe Tait. "He was a decent judge of talent. If I had been running the Indians, he would have been the farm director, and Herb Score would have been general manager. I'd have given Phil an airline credit card with no limit and told him to fly around the country, checking out every young player worth seeing, then come back in the fall and give us a full report. He would have been very good at that job. While Phil could be a very nice person, when he had to make some hard decisions about Kenny Aspromonte and Frank Robinson, he showed that he just wasn't very strong. I guess I shouldn't criticize him too harshly. He did work for Gabe Paul and Charlie Finley in the same lifetime, and that's more crosses than any man should have to bear."

In the middle 1970s, the Indians continued to search out more and more investors. For as little as $50,000 you could be a "partner" in the team. The Indians had forty-seven partners at one point. Many were instant experts. They hung around the press room, often arguing with one another about team policy. As for getting them to agree on anything . . . good luck.

"Here is how bad it got," said broadcaster Joe Tait. "In 1976 we flew Wright Airlines to our games because no major commercial airlines would take us. The Indians' idea of travel was 'fly now, pay later.' Wright was a commuter airline with two-motor prop jobs that usually went between Cleveland and Detroit. These were not jets. The normal flight from Cleveland to Kansas City was ninety minutes. On Wright Airlines it was over three hours. There was a trip where we flew from New York to Milwaukee, and we had to stop and refuel at 3:00 A.M. in Cleveland. They had to send two planes with the team because they were so small they couldn't fit all the players and equipment on one plane and get it off the ground. Half the guys were in mortal fear of these little planes going down. The cabins weren't pressurized, and the plane wasn't powerful enough to fly above storms. So if there was a thunderstorm, you were right in the middle of it, and you got banged around. One night we were struck by lightning. It sounded like someone whacking a frying pan with a soup spoon. It was deafening, and poor Charlie Spikes, he just started crying. John Ellis was one of the toughest guys I had ever been around—later in his life he became a bail bondsman—but when the plane took off and landed, he would put his head in his hands and curl up in the seat, almost in a fetal position. Guys thought they were going to die on those planes."

Even the buses weren't safe.

"We had one in Detroit where at least a third of the seats were gone," said Duane Kuiper. "They had been ripped right out. One of the players yelled, 'Hey, Bussie. Next time do you think you could drive us to the game with a bus that has all the seats in it?'

"The driver turned around and yelled, 'You guys will get a bus with all the seats when you pay your bill for the last three years.' The players heard that, and the bus got very quiet."

The remarkable thing was that in the middle 1970s, the Indians produced young players such as Rick Manning, Dennis Eckersley, Jim Kern, Buddy Bell, and Duane Kuiper. They traded for players such as Andre Thornton, George Hendrick, Oscar Gamble, and Jim Bibby.

"The team we bought at the end of the 1971 season lost 102 games," said Bruce Fine. "We never were anywhere near that bad, and we had a couple of interesting years. We kept the team afloat by getting a few of the owners like myself to meet the cash calls. We also borrowed as much money as we could from the banks, figuring we'd let the next ownership group worry about the loans. People don't remember it now, but with Ken Aspromonte's last team, then Frank Robinson's, we had some exciting seasons."

In the spring of 1978, Jim Bibby became a free agent because the Indians refused or forgot to pay him his $10,000 bonus for the 1977 season. Bibby had had to continually bug the front office for the bonus he was owed from the 1976 season, so this time he really was running out of patience.

"Bibby had a clause in his contract that he would receive an extra $10,000 if he made thirty starts," said Bob Quinn. "Bibby got that thirtieth start on the last day of the 1977 season. But the contract stated that we had to pay him the bonus within thirty days of the end of the regular season. A guy in the accounting department told me that he had the check in his file. Phil Seghi told him that we owed Bobby the ten grand. The guy said, 'Don't worry about it. We're going to be a little late. We don't have the cash.' For heaven's sake, they didn't have ten grand? At forty-five days, I remember Phil Seghi telling the accounting department that we had to get this bonus paid. After sixty days, Bibby's agent filed a grievance. They took the case to arbitration and won, Bibby becoming a free agent."

This came only a year after the Tribe sent Rick Manning a contract cutting him more than the legal level of 20 percent, and Manning became a free agent. The same was true of Don Hood and Tom Buskey, whose contracts were also handled illegally by the front office. The difference was that the Tribe was able to sign Manning, Hood, and Buskey before losing them. Bibby went on the open market and signed with Pittsburgh.

"This isn't a baseball team, it's a production by Ringling Brothers. All you need are the elephants," wrote Bob August in the *Cleveland Press*.

"Phil Seghi took the heat for the Bibby incident," said Bruce Fine. "He was treated like a bobo, but it wasn't his fault. It was an accounting error, pure and simple."

As Bibby departed, several Indians wished they had been in the same position. Jim Kern talked about how it took three months to receive the $150 the team owed him as reimbursement for his luggage being shipped from spring training in Tucson to Cleveland for the regular season.

"For years the Bibby incident became the subject of a little song we made up," said Quinn. "Bibby was long gone, and one day we were talking about it in the press room. It was about 1979. We were pouring down the Coors, and I was there with Danny Coughlin, who was writing for the *Plain Dealer*. We put together words that were sung to the tune of 'Bye, Bye, Blackbird.'"

Quinn was recalling this incident in 1993. He is now the general manager of the San Francisco Giants, but he broke into song:

Pack up all my gear and dough
Here I go
Ho, ho, ho
Bye, bye, Bibby.
No one here loves or understands me,
Look at that late check they tried to hand me . . .
Bye, bye, Bibby.

Quinn said they had about six different verses for the song, and former Indians owner Steve O'Neill loved it. Of course, O'Neill did not own the Indians when the snafu occurred. He bought the team a year later.

"But every Saint Patrick's Day when the O'Neill, Quinn, and Seghi families went out to dinner in Tucson, Steve would ask me to sing the song," said Quinn.

❖   ❖   ❖

In 1973, Gabe Paul took George Steinbrenner and his money and went to New York. With Paul in control, the Yankees won pennants in 1976 and 1977. Paul's fans pointed to New York and said, "Look what happened when Gabe finally had some money to work with."

Paul really did build the great Yankee teams of the late seventies and early eighties. That was especially true because Steinbrenner was new to baseball and didn't always lay his heavy hands on the daily operations of the team. Paul also had a knack for keeping Steinbrenner away from the neck of manager Billy Martin, and that was crucial to New York's success.

But five years with Steinbrenner was enough for Paul, so he returned to Cleveland in 1978. He put together another ownership group, this one headed by Steve O'Neill, a native Clevelander who had made his money in the trucking business with a company called Leaseway Transportation.

"Steve O'Neill was a lovely old fellow," said Pete Franklin. "Old is an understatement. O'Neill was in the George Burns category. He kept saying, 'Oh, I don't know anything about baseball. Gabe knows about baseball. He'll take care of it.'

"Then I realized, 'Gabe, you did it again. You found another one.'

"Perhaps Gabe's greatest asset was to cultivate these rich guys, making them think that Gabe was a baseball genius. Gabe's wife, Mary, a wonderful person, was a real asset in this. She would get to know the owners' wives; they would go out socially. Gabe was a very good schmoozer. He didn't chew tobacco. He wore great, tasteful suits. To this day I have enormous respect for how he operated in this ballpark. And when he came back to the Indians in 1978, having won two pennants, what the hell, we were excited. At least it looked like O'Neill's group had some money. The other guys were flat broke. They were selling off players just to make the payroll. Damn right Gabe looked good in the late 1970s."

Phil Seghi was the general manager when Paul left in 1973, and he remained GM when Paul returned. Of course, Gabe was president and a minority owner, so Seghi was back to being the second banana.

Paul was sixty-eight when he took over the Tribe in 1978. Seghi was listed as sixty, but most considered that to be a baseball age, believing his real age was very close to Paul's. As for O'Neill, he was seventy-eight when he bought the Indians.

With all that age came a bit of desperation. Paul desperately wanted to win a pennant with the Tribe. He also knew that time was running out—on him, on O'Neill, on everything. Maybe that was why he loaded the team with veterans in the late 1970s and early 1980s, veterans such as Bobby Bonds, Cliff Johnson, Toby Harrah, Bert Blyleven, Manny Trillo—some were good and some were not. Paul and Seghi kept shuffling the deck, trade after trade after trade, but the best they could do was a .500 team.

After the 1979 season, they even tried to hire Billy Martin.

"We got very damn close to bringing him here," said Paul. "Instead, Billy went to Oakland. I always thought Billy could have done for us what he did for the A's [who won a division title in 1981] because our talent may have been better than Oakland's."

While Paul and O'Neill did pump more money into the farm system and while they did take on some players with big contracts, there never was the huge influx of cash that many expected.

"The money was there," said Bob Quinn. "They gave me another farm team. We added coaches at every minor league level, and we upgraded our scouts. But I also felt that Gabe and Phil were a little reluctant when it came to Steve O'Neill's money. They really guarded against wasting it."

O'Neill died in 1983. He was eighty-three years old. In other words, for three years the Tribe was owned by a dead man. With O'Neill gone, the team was owned by the estate of the deceased owner, and it remained that way for three years.

O'Neill's sixty-year-old nephew, Pat O'Neill, operated the team. If Steve O'Neill relied on Paul for advice in baseball matters, Pat O'Neill couldn't find the press box unless Gabe led him there.

Eventually, it fell to Pat and Gabe Paul to find a buyer for the team. The profits from the sale were to go to the Catholic Charities of Cleveland—so, technically, they owned the team from 1984 to 1986.

"You can't say that the archbishop ran the club, but I like to think that he prayed for us," said former Indians president Peter Bavasi.

O'Neill could afford to be generous. He was said to be worth $150 million at the time of his death.

"When all this was going on, Gabe and Phil felt a real responsibility not to waste any money and to get a good return on O'Neill's investment," said Bob Quinn. "Gabe had always been ultraprotective of Steve, and he was the same way with Pat O'Neill. He moved very cautiously when it came to making a major financial commitment."

In 1984, Paul opened talks with Donald Trump.

"He was interviewed, he had the money, and he wanted to buy it," said Paul. "There was all this speculation that Trump would move the team to New Jersey, and that just wasn't the case. But the papers kept harping on it, even when Trump said he'd sign a lease to keep the team in Cleveland. Finally, Trump asked Pat O'Neill to let him out of the deal, and he did. That was really a shame. Trump said he was going to use his own money to build a new ballpark and have a hotel right next to it. At that point he had the money to do it, but the local media never gave him a chance."

In December 1986, a potential owner emerged: Dave and Dick Jacobs, originally from Akron but now headquartered in Cleveland. Their company owned forty shopping malls in fourteen states. They owned Wendy's restaurants in New York, six major office buildings, and five hotels across the country. They also were the heavies behind much of the revival of downtown Cleveland, such as the Galleria Shopping Mall and the new Marriott Hotel. They were masters of putting together deals and of convincing cities to give the tax abatements and other financial incentives to build.

Finally, the estate of Steve O'Neill had found someone to buy the Indians. Paul had retired to Tampa in 1985, but it wasn't until the team was sold a year later that he finally was out of the Tribe picture. He made a nice chunk of change; he'd bought a piece of the team in 1979 for $250,000 and reportedly sold it for $1.5 million as part of the $34 million the Jacobs brothers paid to buy a controlling interest in the franchise. They also assumed over $30 million in debts.

With that purchase, the Gabe Paul era in Cleveland finally came to an end. Paul's influence and his ultimate place in Indians' history are the subject of widely divergent views in Cleveland. Part of the reason for this is that the Gabe Paul the public knew was not the same Gabe Paul known by those who were close to him. Listen to these Gabe Paul stories from men who worked with him over the years:

Bruce Fine, a minority owner of the Indians in the 1970s:

"We were playing the Orioles, and Don Baylor was called out on strikes.

As Baylor went back to the dugout, our organist played 'Bye, Bye, Blackbird.'

"Gabe reached for the telephone in his owner's box. He called the Director of Stadium Operations and screamed, 'Did you hear what that guy just played? . . . He's done! . . . Right now. . . . I want him out this second.'

"Gabe had just fired the organist in the middle of the game, and we didn't have any music for the rest of the night. The funny thing was that no one noticed, which I guess told you something about our organist."

Nev Chandler:

"Gabe had a brand-new Cadillac that he had just gotten from Central Cadillac in downtown Cleveland. The car was due for its three-thousand-mile oil change and service, so Gabe had one of the Indians' go-fers drive it to the dealer. He only had to drive it a couple of miles, but the guy gets into an accident and totals the car.

"The Indians were playing the Yankees that day, and it was before the game. Gabe was upstairs in the press room, hanging around with the writers—he especially loved to hold court with the New York guys, because this happened after he had gone to New York, helped build a winner, and now was back in Cleveland. The New York writers loved Gabe.

"Then the phone rang in the press room. Gabe took the call. You'd never have known that anything was wrong. All you heard Gabe say into the phone was 'Umm . . . hmm. . . . Okay, Joe. . . . See you when you get here.' Then he hung up.

"Gabe came back to the table, and one of the writers asked him, 'Is everything okay?'

"Gabe said, 'Everything is fine.'

"The writers eventually began to leave and go to the press box as the game was ready to start. Finally, all the writers were gone, and the only people left were those who worked in the press room. Gabe screamed to no one in particular, 'Do you know what that goddamn kid did to my new car?' Then Gabe picked up a plate that was sitting right in front of him and threw it, smashing it against the wall. Gabe got up and left the press room as if nothing had happened."

✿   ✿   ✿

Rich Rollins, who worked for the Indians in the 1970s:

"Gabe was always very concerned about how his team would appear when we played the Yankees. We had a Saturday game with them at the Stadium. There was only one week left in the season. We were drawing nobody, but the Yankees were in the pennant race and the game was going to be televised nationally. Gabe called a meeting and asked, 'What is our advance sale for the game?' We told him it was about two thousand. At this point in the season, we just weren't getting any more than three thousand fans. Not with the Browns going full blast and us dead last in the standings.

"Then Gabe said, 'We are going to stay in this room until we figure out how to out twenty-five thousand people in the stands.'

"Bruce Fine said, 'Gabe, just how the hell are we supposed to get twenty-five thousand fans?'

"Gabe stood up behind his desk. He walked into the middle of the office, right among us. He took off his glasses and slammed them to the floor. Then he screamed, 'Well, goddamn it, I said we're not leaving here until we figure out how we'll do it.'

"We finally had everyone in the front office giving out free tickets to any group or anyone who wanted them. For a week the entire front office's only obligation was to give out tickets so Gabe could have a decent crowd and wouldn't look bad on national TV. We gave out over twenty-five thousand tickets. We probably had seventeen thousand fans show up, and we announced a crowd of twenty-five thousand, which the TV network said was a very fine crowd for Cleveland considering how late it was in the season and where the Indians were in the standings."

More from Rollins:

"Gabe was incredibly media conscious, down to where he had to know what writers were in the press room even before he got up there. He would have our P.R. people go up there, take a tour of the press room to count heads, see who was there and if they had brought their wives or if there were scouts from other teams. Gabe would take in all the information, then he'd walk into the room himself, knowing exactly who was there and having a good idea what they wanted to hear.

"Gabe was convinced that goodwill began in the press room. When he returned to the Indians in the late 1970s, he ordered that top-shelf booze be served at the Wigwam bar. He said writers liked Jack Daniels, so we always had plenty on hand. And he also wanted a couple of members of the front office to stay up there until the last writer left after games. One night I was there until two in the morning watching some guy from Chicago do dumb magic tricks.

"But that was Gabe, on top of everything when it came to the media. He knew when writers' birthdays were, and he'd send them cards. He would even send flowers to the wives of the writers on *their* birthdays."

Bruce Fine:

"To the people in the front office, Gabe was always 'Mr. Paul,' never Gabe. He ran a very tight ship, but he seldom yelled at any member of the front office in front of other people. He would call them into his office and then would bellow. When Gabe bellowed, you could hear it from a hundred feet away. A closed door didn't matter.

"There was a meeting with a young man who really did have a couple of dumb ideas about promotion. Gabe started screaming at the kid: 'I don't have any confidence in you whatsoever. None. I don't care how small the decision is—whatever it is you want to do, you come to me with it first.'

"Really, Gabe humiliated the kid, and everyone in the office knew it five minutes later."

Gabe's favorite story:

Gabe loved to trade with Brad Corbett, who was the owner of the Texas Rangers in the late 1970s. "It was at the winter meetings. We had been drinking and eating and talking trade all night. Then we went into the men's room together, and we were still talking trade. We were standing next to each other at the urinals, and then we finally got the players in the deal to make it work and bring Bobby Bonds to Cleveland.

"I said, 'Okay, Brad. Now that we've got a deal, let's shake pricks on it.' "

Rich Rollins:

"Gabe hired Harry Jones as his public relations director. Harry had been a baseball writer in town for years. When Harry took the job, he ordered subscriptions to newspapers from every city in both leagues. He wanted to see what people were writing about the Indians.

"But this was just too many papers. Before long there were papers everywhere in Harry's office, which was right outside my door.

"One day I heard Gabe screaming, 'Son of a bitch.' I looked out my door and saw newspapers flying out of the P.R. office. Gabe was throwing them all over the place. He screamed, 'These goddamned newspapers. We don't need all these goddamned newspapers.'

"He took the papers and put them all over the office. I mean there were papers on the receptionist's desk, in the sales office. He cleared out the P.R. office and had about two months of newspapers spread everywhere else in the team's office. Then he told the cleaning crew not to touch them until the next day when Harry Jones was supposed to be back in the office. When Harry Jones arrived, Gabe pointed to the papers everywhere, and then he fired Harry."

My favorite Gabe story:

Gabe once told me, "If you lie once, then you're a liar. That was what Branch Rickey always said, but he's a guy they always used to accuse of lying."

Rich Rollins:

"One day Gabe called me into his office and gave me a $2,000 raise. He said, 'Rich, we are going to give you a new title.'

"I said there was no need to do that since I was keeping the same basic job. I was just happy to get a raise because Gabe just didn't give raises to people in the front office. He threw money around as if it were lead.

"Gabe said, 'No. A guy in your position needs a new title, a good title. That means a lot in baseball.'

"Gabe couldn't decide on a title he liked. Then he had his secretary bring in the Major League Blue Book, which had the names and titles of everyone in baseball.

"Gabe said, 'Before you leave this office, you're going to have a title that no one in baseball ever had before.'

"I tried to tell him that I didn't care, but I could tell this became a challenge to him. I mean, Gabe spent over an hour going through the Blue Book looking at titles. It dawned on me that he had nothing better to do than this. He'd say something, I'd say the title was fine, and Gabe would then reject it.

"Finally he said, 'Rich, I've got it. This is it. You are our new Director of Administration.'

"I told Gabe that was nice, but what did it mean? He said I'd do the same job I always had, which had been in sales. So I became the first Director of Administration in baseball history—and I didn't even know what it was—and now almost every team has one."

My second-favorite Gabe story:

It was the early 1980s. I was interviewing Gabe about Rick Manning. Gabe was mad at Manning about something. Phil Seghi, who was then the general manager, was also there. It was late in the afternoon. Gabe started to say something, then he sort of nodded off. It took a second for me to realize that Gabe Paul had fallen asleep in the middle of a sentence. I looked at Phil Seghi. Phil Seghi looked at Gabe. Gabe's eyes were closed, his mouth slightly open. Then Phil said that we'd continue the interview later.

I quietly left the office as Phil Seghi sat there, apparently waiting for Gabe to wake up.

When Fernando Valenzuela went to the L.A. Dodgers in 1981, Gabe Paul wanted to know why the Indians didn't have reports on the lefty from the Mexican League. They did, from one of their scouts.

"The scout kind of liked Fernando," said Bob Quinn. "But he said that Fernando was a one-pitch pitcher, which was true. It was the Dodgers who taught him the screwball, which was his bread and butter. Also, the scout said we couldn't compete financially to sign him, which may have been the case. But the scout didn't give us a chance to compete. He just passed."

Paul wanted to know what other players were on that report. There was an infielder named Juan Paco. Without cross-checking, Paul ordered the Indians to sign Paco from his Mexican League team. Price was no object. The price was $40,000.

"Gabe and Phil Seghi sent me to the St. Louis airport to pick up Paco," said Bob Quinn. "I couldn't believe it when the kid stepped off the plane. I called Gabe and said, 'If you think I'm small, wait until you see this kid. He can't be more than five feet six.' For us, $40,000 was a lot of money. This kid couldn't play a lick. Gabe used to call him the Mexican Midget. He was convinced that this wasn't the real Juan Paco, that the Mexican team had sent us an imposter."

Rich Rollins:

"The Indians had a game that went long into the night. The next day Gabe was meeting with [Manager] Dave Garcia. My office was about two doors down from Gabe's. Dave Garcia came into my office and said to me, 'It's about Mr. Paul.'

"Think about that. Dave Garcia had spent his life in baseball. He was managing the team, and he was about sixty years old, but he still called Gabe 'Mr. Paul.'

"I asked Garcia what was wrong, and he said, 'Rich, Mr. Paul has just fallen asleep in the middle of our meeting, and I don't know what I should do.'

"I said I had no idea, either.

"Dave and I went back to Gabe's office and sat there until Gabe woke up. We were afraid to say a word in case it might disturb him."

Gabe's own second-favorite story:

"Birdie Tebbetts was my favorite manager because he didn't care what kind of person the player was as long as he could play. Listen, you don't find ballplayers on church doorsteps. That was what I always believed, and so did Birdie.

"But what I loved about Birdie was that one spring he had an apartment in Tucson, and there was a whore in the building next door to Birdie's. He always warned the players not to go there.

"That was the spring where Birdie had his heart attack. He was rushed to the hospital and taken to the emergency room, where there were two beds in this one area. The priest came in to give Birdie the last rites. He looked over at the other bed and saw the whore in it.

"Birdie said to the priest, 'Father, can you believe it? Here I am dying, and I can't even get rid of that bitch!' "

Nev Chandler:
"You know what I liked about Gabe? He truly loved the game of base-ball. When the team was on the road, I know he'd stay up all night, listen-ing to our games no matter where the Indians were playing. Then after our game was done, Gabe would go across the dial until he found another game. He told me a couple of times that he used to fall asleep with the transistor radio next to his pillow, listening to baseball. This from a man in his seventies."

Gabe Paul was directly in charge of the Tribe for eighteen of the twenty-three years from 1961 to 1984. In only three of those eighteen years did the Indians have a record over .500. Their best finish was a distant third place in 1968.

"I don't care what anyone says, Gabe Paul was a good baseball man," said Hank Peters. "He took a lot of criticism, but Gabe did the best he could with what he had, and what he had wasn't much. Financially, he just couldn't compete with the other teams, and when you're strapped for money, it forces you to make moves you ordinarily wouldn't. I give Gabe credit for keeping the Indians in Cleveland during some very tough years."

"There was a line by Dave LeFevre, who once tried to buy the team in the 1980s," said Pete Franklin. "He said, 'I want to stand next to Gabe Paul when they drop the atomic bomb.' Boy, was that the truth. Gabe was the ultimate baseball survivor. He was a very intelligent man, a great self-promoter, and a guy who knew how to get next to people with money. When an owner needed money, Gabe knew where to find it. He was al-ways the point man, and he'd listen when guys from other cities would talk to him about moving the Indians there. Then the deal would fall apart, and Gabe would take credit for keeping the Indians in Cleveland. For a long time he ran a shell game. He was a marvel because you weren't always sure where Gabe was coming from or what he had planned. He liked to keep people guessing. But when it came time for him to retire, they had a ban-quet. He stood up and said that he was proudest of the fact that he made sure the Indians didn't move. Then he got a huge standing ovation. It was amazing. He had convinced these folks that he was a hero even though he ran one of the worst damn franchises in the history of professional sports, and he ran it for twenty years. Think of all the owners he outlasted. He knew where the bodies were buried. He knew how to make the system work for him. The fact that he was the captain of the *Titanic* for so long tells you a lot about the man, and he probably would still be running the Indians today if the calendar hadn't caught up with him."

Whatever Happened to
Super Joe?

The first time I saw Joe Charboneau was in the spring of 1980, my first year on the Indians beat for the *Plain Dealer*. Charboneau was taking batting practice, launching one rocket after another deep into the gaps in right- and left-center fields. He had a wonderful swing, technically flawless. It was a powerful swing but not the swing of a pure power hitter. Charboneau hit more line drives than deep flies, but those line drives . . . No other Indian hit the ball as hard as Charboneau in 1980. His line drives made the ball beg for mercy.

I have to admit, I wanted him to be something special. I knew that Charboneau came to the Indians camp having hit .350 in 1978 and 1979, winning batting titles at Class A Visalia and Class AA Chattanooga. I was looking for a phenom to spice up the March spring training stories from Tucson, and Charboneau was the best candidate.

Then I talked to him, and he went on about being able to bench-press four hundred pounds and do two hundred sit-ups, and something clicked.

Super Joe.

Never before had I given a player a nickname, but that just came into my head. Really, it was like he was Superman. Super Joe. Then I remembered the musical *Damn Yankees* with Super Joe Hardy from Hannibal, Mo. Actually, his nickname was "Shoeless Joe," so I had my literary references all messed up.

I called him Super Joe even before I knew that he could drink beer through his nose or open a bottle with his eye socket. At the time I didn't know it, but I wanted to create a hero because I decided that the Indians desperately needed one. I didn't realize this until talking with Andre Thornton years later

"What you wanted was another Rocky Colavito," said Thornton. "That was what the front office and the fans dreamed Joe would become. Rocky was a good person, had charisma, hit a ton of homers, and had a great arm. Really, Rocky had far more ability and a lot more maturity than Charboneau. But Joe could have become an icon in Cleveland anyway. This is a blue-collar, shot-and-a-beer town. He was the latest great white hope. The fans tried to make Buddy Bell into that guy, but Buddy didn't have the outgoing personality. They wanted Rick Manning to be him, but Rick just didn't have the ability. So they turned to Joe."

Actually, the closest thing the Indians had to Colavito, at least in terms of hitting home runs, was Thornton. But he was black, religious, and, in his own way, rather shy. Fans loved Colavito; they respected Thornton.

They wanted to love Charboneau.

"Joe fit the image in many fans' minds of what an athlete should be," said Thornton. "They don't want him to be too smart, but they want him to be a little eccentric. They really don't want the athlete to be someone they have to look up to because of his character or integrity. Rather, they would like the guy to be someone they could laugh about, someone whose personality entertains them. That was Joe. He had all the wild stories. He came from the wrong side of the tracks. He had such a hot temper that Philadelphia had given up on him, and the Indians picked him up because they always gave guys second chances. Then he went to spring training in 1980, and while he would never be a great player, he did have a great spring. Say this for Joe: He could hit a baseball. He probably didn't know why he could hit it, but he could hit it."

Charboneau indeed had a super spring—and a strange one. The Indians played an exhibition game in Mexico City. They were waiting outside their hotel for the team bus when a grimy little guy who looked like Charles Manson came up to Charboneau. He had a pen and a piece of paper in his hand.

"Where are you from?" he asked Charboneau.

"California," said Charboneau, reaching out to take the pen because he assumed the guy wanted his autograph. Instead, the guy stabbed Charboneau in the gut—with a Bic pen.

"He's got a knife," screamed Charboneau, holding his stomach as he was falling down. Several Indians jumped the guy and pinned him down until police arrived. Then it was discovered that Super Joe had been stabbed with a Bic.

Charboneau was taken to something called the ABC Hospital, which was supposed to be the premier medical facility in Mexico City.

"The place was awful," he said. "I walked down the hallway, looked into one of the rooms, and they had this guy's skull cut open. They were doing brain surgery, and they didn't even bother to shut the door."

Charboneau was treated and released from the hospital. He had a cut and nothing more. Then he went to the police station and picked his attacker out of a lineup.

"They fined the guy fifty pesos, which was $2.27," said Charboneau. "Then they let him go. The closest I ever want to get to that country again is a Mexican restaurant."

This made for a great story back in Cleveland, and it was the start of the legend of Super Joe.

Nonetheless, Charboneau was not expected to make the final roster in 1980, but in the final week of the spring, Thornton ripped up his knee and required surgery.

"I know for a fact that I was supposed to go play every day at Class AAA," said Charboneau. "The Indians had brought in Andres Mora from Mexico, where he had hit a million homers or something. They wanted him to be the starting left fielder. I would go home at night, and my wife and I would get out the roster, trying to figure out how I'd make the team. By the end of spring training, I was throwing up before exhibition games because I was so nervous."

Mora had a lousy spring, and when the regular season opened, Thornton was on the injured list, Mora was on the bench, and Charboneau found himself in left field. The Indians' first game was in Anaheim.

"I remember walking into that dressing room and thinking about when I was a kid and I used to catch frogs and sell them for a quarter each so I could get enough money for my first pair of spikes," said Charboneau

Along with his bizarre tales, it was Charboneau's willingness to express his sheer delight and awe at being in the majors that endeared him to the Cleveland fans and the media. The bats he used belonged to Cito Gaston, who was a veteran outfielder trying to hang on with the Indians. He was cut late in the spring and left his bats behind; Charboneau didn't have a contract with any bat company, so he gladly made Gaston's bats his own.

"In my second big-league at bat, I hit a home run into the right-center field bleachers [off the Angels' Dave Frost]," said Charboneau. "That was back when they were constructing the football seats at Anaheim Stadium. I know that Sid Monge spent a half-hour looking through all the construction until he found that ball. I still have it. I have two baseballs. That's one. The other is when I hit a grand slam in Seattle, my only grand slam."

When Charboneau returned to his Anaheim hotel after that first game, he found about six men claiming to be agents. They were waiting for him, wanting to represent him.

"I was walking next to Joe into the lobby when the agents mobbed him," said Nev Chandler. "Joe was befuddled by all this attention. He said to me, 'Do you know any of these guys?' I said I didn't. Joe said, 'They all want to take me to dinner, but I can't go with six guys at once. You've got to help me, I don't know what to do.'

"Whenever we broadcast a game, Herb Score and I shared a rental car. I said that we could drive somewhere, and I'd take Joe to dinner.

"Joe said, 'Come with me.' He took me over to the agents and said, 'This is my friend Nev Chandler. He is one of the Indians radio broadcasters, and we're going to talk about this. In fact, I might make Nev my agent.'

"I stood there with my mouth open. This was also my first big-league game as a broadcaster, and now I was supposed to be Joe Charboneau's agent. Anyway, I led Joe out of the hotel, and we went to eat. We talked about agents, and I told Joe that he needed to get an experienced guy, one who knew the baseball business and was smart about investing money.

"Joe told me that I gave him great advice. Then he went out and hired Dan Donnelly as his agent. Dan was a heating and cooling guy who had never represented a player in his life until Joe."

Charboneau wouldn't sign with Donnelly until later, after the Indians arrived in Cleveland with a 1–5 record on the road. Charboneau was only 2-for-14 when the Indians took the field for the home opener.

It was on this date—April 19, 1980—that Charboneau truly became Super Joe to the fans.

"The weather was perfect, about 65 degrees and sunny," said Charboneau. "It doesn't get much better than that in Cleveland in April. The stands were packed [61,753 fans]. I got a huge cheer in my first at bat, and I hadn't even played in Cleveland yet. I hit a three-run homer. We won the game, and I honestly thought that every day would be like that one. That day and that game is my favorite baseball memory."

Charboneau walked in his first at bat, doubled his second time up, and homered in his third appearance. He received a standing ovation following the home run, then he came out of the dugout to tip his cap.

"I was really surprised about how the fans cheered me," he said. "I also know that some of the other guys on the team were wondering, 'Why are they all excited about him? What did he do? He just got here.' I was thinking those same things myself."

The real Super Joe stories were told after the home opener, as reporters began to ask questions and Charboneau responded with truly astounding answers.

First of all, he was from a broken home and had lived in four houses and a dozen different apartments while growing up in Santa Clara, California. Each year the financial condition of the family worsened, and each year his mother moved them to a place where the rent was lower. At the end, the furniture came from the Salvation Army and from rummage sales. His mother was a receptionist at a local hospital, where she often worked at least six days a week to try to support her six children. His father had left the family and moved to Oregon.

Charboneau signed with the Phillies for a $5,000 bonus in 1976. He batted .198 at Class A Spartanburg, and his memories of that first season are pure Charboneau. Making $500 a month, Charboneau shared a two-bedroom apartment with four other players. He would stay up until 4:00 A.M. after games, then set his alarm to get up at 3:00 P.M. so he could watch "General Hospital."

"I used to sleep on the couch," he said. "The carpet had never been vacuumed. You couldn't even see the rug because of all the newspapers, old pizzas, chicken bones, candy wrappers, and other junk we threw all over the place. In the bathroom, the floor mat was pictures from an old *Playboy*. We took in a stray dog called Rat. For a week he slept with me on the couch, then he left. The place was so filthy, even he couldn't stand it, and Rat had mange."

Charboneau said that they once made mashed potatoes. They came out like paste. Not only would no one eat them, but the guys got into an argument about who should clean the table.

"We just left the potatoes sitting there for a month," he said. "When Cindi [his girlfriend and later his wife] came to see me, she threw out the potatoes, and they had mold and green hairs hanging from them."

As you can see, Joe Charboneau stories are not for the weak of nose— which brings up the nose story.

Some players were in a bar, and Charboneau was doing his tricks. He had opened a beer bottle with his forearm. "I once did it with my eye socket, but that hurt like hell and left a scar under my right eyebrow. I never did it again."

Then Charboneau had another brainstorm: "I can drink beer through my nose." Then he took a straw and drank beer through his nose.

That was all in 1976, Charboneau's rookie year as a pro, when he batted .298 with 4 homers in forty-three games. Early the next season he wasn't playing; he pouted, and the Philadelphia front office suspended him for insubordination. He quit, went home, and sat out the rest of the 1977 season, working at a Toys "Я" Us warehouse. In 1978 the Phillies gave him another chance, and he batted .350 at Class A Visalia.

Indians farm director Bob Quinn knew that the Phillies liked Charboneau's bat but worried about his head. He had a terrible temper, was easily depressed, and they thought he had a lot in common with an eight-year-old. Quinn believed Charboneau could hit, and he'd worry about the rest later. He approached the Phillies. They expressed an interest in a pitcher named Cardell Camper, and the deal was done.

In 1979, Charboneau set a Class AA Southern League record by hitting .352 at Chattanooga.

"He outhit anyone else in the rest of the league by nearly forty points," said Quinn. "He also had charisma. There was a picture of him in the local paper where Joe was sitting at a table in the outfield. There was a white linen tablecloth. Instead of wearing a baseball uniform, Joe had on a tuxedo and he was sipping from a glass of champagne."

Charboneau delighted photographers because he'd wear anything and stand anywhere they asked. He just enjoyed the fact that someone wanted to take his picture.

And there were more stories.

- *A Bad Boxer:* He was a bare-fisted fighter in boxcars on the wrong side of the tracks near the migrant workers camp outside of Santa Clara. He fought about twenty-five times for a $30 prize and usually lost.
- *A Bad Eater:* He was watching TV and saw a snake swallow a whole egg, one big gulp. Charboneau told his friends he could do it. They bet against him. He went to his refrigerator, took out an egg, stuffed it in his mouth, and nearly gagged to death. "My buddies kept whacking me on the back until the eggshell broke and I could swallow it," he said. "I never did that again." But he did eat cigarettes for money. "I ate six, nonfiltered. Threw up and collected five bucks for it." He tried to eat a shot glass but cut up his gums and had to spit it out.
- *A Bad Doctor:* He got cut while climbing a fence and didn't want to go to the doctor. He tried to sew up the cut with a needle and fishing line. He also once fixed his broken nose with a pair of pliers.
- *A Bad Dentist:* He once pulled out a tooth with a pair of pliers. He used a bottle of whiskey to dull the pain.
- *A Bad Dresser:* When the Indians came to Cleveland for their Meet the Tribe banquet, Charboneau was supposed to wear a suit and tie. All he had was a shirt and a pair of pants he'd bought from the Salvation Army for $20. He also wore a ninety-nine-cent tie with a shark on it.

"I first met Joe in spring training," said Dan Donnelly. "I owned a heating and cooling business, and I was a season ticket holder and I went to spring training. I also was friends with [Indians coach] Dave Duncan, and through him I got to know Joe. When Joe and his wife and young son came to Cleveland to open the season, they didn't know anyone. I was his first friend here, and I helped him find an apartment, buy some clothes, and get settled in. I wasn't even thinking about being an agent. Right after the opener, Joe started getting requests to make appearances. People wanted to pay him $500 for two hours. That was huge money for Joe because he made only $24,000 as a rookie. He didn't know where these places were, so I drove him to his appearances. Then I started setting up a schedule for him. Other agents wanted to represent him. One day he said to me, 'Dan, I don't know those other guys. I know you. Why don't you be my agent?' I agreed to help him."

Think about this for a moment: Charboneau was literally lost in the big city. He didn't know where to live, where to go to the store, or what to do. He ran into Donnelly, who was a super-fan, a guy with season tickets to every Cleveland pro team. Donnelly had spent a lifetime on the sidelines, watching the games. But suddenly he had a chance to be a part of the game, an agent. And his first client was the hottest athlete in town, a guy who had his own song, with the main verse being "Go, go, Joe Charboneau."

"It's a punk rock song, and I'm a punk rock ballplayer," said Charboneau, who drove a 1955 pickup to the games each day. Donnelly was ready to junk the truck from his heating and cooling business, but Charboneau took it home and got it running.

"This became kind of a fantasy for me," said Donnelly. "That 1980 season was an unbelievable ride for Joe and me. The media was gobbling up Joe. He was featured in *People, Sports Illustrated, Us* magazine, and a lot of others. They all wanted the crazy stories, the eating raw eggs and drinking beer through his nose. Joe liked to give people what they wanted. Was some of it embellished? I don't know. I never saw him do that stuff, but maybe he did. He was a wild kid. I used to tell Joe that it was time to wipe the slate clean, to not dwell on those crazy stunts. I kept telling him that he was living what every kid dreamed, and he had to be careful not to screw it up."

Charboneau finished with a .289 batting average, 23 homers, and 87 RBI. He pulled a groin muscle and was limited to pinch-hitting in the final three weeks, but he still was 5-for-8, and he led the team in game-winning hits. He also became the third player in history to hit a home run into the third deck in left field at Yankee Stadium.

Through it all, Charboneau was embraced by the fans.

"I know that some of the players wondered why I'd go out an hour before a game and sign autographs," said Charboneau. "Then I'd sign for an hour afterward. I wasn't trying to impress anyone. I enjoyed it. I was surprised that so many people wanted my autograph. It never costs you anything to take a couple of seconds to sign your name and be nice to people. It is something you can do to make people feel good."

What made Charboneau special was that those emotions were genuine.

"It was funny how Gabe Paul and Phil Seghi reacted to Joe," said Donnelly. "They liked the fact that he was popular because it helped sell tickets. But during games they would send a go-fer down to my seat to get me and take me up to their box. It would take three innings for Gabe to get around to what he wanted to say, but usually it was something like he was furious with Joe for picking up baseballs that had been hit into foul territory and tossing them to the fans. I know now that they were also cultivating me. I was the rookie agent; they were the veteran baseball men. They didn't want me to forget that, and they loved to lecture me."

At the end of the season, Charboneau was named the American League Rookie of the Year. While he was a below-average outfielder with a lousy arm, he was a strong hitter who didn't seem prone to strikeouts.

"He was a legitimate Rookie of the Year," said Herb Score. "He had the tools to be an excellent hitter for a long time."

There would be only one year, but it was some year. At the end of the 1980 season, he did a Super Joe book. He had several endorsements with Cleveland-area companies. Everyone wanted a piece of Super Joe.

"It was a real whirlwind, one banquet after another," said Donnelly. "Joe was overwhelmed by the adulation. Being his agent was almost a full-time job."

And Donnelly was making a serious move into the agent business. He signed up Indians pitcher Mike Stanton and fielder Von Hayes, the top prospect in the Cleveland farm system. He also represented a couple of second-line football players.

"The Indians thought they had hit gold in Joe," said Thornton. "But anyone who knew Joe knew he was a walking time bomb. Gabe Paul saw Joe as a meal ticket, and he didn't work with Joe on the mental part of the game. But that was because the front office was so desperate for anything they could sell."

Paul and Seghi wanted Charboneau to play winter ball in Puerto Rico.

"They worried that Joe would get fat by sitting on his butt all winter eating and drinking," said Donnelly. "He had weight problems earlier in his career. I thought they had a point, but Joe didn't want to go to winter ball. He had played in Mexico once before and hated it. That was still an issue when we were talking contract. They wanted to pay Joe only $40,000, which was an insult. Phil Seghi told me a story about how he once had a player in his office who wouldn't take the contract offer. Phil told the player that he would put the contract in his desk drawer. When he came to his senses, he could come back and sign the contract, but he should know right now that nothing on the contract would change.

"Then Seghi said, 'And that player came back the next day and signed. His name was Pete Rose.' "

Charboneau ended up signing for a base of $75,000, which was a good deal for a second-year player in 1981 who had absolutely no leverage.

"If the Indians had drawn 1.2 million and if Joe had five hundred plate appearances, he would have made $100,000," said Donnelly. "But this was 1981, the strike year. So all those incentives went out the window."

And so did Charboneau's career.

Some people want to blame it on his swollen head. Others said he drank too much and exercised too little. Joe Charboneau said it was his back that made him the answer to this trivia question: "Who was the first major league player to win the Rookie of the Year Award and then go back to the minors the following season?"

"I thought I went to spring training in 1981 in good shape," said Charboneau. "We were playing an exhibition game in Tucson, and I slid head-first into second base. I felt something pop in my back. Originally, the Indians thought I just strained something. I hoped that was the case when I left the park that day, but by the time I went to bed, my back was so bad I couldn't move. The next day Cindi had to drive me to the park, and all I could do was lie down on the backseat. The first doctor who examined me said that I had ruptured a disc. But the Indians wanted a second opinion, and that doctor didn't think there was a rupture. He said I had strained it, and in a few days I was cleared to play."

But anyone who saw Charboneau knew one of two things:

A. There was something seriously wrong with his back.

B. He was walking around with an ironing board for a spine.

"I knew that there was a bad problem," said Charboneau, "but I was making $75,000, and for that kind of money, I felt I had to play. People don't want to read about injuries. It sounds like a guy is making excuses."

Charboneau batted only .210 in the first half of the season, which came to an end on June 11 because of the baseball strike. At the plate, he stood stiffly and swung weakly, all arms. He looked like a seventy-year-old man with arthritis.

"Joe was feeling even more pressure because Von Hayes had made the team as an outfielder," said Donnelly. "Garcia was playing Rick Manning, Miguel Dilone, and Hayes in the outfield, Mike Hargrove at first base, and

Andre Thornton as the DH. Joe was filling in. His back was killing him. He was really frustrated. He kept saying that he wanted to avoid the sopho-more jinx, but that was exactly what was happening to him."

During the strike, Charboneau played softball for a couple of amateur teams. He continued to make personal appearances. He was still Super Joe to most fans. His daughter was born, and he named her Dannon—after his favorite yogurt.

"The bad thing was that Joe didn't work out during the strike," said Donnelly. "A couple of people who were leeches hooked onto him, and they turned his head around. When the season resumed, Joe was probably twenty pounds overweight."

He looked it and played like it.

"I went to Gabe Paul and suggested that we get Joe a psychiatrist," said Donnelly. "Gabe told me, 'You're his psychiatrist.' So I went to Joe to try to get him to see a doctor on his own. But he told me, 'No, Dan. We can work this out together. You give me good advice. I don't need anyone else.' I knew there was trouble coming because the Indians were pretty disgruntled with Joe."

In early August they sent Charboneau to Class AAA Charleston. He continued to insist that his back was fine.

"Joe told us he wanted to go to the minors," said Quinn. "He wasn't playing that much, and he wanted to play every day. You would watch Joe swing, and you could tell that he had lost all confidence in his ability. Cou-ple that with his back problems, which were very real, and you have a recipe for disaster."

Quinn took Charboneau's fall harder than any member of the Indians front office. Super Joe was Quinn's discovery.

"That first year, Joe was a man among boys," said Quinn. "He was Paul Bunyan. This man hit a home run off the third deck in Yankee Stadium. It was storybook stuff. He could have been Jose Canseco. Then it was gone. He probably lost his stardom as fast as anyone in the history of the game."

Charboneau was a sad case by the end of 1981. He was sleeping on an army cot in the back of the Charleston clubhouse "because I really want to get back into baseball," he said at the time. He had a $1,500 a month mortgage on a new home in the Cleveland suburb of Avon Lake. He also had bought a new Corvette.

"I was probably $15,000 in debt from the minors," said Charboneau.

"While I was supposed to make $75,000 in 1981, I actually made only $38,000 because of the strike. That would be the most I ever made in baseball—$38,000."

Charboneau had back surgery to repair disc damage after the 1981 season, and he even made the Cleveland roster after hitting .330 in the spring of 1982. But that didn't last. He played little and suddenly discovered that he was no longer the center of attention. That bothered him, too. Remembering that he was "a punk rock player," he streaked his hair with red dye. The Indians sent him to Class AAA Charleston. He didn't like it there and asked to go to Class AA Chattanooga, where he had batted .352 in 1979. He thought he might regain what was lost in the town where he believed his baseball career had really begun. But he went 0-for-13 and then shaved his punk rock cut—along with the rest of his hair. His right wrist was sore, and he spent much of 1982 as a bald-headed first-base coach in Class AA.

He was the kid no one expected to amount to anything, the poor kid from Santa Clara who was an underachieving student and a punching bag for migrant farmers in boxcars. Then he surprised everyone, especially himself. When it was gone, he couldn't understand what had happened. *Why don't people like me? I'm the same person I was before.* He did things to bring the spotlight on himself. The shaved head and other stunts were just the newest version of eating raw eggs to impress his friends.

"I know some people said I lost my career because I was a head case," said Charboneau. "But after my back operation, I was a singles hitter. My last year in pro ball, I hit only 4 homers. I ran the sixty-yard dash in something like eight seconds. I had no power, no speed. I'd make what I thought was good contact, but the ball wouldn't go anywhere."

The Indians released Charboneau early in the 1983 season. He was at Class AA Buffalo. His final stunt was to enter a contest with a bunch of Buffalo fans and the San Diego Chicken. At first base were chicken wings, at second base were ribs, at third base were chicken legs, and at home plate were cans of beer. Each contestant was timed, and the one who covered the ground the fastest won all the food and beer.

Charboneau was the best—by thirty seconds. He slid headfirst into the beer, drawing a huge cheer. When it came time to play, Charboneau tapped a ground ball to the pitcher. He walked to first base, was booed by the fans, and then made an obscene gesture at the crowd. He was released a few days later.

"I called several teams about Joe," Phil Seghi said at the time, "but no one would touch him. They had all seen Joe play."

The Pirates signed Charboneau, and he played in their farm system in 1984. He went to spring training in 1985 but was cut. He also shattered his left ankle.

"My body broke down," he said. "Once you've had major back surgery, you're more or less done. I've had two back operations and surgery on four discs. I've had two ankle operations, and have a pin and a plate in my left ankle. I had elbow surgery and wrist surgery. I once added it up, and I have about twenty screws in my body. I don't know why I started getting hurt. As a kid, I was so resilient. Recently, I ran into a guy who was a high school teammate, and he couldn't believe what had happened to me. He said, 'You were so much stronger than everyone else in high school.' I was. I was stronger than a lot of guys in the big leagues, too."

Charboneau said he has only one video of his days with the Indians.

"It's the home run in Yankee Stadium," he said. "Tom Underwood was pitching. The count was 3 and 1, and it was an inside fastball."

Charboneau and Donnelly had a falling out in 1983. Donnelly was dropping out of the agent business. Like Charboneau, his ride was wild but quick.

"Those were tough years for Joe," said Donnelly. "He went from everything he did being right to not being able to do anything right. When he went sour, no one wanted to help him. The bank foreclosed on his house. He had no money. He owed me money. I had signed documents. I could have gone after him legally, but why do it? He had nothing. Because of Joe, I got to do things and meet people I never would have otherwise."

For a while Charboneau was a host and a bouncer in a Buffalo bar. Then he became a liquor salesman in Arizona. He returned to Cleveland in 1990 and started the Joe Charboneau Batting School, which he later sold. Now he gives private hitting lessons to individuals or teams. He also makes a lot of appearances at baseball card shows and for the Major League Baseball Alumni Association.

"We've traveled with troops overseas," said Charboneau. "I've been with the guys in bunkers when they practiced throwing hand grenades. I've dressed up in a helmet and the gear and gone out in the field. I've played softball on the deck of aircraft carriers with navy guys. This has been a lot of fun."

Charboneau is still married to Cindi, but she is suffering from multiple sclerosis.

"I know that Joe has had some tough times," said Donnelly. "We haven't spoken since 1983. For a long time I searched my mind, wondering if there was anything I could have done. But whatever I tried, nothing seemed to help Joe. I don't know. I just wish there was something I could do."

Today, Dan Donnelly is what he was before he met Joe Charboneau—a heating and cooling man and a season ticket holder.

"I was a baseball fan who grew up in Cleveland," he said. "I thought I had the next Rocky Colavito. That 1980 season was a dream for me. But would I do it again? No, not knowing what I do now. The agent business is shark-infested waters. Being an agent hurt my regular business. It may have cost me my marriage. I paid a real price. But at least once a week someone still remembers and asks me if I was the guy who used to be Joe Charboneau's agent. Then they want to know whatever happened to him. But when you think about it, everything in Joe's life was very short-lived."

Charboneau agrees.

"I felt like I was in a dream in 1980," he said. "But it happened so fast. I didn't enjoy it as much as people would think. I was worrying about staying in the majors, taking care of my family, trying not to mess up. I like it better now when I think back on it rather than when it was actually happening to me."

In Cleveland he is still known as Super Joe Charboneau.

"I was very uncomfortable with that nickname at first," he said. "How could I live up to being Super Joe? But then I realized that the fans liked it and thought it was fun, so I found I enjoyed it. I'm almost forty now, and 1980 was a long time ago. I really only had the one year, but so many people still remember, and I get to make a lot of personal appearances and do some radio and TV. That's the nicest part, that people still remember."

Watch What You Wish For

I grew up in Cleveland. I went to Benedictine High School on the east side and Cleveland State University. I didn't need an advertising campaign to tell me that I loved baseball and I loved the Indians.

But sometimes you shouldn't get too close to those you love. So it was for me when I covered the Tribe from 1980 to 1984 for the *Plain Dealer*. It was five long years. Here are some stories from the front lines.

At the end of the 1982 season, Andre Thornton pinch-hit for Miguel Dilone with the bases loaded. Not a bad idea by Manager Dave Garcia, given the fact that Thornton already had more RBI that season than Dilone did in his career. When Dilone protested the move by throwing about a dozen bats out of the dugout and onto the field, I felt he was acting like a spoiled brat and I spanked him in print the next morning, mentioning his RBI totals compared to Thornton's.

The next day, I was in the dugout and Dilone came toward me with a fungo bat.

"Take off your glasses. We fight," he said.

I had no intention of taking off my glasses or fighting. Dilone called me a bunch of nasty names. I told him to cool it. That was when I noticed Garcia at the other end of the dugout. Dilone continued to scream obscenities at me. I thought Garcia might stick up for me since I had done the same for him in the paper, and especially since Dilone was waving the fungo bat around as if he wanted to smash my forehead. Then I saw Garcia get up, turn his back, and head into the tunnel leading from the dugout to the clubhouse. About that time, Sheldon Ocker from the *Akron Beacon Journal* arrived, and he calmed Dilone.

I was more upset at Garcia than at Dilone, who was a poor, uneducated kid who didn't know any better. It didn't make it right, but today I can understand it.

I can also understand what happened to Garcia. His tank was empty. He was like Chief Joseph surrendering. He would fight no more. In his nearly four years as manager, Garcia was often second-guessed by Phil Seghi. Gabe Paul never seemed especially thrilled with him, either.

Garcia would not be rehired for 1983. Instead, Paul turned to Mike Ferraro, a third-base coach with the Yankees best known for being blasted by George Steinbrenner in the 1980 playoffs. Ferraro had waved home Willie Randolph, but two perfect throws by the Kansas City Royals nailed Randolph at the plate. It was a classic case of an owner bullying a hired hand.

Ferraro had a 331–221 record as a minor league manager and, contrary to Steinbrenner's opinion, was considered a terrific third-base coach. He looked like a good candidate for the Cleveland job.

But looks can be very deceiving. Ferraro was hired to manage the Indians in November 1982. Three months later he had surgery to remove a cancerous kidney.

The Cleveland curse?

Ferraro began to wonder, especially when pitching coach Don McMahon had a heart attack. And when Bert Blyleven fell off his roof and was a walking bruise, nearly the same accident as Toby Harrah's two years before. And right before the 1983 season, Harrah's house burned down, his father was killed in an auto accident, and Toby had what turned out to be minor heart surgery of his own.

"I never saw so many bad things happen to one team," said Ferraro, and he said that before he began to manage.

Then it got worse. Nothing that Ferraro had learned with the Yankees prepared him for the Indians.

"The umpires give us no respect, absolutely none," he said. "It's as if they can't wait until they get our half of the inning over with."

When Seghi and Paul called up the immortal Otto Velez from the minors, "the least they could have done was tell me before he got here," said Ferraro.

Velez gave the 1983 Tribe about 33 DHs on the roster. So why promote him?

"He was a house afire," said Seghi, causing reporters to wonder what exactly he was puffing on in his pipe.

Well, Velez was just smoldering by the time he got to Cleveland. Otto was supposed to be a "good pinch hitter," according to Seghi. He was 2-for-25 when the Indians released him. Meanwhile, Ferraro said that Paul and Seghi weren't interested in his problems: "It's always two against one."

Mike, welcome to the Tribe.

The first player to test Ferraro was Broderick Perkins. What the Indians were doing with Broderick Perkins is another question for which only the late Phil Seghi has the answer. For whatever reason, Seghi always loved Juan Tyrone Eichelberger and Broderick Phillip Perkins III. He loved them enough to trade Ed Whitson to San Diego for them.

This was not a good idea.

Eichelberger was a raw athlete someone tried to make into a pitcher. He once told traveling secretary Mike [son of Phil] Seghi that he didn't want a window seat on the plane.

"Why not?" asked Seghi.

"Because I don't want to catch a draft on my arm," he said.

Let's just say Eichelberger seemed to detest everyone with the Indians except Perkins.

As for Perkins, he was a first baseman who never hit more than 2 home runs in a season. The Indians already had a left-handed hitting first baseman in Mike Hargrove, who was a .300 hitter. They also had a million guys who could DH. So why trade for Perkins?

"He's a helluva pinch hitter," said Seghi.

That was supposed to make things better for the Indians? It was like a doctor telling a patient to take two aspirins for a brain hemorrhage. What did it matter if Perkins was a good pinch hitter? Where was he supposed to play? The answer was nowhere, and Perkins didn't like it.

After sitting out the first three games of the season, Perkins taped a paper plate to his locker and wrote "Day III." When he didn't play the next game, he changed the sign to "Day IIII." With each passing game, Perkins added another stroke.

"I guess Perkins thinks he's being held hostage," said Ferraro. "If he keeps that up, he'll need a pizza platter to keep track of all the games."

After six games, Perkins took down the sign. On the seventh day he played, but not well. As for the rest of the year, he rested—when he wasn't fighting.

Yes, fighting.

In the second week of the season, Hargrove was called out on strikes. He went back to the bench, screaming at the umpire. Most of the Tribe players yelled, too.

Perkins told Hargrove, "That was a good pitch."

Hargrove just stared at Perkins, fighting the urge to grab Perkins and turn him into a potted plant. Of course, Perkins saw Hargrove as the guy taking his place in the lineup, and he wanted to annoy Hargrove.

He did. But that didn't get Perkins any more at bats.

A few weeks later, Perkins went into the clubhouse and heard country music. Rick Sutcliffe was playing it. Sutcliffe was the starting pitcher and the starting pitcher had the right to pick the pre-game music. Perkins didn't think so. Words were exchanged—foul, unprintable words. Suddenly, Sutcliffe stood up and went nose-to-nose with Perkins. Then they were in a bear hug, only they were serious. They wrestled across the dressing room until they both fell into Bert Blyleven's locker, and Blyleven and Dan Spillner pulled them apart.

Seghi was not fazed by this.

"It used to happen every day to the old Oakland A's when they were in the World Series," he said.

But we had seen the old A's. They were not the 1983 Indians.

A week after the Sutcliffe incident, Perkins was joking with Len Barker. He threw some ice at Barker. Barker waited until Perkins went into the shower, then he tossed some ice at Perkins.

Perkins screamed that the ice Barker threw had hit him in his eye and that he may never see again.

Barker laughed and went into the trainer's room.

Perkins showed up at the door of the trainer's room, waving a bat and wanting to tee-up Barker's head and knock it across the room.

Barker had about six inches and fifty pounds on Perkins. He charged at Perkins headfirst. They were on the floor when teammates broke up the fight.

The bottom line on Perkins? In two years with the Indians, he batted .271. As a pinch hitter, he was 11-for-69 (.160).

You may have wondered where Mike Ferraro was during all of these incidents. Well, he was in his office. As the season went on, Ferraro stayed longer and longer behind closed doors. He would even send traveling secretary Mike Seghi into the dressing room to get a sandwich and something to drink, because Ferraro didn't want to venture out among the players. He preferred to talk to the writers, telling us stories about George Steinbrenner and Yogi Berra. They were good stories, and we were glad to listen. Besides, we understood exactly how Ferraro felt. He didn't like the Indians players any more than we did.

When you're around a baseball team every day, the players become sick of the writers, and the writers get weary of the players. They begin to pick at one another. You take a jab at them in the paper, saying something factual like "Wayne Garland has a 7.88 ERA in his last five starts." Garland can't debate the truth of the numbers, but he sure could scream at you for printing them.

"Why pick on me?" was the defense used by many players.

Sometimes players screamed for no reason. One day I was interviewing Mike Hargrove. I was sitting in Toby Harrah's chair. Harrah was a hundred feet away, lying on his stomach getting a rubdown from trainer Jimmy Warfield. Harrah screamed obscenities at me for five minutes until I finally got up. He just didn't want some ink-stained wretch sitting in his chair even though he had no intention of sitting there.

"You've got to understand, Toby just has the red-ass," said Hargrove. Having the red-ass was supposed to cover a multitude of sins. A ballplayer could act like the biggest jerk in the Western Hemisphere, but it was okay because he had the red-ass—especially if the schmuck on the end of the tirade was a sportswriter.

If you put your bag and computer down for a moment in the clubhouse, one of the ballplayers would snatch it and hide it, usually in a garbage can. Great fun for them as they watched you desperately look for it. They would drink on commercial flights and become rowdy and profane in front of regular airline customers. I was on one plane when Ed Whitson grabbed Rick Manning by the shoulders and ripped off his shirt. The guys were just playing around, although the nonbaseball passengers probably had other ideas. Another wonderful activity was for one ballplayer to distract a stewardess while another player stole miniature liquor bottles from her cart.

It reached the point where I had a queasy feeling in my stomach whenever I walked into the dressing room, wondering what clod would insult me today and if I should bother arguing with this lower life form or ignore him and try to do my job.

Yes, I understood why Ferraro didn't want to leave his office.

I first met Wayne Garland in 1980, and I thought he was perhaps the most miserable human being I'd encountered in baseball. Baseball clubhouses are often the breeding grounds for guys who act as if they're beginning a life sentence on Devil's Island. They complain about everything, and then they complain because somebody else is complaining too much.

But no one quite complained like Wayne Garland. He never talked, he growled. His face was frozen in a scowl, and he looked at most people as if they were lice.

Garland never liked anything. I thought it was due to the fact that he signed a ten-year, $2.3 million contract with the Tribe in 1977 and then blew out his shoulder. He was one of the first huge free agents, and he was certainly the first free agent bust.

"Nah, that isn't why Wayne acts like he does," Baltimore manager Earl Weaver told me. "You know what his nickname was with us? We called him 'Grumpy.' This guy was a big grouch when he was winning twenty games for me in 1976. I had to run him to the mound four times in September so he'd win that twentieth game, and he bitched about it the whole time."

"About what?" I asked.

"Everything. . . . anything. . . . With Wayne, who knows? And I found it better not to listen," Weaver said with a laugh. "He's really not a bad guy, but he just acts so unhappy all the time."

From 1969 to 1975, Garland pitched for Baltimore, primarily in the Orioles farm system. In those six years his major league record was 7–11.

But in 1976 he perfected his screwball and moved into the Oriole starting rotation. He had a 20–7 record and a 2.68 ERA, completing fourteen of his twenty-five starts. He was only twenty-six years old, and he was a free agent.

"Before the 1977 season, we wanted to do something dramatic," said former Tribe president Ted Bonda. "Free agency was coming, and we needed a starting pitcher. We tried like hell to get Catfish Hunter [in 1975]. We made trips to his home. We had Gaylord Perry call him on our behalf, because Gaylord and Catfish were good friends from North Carolina."

But Hunter signed with the Yankees—with George Steinbrenner, Gabe Paul, and the Yankees.

"We really finished second to New York in signing Catfish," said Bonda.

Maybe the Indians did. But free agency is not like hand grenades—close isn't good enough, although being "second" to another team in the bidding would become a common theme for the Indians in the free agent era. Supposedly they were second on Dave Winfield (who went to New York) and even second in line to hire Billy Martin as manager (to Oakland).

So the Indians wanted Garland, who had earned $19,000 in 1976 when he won the twenty games. He was hoping to make about $40,000 the next season before he discovered the free agency game. Each team was asked to make one sealed bid to Garland's agent, and he'd accept the best one. The Indians wrote the numbers $230,000 and ten years on a contract. It was $230,000 annually for ten years, a total of $2.3 million. This was when the average salary was $50,000 and an All-Star hoped to make $100,000.

"I was flabbergasted," said Garland. "The last thing I expected was that kind of money. I never asked for that much. I never even dreamed I'd make that much. But what was I supposed to do, give it back?"

Garland signed.

He dismissed jokes about playing in Cleveland by saying, "For that kind of money, I'd have played in Siberia."

When the signing was announced, Phil Seghi said, "No one is worth $2 million, but we could spend $2 million on our farm system and not come up with a twenty-game winner."

The question was: Where did the Indians find the cash? Remember, these were Nick Mileti's Indians.

"We could be somewhat reckless about it," said Bonda. "We'd get it, then think about paying it back later."

Bruce Fine offered this explanation: "Ted Bonda never worried about a big contract that went out for a long time. He'd say, 'Why worry? We won't be around to pay it all anyway.' We operated by borrowing money and figuring that the next owner would pay it back. Besides, Garland looked like a good investment. He was only twenty-six, he had already won twenty games, and we thought he'd be a twenty-game winner for the next ten years."

As usual, the Indians thought wrong. Garland injured his arm in his first spring training game with the Indians. Yes, his first *spring training* game!

It was a windy, cold day in Tucson. As Garland warmed up, his arm felt stiff. He thought he'd "throw through it." He pitched, and the arm went from stiff to sore. But Garland kept pitching, and his arm kept getting weaker and worse.

He was the two-million-dollar man when those numbers meant something. He even wore number 23 for a while, which fans immediately associated with the $2.3 million contract. He was booed, and his gloomy personality turned to one of doom.

One of the best Garland stories involved his former wife, Mary. A fan screamed, "Hey, Wayne, give me a buck." It went on all night, and the fan was only a few rows away from Mary Garland at the Stadium.

He yelled, "Hey, Wayne, give me a buck," for about the hundredth time as Garland walked off the mound at the end of an inning.

Mary Garland had heard enough. She approached the man, handed him a dollar, and said, "Here. I'm Wayne's wife."

Garland had another nickname, "Bulldog," because the man could be very stubborn, and that was the case in 1977. He pitched with a bad arm, and he kept pitching. Garland started thirty-eight games, completed twenty-one of them, and somehow gritted his teeth and threw 283 painful innings. His final record was 13–19 with a 3.59 ERA. A sidelight was that he made three late-season starts that could have meant defeat number twenty. He didn't lose any of those games because he was determined not to go from a twenty-game winner to a twenty-game loser in one season.

Given his physical condition, that 1977 performance was more impressive than his twenty wins in 1976. But it probably cost him his career. By the end of the season his arm was a slab of meat. It required major rotator cuff surgery. If he had stopped pitching early in 1977 and had the operation sooner, would it have made a difference? Would the damage have been less severe and more likely to heal? Garland could never answer those questions. Nor did he think about them in 1977. All he wanted to do was prove that he was worth the money. If he couldn't be a $2.3 million pitcher in terms of production, he could give $2.3 million in effort.

Coming back from the surgery, Garland was 15–29 in four years before being released at the end of the 1981 season. He tried everything: starting, relieving, even a knuckleball. At first the Cleveland fans were highly critical of him, especially after buying a $775,000 mansion in the exclusive Cleveland suburb of Gates Mills. It was a fifteen-room stone home on twenty-two acres. He had a tennis court, swimming pool, riding stables, and two smaller homes where maids could live. His down payment was $250,000. He put $65,000 in escrow and had a $450,000 mortgage. The house became as much a burden to Garland as his arm. He ended up in a nasty lawsuit with the former owners, and it served as a sign to Tribe fans that Garland had let the money spoil him.

But when the fans saw him coming back and coming back, they cheered the few good moments he had and usually shrugged at the failures. When the Indians cut him loose, it was regarded more as a tragedy than a mistake, another rotten piece of Cleveland luck.

While he was still a miserable S.O.B. to deal with, I found myself looking at him with a feeling of grudging admiration.

The Indians had quite a few guys whose elevators got stuck between floors, guys like Jerry Willard. He was one of five players the Indians received from Philadelphia in the Von Hayes deal of 1982. He played parts of 1984 and 1985 with the Tribe and didn't exactly distinguish himself—at least not unless you knew Willard.

When he complained of a sore throat and was told to gargle with salt and lukewarm water, Willard asked, "Where do you get lukewarm water?"

When Willard was told that a bond issue was on the ballot for June to raise money for a domed stadium, he asked, "If it passes, can we play in it by the end of the season?"

✧   ✧   ✧

In Kevin Rhomberg, the Indians may have had the most touchy-feely player in the history of baseball. Rhomberg had these eccentricities:

"He wouldn't make a right turn," said Mike Hargrove. "I mean when he was walking or running. I never saw him drive, but if he had to go right, he would make several lefts until he got there. I guess making left turns was okay because he needed to make left turns to run the bases."

There was more.

"He had this thing where if you touched him, then he would have to touch you back," said Hargrove. "It got out of hand. Guys would run up to Kevin, touch him, and run away, and Kevin would have to run them down to touch them back; he couldn't go on with what he was doing until he touched them. All this touching and not touching, and no left turns, it made me really nervous. I liked Kevin as a person, but when I saw him coming toward me, I went to the other side of the room."

There was even more.

"If you touched Rhomberg and he didn't get you back and it was the end of the season, then you'd get a letter from him," said Sheldon Ocker of the *Akron Beacon Journal*. "The letter would say, 'Because I touched this letter and now you have it in your hands, consider yourself touched back.'"

The Indians brought up a player from the minors named Rodney Craig. He wore a batting helmet that was something like a size 9.

The players called him "Buckethead."

He was also supposed to be a great pinch hitter—he went 2-for-19.

The Indians once had a pitcher named Bob Lacey who got fat during the 1981 baseball strike. His plan for losing weight was to drive to the Stadium in August with the windows of his car rolled up and the heat on full blast, making it a sauna on wheels.

Right before the Indians traded for Lacey, Oakland manager Billy Martin was so fed up with the lefty that he would not pitch him in spring training. In fact, he ordered that no one even play catch with Lacey.

So during an exhibition game, Lacey went to the bullpen, put on his glove, and pretended he was warming up. He wound up, mimed throwing the baseball, then pretended to receive a throw back from the catcher. Then he did it again and again and again.

The Indians had a utility man named Ron Pruitt. One day Pruitt stood up for the national anthem; when he took off his cap, he was wearing a rubber conehead.

Pruitt and a pitcher named Victor Cruz once got into a fight in the back of an airplane. They were playfully pushing each other, then started throwing punches while normal passengers (it was a commercial flight) watched in fascination.

Manager Dave Garcia was sitting at the front of the plane. Later, he said, "I never saw it, so as far as I'm concerned, it never happened."

That often was Garcia's approach to discipline.

As for Cruz, he once told me, "You know, umpires never like me. Those umpires, they are vampires."

Cruz was also the only ballplayer I ever saw who had tattoos on the inside of his fingers and the tops of his thighs.

The Indians had a pitcher named Ray Searage. His nickname was, naturally, "Raw Sewage." And that wasn't even the worst pitcher's-name story.

They also had a pitcher named Bob Owchinko. When they played an exhibition game against a Japanese team, the Japanese reporters broke into loud laughter when Owchinko was announced.

Why?

"Because his name means 'little penis' in Japanese," said a Japanese scribe.

The Indians had a second baseman named Jack Perconte who had problems in the field. Coach John Goryl blamed it on Perconte's "stubby fingers." When Perconte was traded to Seattle, Gabe Paul told reporters that Perconte struggled "because he has a mental block."

"Yeah, and that block is right in the middle of his glove," said Manager Pat Corrales.

Paul just glared at Corrales as reporters wrote down the exchange.

The only Indian who loved to second-guess managers more than Phil Seghi was Toby Harrah. One day Ferraro found Harrah in his street clothes in the clubhouse while the rest of the team was on the field for batting practice.

"Hey, Toby, get dressed and get out there," said Ferraro.

"No rookie manager is going to tell me what to do," said Harrah.

The two men screamed at each other for a while. Then Harrah delivered the killer line: "I'll be around here longer than you."

He was right.

Later, Harrah would say, "There is a fog over this team."

He would be right about that, too.

The Indians hired former Cleveland Browns wide receiver Reggie Rucker to supply expert analysis on their TV broadcasts.

Only the Indians would do that.

And only Rucker would second-guess Ferraro by saying, "When there is a runner on third, I'd put an outfielder *behind* the catcher in order to prevent a wild pitch."

The idea is not only stupid, it's illegal; only the catcher may line up in foul territory.

Rucker's broadcasting partner, Joe Tait, could only shake his head and pretend he didn't hear it.

I couldn't exactly say I had any terrific times covering the Indians. I can say that when I think about covering baseball at its absolute worst, I think about 1983. I hated even thinking about going out to the Stadium every day. The team wasn't just bad, it was a miserable group of human beings. The manager, Mike Ferraro, was in an almost constant state of depression. "Of course, the poor guy had just lost a kidney to cancer," points out Mike Hargrove, "so who knows what that did to his state of mind."

Ferraro must have known things were slipping away from him almost from the start. "We had just lost a Sunday game," Hargrove recalls, "and before the Monday night game, Ferraro called a team meeting, and he really chewed us out. Right out of the clear blue sky, he said we were a bunch of losers, that we didn't dress like big leaguers and we didn't play like big leaguers. He went on and on. He said we had no team leaders, that none of us had the guts to be a leader." The team's record at that point was 4–4.

"It was the kind of speech you give when your team is in trouble, not when it's 4–4," Hargrove continued. "That really fried me, and the guys on the team lost a lot of respect for Ferraro that day. It was the only time in my career that I wanted to challenge a manager, and to this day I wish I had."

The fall of Mike Ferraro was one of the saddest things I saw with the Tribe. The end came on July 6 in Kansas City. The Indians lost to the Royals, 6–1. But what astounded Ferraro was that his entire team ran off the field with two outs in the sixth inning. Neal Heaton walked lead-off hitter Hal McRae. Then Amos Otis grounded into a double play, and the Indians ran for the dugout. But that was only two batters and two outs.

"It was the kind of double play that usually ends an inning," Hargrove recalled ten years later. "I caught the ball at first, rolled it to the mound, and the whole team just followed me into the dugout. They had to call us back on the field. I told [coach] Johnny Goryl, 'That has to change Ferraro's mind about us having no leaders. I led the whole team right off the field.' It was just crazy."

Ferraro agreed.

After that July 26 game, he sat quietly in his clubhouse office. He had a deck of cards in front of him, and he was playing solitaire.

"How are you supposed to win when you don't know how many outs there are?" asked Ferraro, flipping down two cards.

"From the dugout we were shouting that there were only two outs," he said, flipping over another card.

"I know we have a lot of unhappy guys, guys who would rather play somewhere else," he said, "but that is out of my hands. In New York we had a take-charge guy like Graig Nettles in the infield. He constantly reminded guys of the situation. But here . . ."

Then Ferraro put down the cards and looked at me.

"After a while," he said, "when you lose so much, it becomes almost like winning. Some of these guys have been in Cleveland a long time. It has been losing and more losing. You begin to feel like you're in a traveling circus, just going from one town to another. Winning, losing, it doesn't matter."

Ferraro kept talking about the lines blurring between winning and losing. It sounded like Zen. Winning is losing. Losing is winning. Everything means something. Everything means nothing.

Then he stared at the cards and said, "I can't even win at this game."

Three days later Gabe Paul mercifully fired Ferraro. I wish I could have gone out the door with him.

Ferraro was put out of his misery after a hundred games, and Pat Corrales took over as manager for the rest of the '83 season. The team played nearly .500 ball the rest of the way, but it did nothing to lighten the gloom. Nearly everyone on the roster wanted to be traded. Bert Blyleven was only the first to go public. Then came my good friend Miguel Dilone, who said, "I bat .341, and they treat me like a nobody." Then the man cried. He honest to goodness broke down and wept. "Get me out of here," he pleaded.

It was back in 1980 that Dilone hit .341. In 1983 he was batting .191. The Indians did get him out of there; they sent him to the Class AAA Charleston Charlies.

Then Len Barker said he wanted to be traded. The next day Lary Sorensen said, "You can take everything Lenny just said about wanting to be traded and put my name on it."

That's when you know a team is dismal—when they can't come up with their own "trade me" quotes.

Mention Lenny Barker and two great contributions come to mind. The first is that, for one game, Barker was perfect.

The night was Friday, May 15, 1981. The Indians were playing the Toronto Blue Jays. At this point in his career, Barker was one of the best young pitchers in baseball. In 1980 he was 19–12 with a 4.17 ERA and led the league with 187 strikeouts in 246 innings. He was only twenty-five years old.

The Indians thought that one day he might throw a no-hitter because his fastball was clocked at ninety-five miles per hour.

But a perfect game? As in no walks?

Only three years before his perfect game, Barker uncorked a fastball that landed halfway up the screen behind home plate at Fenway Park. And when he was in the Texas farm system, he unleashed a pitch that flew *over* the backstop and banged against the tower that stood in the middle of four diamonds at the Rangers' minor league complex. There was also the pitch that ended up in the press box at Sacramento.

A perfect game from Lenny Barker?

For a while there was some doubt about Barker even making the majors. He was a guy who liked to party and liked to drink. One night in a Plant City, Florida, watering hole, Barker had a few beers. Okay, a lot of beers. Then he picked up a huge bar and threw it against the door, knocking the door down. Legend was that Barker hid under a bed when the police arrived at the Rangers' spring training hotel looking for him.

In one of his best deals with Texas, Gabe Paul picked up Barker and Bobby Bonds for Larvell Blanks and Jim Kern after the 1978 season. The irony was that the Indians wanted Dock Ellis instead of Barker, but Pat Corrales was managing Texas and wanted to keep Ellis. So Barker was shipped out, primarily because he was a wild man on and off the field.

By the time of Barker's perfect game, Dock Ellis was out of baseball.

"Lenny went into that night as a guy who was known as a great seven-inning pitcher," said Nev Chandler. "Then he'd get tired, and they'd have to get him out of there. I broadcast the perfect game with Herb Score. Herb and I had talked about Lenny throwing a no-hitter one day. It was not uncommon for him to go into the fifth or sixth inning without allowing a hit, but then something would always happen to him."

But not on May 15, 1981.

"It was cold and gray with a slight drizzle when the game began," said Chandler. "Lenny was throwing hard as usual, but what was making him a good pitcher was that he had developed a sharp curve."

"Not only was it a good curve," said Score, "he found how to get it over the plate. The night of the perfect game, it was the curve that was his bread-and-butter pitch."

There were only 7,290 at the Stadium that night. The Indians and Blue Jays were the two worst teams in the American League East. The weather was awful, game-time temperature being 47 degrees and dropping into the thirties before the final out.

Why go, especially since the game was carried on local Cleveland TV? Who would have believed, Lenny Barker, a perfect game?

"Not me," said Barker. "That was one of the most unreal days of my life. I knew that I had good stuff, maybe even awesome stuff, when I began the game. But as the game went on, I had total command. I could throw anything, anywhere I wanted."

Barker's fastball averaged ninety-one miles per hour.

"For me, that wasn't anything special," he said. "But my curveball, my curveball was something else."

That's because his curveball was nearly eighty miles per hour. Not only did it break big, it broke hard. Over 70 percent of Barker's pitches were curveballs. His control was so astounding that he never had three balls on a batter, nor did he throw more than five pitches out of the strike zone in any inning. None of the balls was hit hard off him. He fanned eleven, all of them swinging. Instead of getting tired, he struck out eleven of the final seventeen men he faced. None of his first ten outs was a strikeout. Forty of his last fifty-seven pitches were curves as the Indians won, 3–0.

"When I went out to the mound for the ninth inning, my legs were shaking," said Barker. "I kept telling myself to throw strikes and keep the ball low." The final three outs were a pop-up to third by Rick Bosetti, a strikeout by pinch hitter Al Woods, and, finally, pinch hitter Ernie Whitt hit a fly ball that was caught by an excited Rick Manning in center.

"I never even looked back over my shoulder when I saw the ball was going to center," said Barker. "I knew Rick would catch it. He caught everything hit to center field."

"I wanted that ball to be hit to me," said Manning. "I was begging for it, especially when Lenny needed one more out. I knew if it was hit anywhere close to me, I'd get it. As the ball came down into my glove, I caught it and said out loud, 'Thank you very much.' "

In the dressing room, the Indians made a path to his locker out of towels, the poor man's red-carpet treatment. On his chair were six beer cans shaped in a huge O. At his locker were three bottles of champagne. Barker opened each bottle, took a slug, and then passed it around—three up, three down, just as in the ball game.

That was the twelfth perfect game in major league history, the first since Catfish Hunter's in 1968. For Lenny Barker, it never came anywhere close to being that good again.

He was 8–7 for the Indians in the strike-marred 1981 season, then 15–11 in 1982. By the end of that season, he began having elbow problems but wouldn't admit it. Manager Dave Garcia called Barker the "Big Donkey," and his stubbornness was evident on this subject. He had a bone spur in his elbow but was reluctant to have it surgically removed when it first appeared. Even in the good years of 1980–82 when his record was 42–30 for a sixth-place team, Barker's right elbow was always swollen. But he'd insist that it "only hurt after I pitched." Then his fastball dropped from over ninety miles per hour in 1982 to the middle eighties in 1983.

I mentioned two contributions. The second one was in late August 1983 when Gabe Paul and Phil Seghi traded Barker to Atlanta for Brett Butler, Brook Jacoby, and Rick Behenna in one of their best deals ever. Barker was on the verge of free agency and not interested in re-signing with the Indians. Nor was the Tribe excited about paying big bucks to a guy with a bum arm.

Atlanta figured one more pitcher would make the difference in a tight pennant race. Barker went 1–3 for them, and they finished three games behind the Dodgers. The Braves gave Barker a four-year, $4 million contract. He eventually had elbow surgery, pitched erratically for a few years, and then his career was over.

The day after Barker's perfect game, a Dallas scribe wrote, "How can it be perfect if it happened in Cleveland?" That was a cheap shot, but it is truly a wonder that it happened to Lenny Barker.

What was the worst trade Gabe Paul ever made with the Indians?

"It was the Cliff Johnson deal," said Paul.

Say what, Gabe? Cliff Johnson for Karl Pagel wasn't great, but what about the Dennis Eckersley deal? Or even Ed Whitson for Broderick Perkins and Juan Eichelberger?

No matter. That's Gabe's opinion.

"Whenever I saw Cliff, he'd put his arm around me and say how he loved listening to me," said Pete Franklin. "He said that I became his hero when he heard me call a woman a 'bitch' on the air one night."

Johnson missed the first month of spring training in 1980 when he broke his right middle finger unloading a barrel of oats off a truck at his ranch in San Antonio. Johnson said he was hurt and refused to report to camp. When he finally did show up, the right middle finger was in a splint, pointing straight up as if it were his message to the world.

Johnson was the Indians' DH for about a year, and his idea of a pregame workout was to sit in the dugout with a cup of coffee and a cigarette and watch batting practice. I don't think he even owned a glove. No one in Cleveland ever saw him wear one.

"Cliff used to call me Uncle Ugly," said Mike Hargrove, "but I always thought about what Graig Nettles told me. He said that Cliff was 'the only man on earth who needed to have his eyes circumcised.' "

Duane Kuiper had three favorite Cliff Johnson stories:

Number One: "We had a Saturday afternoon game in Cleveland. It was raining, and there were only a few thousand people in the stands. About ten rows behind the dugout there was this puny, nerdy guy, and he was all over Cliff. The guy had an umbrella. Cliff struck out a couple of times in the game, and when he came back to the dugout, the fan was standing up, screaming and pointing his umbrella at Cliff. In the eighth inning, Cliff was taken out of the game. He went into the dressing room, changed into his street clothes, and then went into the stands. He sat right behind the guy with the umbrella. The guy had the umbrella hooked on the railing. Cliff took the umbrella, snapped it over his leg, and handed it to the guy, who was about ready to die. He told the guy, 'Young man, when Cliff Johnson is batting, he needs all the concentration he can. He doesn't need you yelling names at him.' Then Cliff got up and walked back into the clubhouse."

Number Two: "There was another game where the fans were all over Cliff. When Cliff made an out, he would jog back to the dugout right next to the stands on the first base side, almost daring the fans to say something. In this game they were screaming at him for popping out to end an inning. But there was a little girl in the first row who said something nice as Cliff went by. He stopped, picked her up, and said, 'Young lady, you are the breath of fresh air that I need.' Then he gave her a kiss and put her back down."

Number Three: "It was 1979, and Dave Garcia had been named manager at mid-season, taking over for Jeff Torborg. Dave called a team meeting, and he was telling us what he expected from the team. Throughout his speech Cliff was mumbling about not playing enough, just trying to agitate as Cliff liked to do. Garcia said something to Cliff. Then Cliff stood up and took a step toward Garcia. At that moment [pitching coach] Dave Duncan charged Johnson, tackled him, and threw Cliff right into his locker. Cliff was on his back and Duncan was standing over him, daring Cliff to do something. Cliff shut up, and that was the day that Dave Duncan became Dave Garcia's very best friend in the world."

One last Cliff Johnson story:

He was upset at me for daring to write that a player should know how many outs there are. Cliff had forgotten to tag up at third base. He could have scored the winning run on a sacrifice fly if he had tagged up; instead, he simply jogged home, believing there were already two outs when the ball was hit. Well, there was only one out, and he was doubled off third base to end the inning.

The next day, the six-foot-six Johnson loomed over me. I could feel his hot breath on my face.

"Pluto," he said. "I just want you to know that I've been ripped by a whole lot better writers than you." Then he turned and walked away, and that pretty much summed up my experiences covering my hometown team.

16

The Conscience of the Indians

On the Indian teams I covered, the essence of class was designated hitter Andre Thornton. Thornton still receives telephone calls from reporters and fans who assume that he is part of the Indians' organization. He's not, but that's the Indians' fault—and an indictment of their organization.

Thornton played for the Tribe from 1977 to 1987. He is fourth on the team's all-time home run list, only twelve behind leader Earl Averill.

But home runs are not the point about Thornton. Rather, Thornton deserved a chance to pursue another career after he retired as a player, a career in the front office. Baseball supposedly has been encouraging minorities to assume prominent roles with teams off the field. The fact that Thornton is black really is a side issue; rather, the fact that Thornton is intelligent—but wait a minute. If Frank Lane could run the Indians, if Ken Harrelson could do a tour of duty as general manager of the Chicago White Sox, if Gabe Paul could be in charge of the Indians for so long, certainly a man like Thornton deserved a chance to be a general manager after serving a front-office apprenticeship.

That never happened. Here is why, and it requires a history lesson.

The Beginning

Thornton loved to play pool.

"There was a pool hall not far from an army base near my hometown [Phoenixville, Pennsylvania]," said Thornton. "This was during the Vietnam War, and a lot of soldiers used to hang out at the pool hall. The owner would back me, and I had my own cue stick. What I did was take the soldiers' money. It was how I was able to have some spending money in high school and buy my class ring. I started playing when I was twelve years old for $5 or $10. By the time I was a senior in high school, I was involved in games where the pot was several hundred dollars."

Thornton's father had been a semi-pro baseball player, but in his real job he was a machinist. His mother cleaned other people's homes a few days each week.

"Combined, they never earned $10,000 a year," said Thornton. "They couldn't believe it when I got $10,000 to sign with the Phillies [in 1967]."

Sports were Thornton's life. He played the big three—basketball, baseball, and football.

He was six feet two and about two hundred pounds, and he could hit a baseball a long way, as was noticed by Philadelphia scout John Odgen.

"Mr. Odgen came down to the Golden Q (the pool hall) and waited until I finished my game, which was for a $200 pot," said Thornton. "John Odgen had signed Dick Allen, and he was highly respected. He was about seventy-two years old and had recently had a stroke. He walked with a limp and held his head at an odd angle. He took me to Connie Mack Stadium in Philadelphia for a tryout. [Manager] Gene Mauch was there. So was [owner] Ruly Carpenter. I was only seventeen. Larry Shepard threw batting practice to me, and there I was hitting balls out of Connie Mack Stadium. The Phillies invited my father and me to watch a game from the press box and then sign a contract.

"My father took Nebs Griffith with him to the game. Nebs had been my Little League coach and was a very good friend, but Nebs also was a former drinker who lost half his stomach because he drank so much. And my father, he was a drinker all his life, an alcoholic. These two guys were pouring down the beers and eating hot dogs in the press box. They kept saying, 'Now this is the life.' My father also had to sign the contract because I was under eighteen. When we went home, I remember it was really hard to get Nebs and my father down all the concrete steps from the press box because they'd had too many beers."

Thornton said he took his $10,000 bonus and bought a 1968 green GTO "with the rear end hiked up and the big air shocks. It cost me about $4,300, and I put the rest in the bank."

While Thornton was a pool hustler and cigarette smoker, he was unlike the children of most alcoholics.

"I never drank much at all," he said. "Watching my dad had the opposite effect on me. I also lost a friend at nineteen. He had just gotten married. One day he went home drunk and was beating up his wife when she stabbed and killed him. I saw how some of my father's friends treated him when he was drinking. I just never wanted to lose control, so other than having a few beers a couple of times in high school, I never drank."

Thornton's path to Cleveland went from Philadelphia to Atlanta to Chicago to Montreal, before he finally became an Indian in 1977 in the Jackie Brown deal with the Expos. Thornton was twenty-seven years old. While he showed some power in the minors, he hit more than 20 homers only once. He also had terrible luck with injuries—broken hands, broken fingers, strained knees—that continually stalled his career and caused four organizations to give up on him.

Even when he came to the Indians in 1977, he got off to a horrible start. Later, Tribe fans would learn that Thornton was just a miserable spring hitter. But since he had never done anything in the majors before, who was to know that the Andre Thornton in April would be different in July?

"It got so bad in my first year with the Indians that Frank Robinson benched me and was playing Bill Melton," said Thornton. "The only reason I didn't go back to the minors was that Phil Seghi really liked me, and he had signed me to a three-year contract. Cleveland was so strapped for money, and I was making $60,000 that first season; they weren't going to give up on me. From about June 7 to the end of the year, they couldn't get me out. Before that, I was hitting about .150. Things came to me later because I was never considered a top prospect in the minors. In 1975 I spent the entire year with the Cubs and put up good numbers [18 homers, .293], but they traded me to Montreal. Really, I needed one team just to stick with me, and the Indians became that team."

Thornton finished the 1977 season with 28 homers and 70 RBI. The next year he batted .262 with 33 homers and 105 RBI.

"People always talk about the Indians' bad trades," said Nev Chandler. "But Jackie Brown for Andre Thornton ranks as perhaps the best in the history of the franchise."

The Tragedy

In October 1977, Thornton, his wife, Gertrude, and their two children were on the Pennsylvania Turnpike. Thornton was driving the family's new van when a sudden snowstorm and fierce winds began to push the vehicle around the road. Thornton's two-year-old daughter, Theresa, was sleeping in her mother's arms in the front seat. Four-year-old Andre, Jr., was in the back. Thornton's van skidded out of control. It went off the turnpike into a ditch and flipped over.

Thornton was stunned. All he remembered was hearing a scream, then there was silence. It was dark, and he couldn't find his family in the van, which was turned over on the roof. Thornton recalled someone stopping to help, and then they discovered his son, who was under a pile of suitcases. He kept yelling that he needed to find his wife and daughter, but the police told him that they had everything under control. He was taken to a hospital, and it was only then that he learned from a nurse that his wife and daughter had died in the accident.

"I felt my stomach go into a knot, but all I could do was sit there, absolutely numb," said Thornton. He asked for a Bible and a preacher. Then he prayed.

"It was then that I truly felt the power of God," said Thornton. "I sensed him telling me, 'I will never leave you or forsake you.' I told my son that it was just him and me now, but I didn't know he if understood because he was so young."

Thornton had turned to Christ after high school when he was doing four months of reserve duty with the Pennsylvania National Guard in 1969. The faith he found in the barracks of Fort Dix is what carried him through the tragedy on the turnpike eight years later.

"I believe that the Lord used the death of my wife in ways I'll never fully understand," said Thornton. "It made me more well known in baseball than anything I could ever have done on the field. The death of my wife solidified my position in baseball. By that I mean that people saw my faith and knew that it wasn't a game. It was heartfelt."

Manager Jeff Torborg, Duane Kuiper, and Buddy Bell represented the Indians at the funeral.

"I have two vivid memories of that day," said Kuiper. "One was that Andy and his son were both pretty banged up. They had bandages on their faces. The second thing was that right before they took the caskets out, everyone in the church was emotionally spent. Then Andy stood up and spoke. He didn't talk for long and I don't remember what was said, but he was so calm that it calmed everyone else down. It was hard to believe the strength he showed that day."

Thornton was also the leader of the Indians' chapel movement, which wasn't well received by everyone in the dressing room.

"I never tried to shove religion down anyone's throat," said Thornton. "When I was with the Cubs, we had veterans such as Don Kessinger and Randy Hundley who weren't afraid to speak out about their faith. But with the Indians, it was not the thing to do, to stand up and say you were a Christian. They had the old-line thinking that baseball and religion don't mix. I'm a big guy, so no one was going to get in my face and say anything bad about the chapel. I remember when I was off to one of my bad starts, [the *Plain Dealer*'s] Danny Coughlin wrote something like, 'Thornton is a nice guy. He reads his Bible, but he can't hit.' Players never said anything directly, but we'd have a service, and some of the guys would walk by and scream a curse word or sit at the other end of the room and intentionally use a lot of foul language just to annoy us."

Kuiper said that there was a danger of the team's splitting "between those who went to chapel and those who thought it was ridiculous. Sometimes it would run long and bump into batting practice. After a while we just stopped having batting practice on Sunday."

In the early 1980s, a lot of players claimed to be Christians, but they often used their faith as a crutch for a poor performance. Thornton had little patience for these people; his opinion was that God didn't pop out with the bases loaded, you did.

"When you are around someone every day, as is the case on a baseball team, you know if his faith is genuine," said Thornton. "Players started to come to me with their problems. This was when baseball was going from a drinking culture to where the guys were also using drugs and pills, sometimes mixing all three together. For some it was a progression from alcohol to pills to marijuana to cocaine. My own brother had a drinking problem, then used drugs, and went to jail for a few years. When David Clyde was on the team, he came to me when he was on the verge of suicide. He was a mess. He had been divorced. He was drinking. His career was going down. That happened to lots of guys, especially since the players in the late 1970s were the first to really get into big money. They made a lot of mistakes."

Thornton's ministry grew, not just with the Indians but in the entire community. He organized youth groups and worked with various churches.

"Andy probably had as big an impact on my life as anyone I've ever met because of how he lives his faith," said Mike Hargrove. "They tell you that Christians are passive, but Andy is just the opposite. Andy would say that God gave you a special talent, and it was up to you to play as hard as you could. And how he continued to play after the tragedy—that was an inspiration to me."

Those who know Thornton realize that he can be intimidating because he is so honest and has almost a spiritual presence.

"When I introduced my wife to Andy for the first time, she told me that she wasn't sure if she ever wanted to see him again," said Kuiper. "I asked her why. She said, 'It's those eyes. He looked right through me.' That is how it is with Andy. When you meet him, he looks you right in the eye, almost as if he's looking right into your soul."

The Trials

The Tribe's front office, especially Gabe Paul, was never very comfortable with Thornton. They didn't think players had the right to speak their minds. But if you asked Thornton what was wrong with the team, you received an intelligent answer.

Over the years, he said, "the ballpark and the condition of the field have made us the laughingstock of baseball. We have a poor image, an image as the worst situation in the majors. We need one man, one vision. We can't have fifty visions or ten visions. We keep going back and forth. One year we trade the hitters for pitchers. Then we turn around and trade the pitchers for hitters. We can't decide what kind of team we want."

In 1980, Thornton tore up his knee in spring training. The team was playing San Diego in Yuma. The Padres' doctor looked at it and said Thornton needed surgery; the Tribe's front office pressured Thornton to have it done right then and there with the Padre doctors.

"That was the beginning of the whole mess," said Thornton. "I had the operation, but the knee wasn't responding. I kept hearing that I wasn't rehabbing correctly or that I wasn't working to come back. My knee never felt right. Gabe Paul put me on the active roster even though I told him that I couldn't bend my knee. I got as far as the on-deck circle to pinch-hit when someone made an out to end the inning. I never did play. Finally, I convinced the front office to let me get the knee reexamined, and they discovered that the first doctor had left a piece of damaged cartilage in the knee. I had another operation to have the cartilage removed. In the meantime, the front office had implied that I wasn't in shape and that I was not a good representative of the organization, even though I was one of the few players to live in the Cleveland area year-round. Gabe Paul said some things about me that I'll never forget."

"The Indians really screwed up Andy's knee," said Kuiper. "They couldn't wait a few more days for him to go back to Cleveland and have it done at Cleveland Clinic, which is what I did when I hurt my knee. They pressured him into having the operation in San Diego. Then they didn't believe him when he said something was still wrong. It was terrible how they treated Andy."

In 1981, Thornton's knee was fine, but he fractured his hand while breaking up a fight between Don Baylor and Rick Waits.

"I had two lost seasons," said Thornton. "Then at the start of 1982, I was booed on opening day. I couldn't believe it. Joe Charboneau was trying to make another comeback, and the fans wanted him to DH instead of me. It was like they were pitting Joe against me. The fans loved Joe, and the front office would have loved to have gotten rid of me at that point. I always felt that they downplayed my accomplishments, but I never understood why. Had Charboneau stayed healthy, they would have run me out on a rail, but Joe was sinking."

A healthy Thornton was rising. He hit 32 homers and drove in 116 runs while making the 1982 All-Star team. He was an All-Star again in 1984.

"I loved playing in Cleveland, but I always felt that I gave the front office more than they gave me in return," said Thornton.

The Contract

After the 1984 season, Thornton became a free agent. He had hit 33 homers with 99 RBI and batted .271 as a thirty-five-year-old designated hitter.

"I was looking for a five-year contract worth about $900,000 a year," said Thornton. "That was the salary range of Don Baylor and Hal McRae, two DHs who had numbers similar to mine. After the 1983 season, we went to the Indians and asked for a three-year, $2.7 million deal. Gabe Paul turned it down, and he never made a serious counteroffer. So I went into the 1984 season knowing I was about to become a free agent, and I had a monster year. When the season was over, I figured that I was done in Cleveland because the Indians still hadn't made a real effort to re-sign me. Then Peter Bavasi replaced Gabe, and there was an uproar from the fans and media about letting me get away. Several teams were interested in me, but it appeared that I was going to sign with Baltimore."

Bavasi did not want to lose Thornton, not so much because of his value as a player but for what Thornton meant to the franchise.

"The 1984 winter meetings were in Houston, and the team was owned by Steve O'Neill's estate, with Pat O'Neill in charge," said Bavasi. "I told O'Neill that we had to keep Thornton.

"O'Neill said, 'What are you going to pay him?'

"I said, 'Whatever he wants. We're going to hand him a blank contract.' O'Neill's mouth dropped open.

"I said, 'Andy is an honorable guy, and so are his agents. We have a bidding war going on now between Kansas City and Baltimore. The price will just keep going up, especially if we get involved. The only way to stop it is to approach Andy and ask him what he wants.'

"O'Neill said, 'That's a big gamble.'

"I said, 'It's a bigger gamble if we lose him. If we are serious about restoring this franchise, if we want to send the right message to the fans and media, we sign Andy. Look, I know he's going to get barrel-chested and that he'll put on weight. His knees are bad. If he plays out only two years of the contract, we'll be lucky. But we have to do this.' Pat O'Neill agreed with me."

Thornton had met with Baltimore and told the Orioles that he wanted a $4.4 million contract for four years. But he wanted it to be paid out over fifteen years, which sounded very good to the Orioles. Then Thornton's agent said they wanted the $2.8 million of deferred money over those fifteen years to be paid at 9.5 percent interest.

"Add it all up, and after fifteen years I'd get over $7 million," said Thornton. "Edward Bennett Williams owned the Orioles back then. Hank Peters was the general manager. Williams wanted me badly. He had even approached my brother-in-law [former Oriole outfielder Pat Kelly] and said he'd donate money to Pat's Christian ministries if Pat could convince me to sign with Baltimore. Anyway, the Orioles agreed to do it, but only over three years. We told them we'd think about it. As we walked out of their hotel suite, we ran into Peter Bavasi."

Bavasi knew what Thornton wanted and said he'd pay it.

"I was tempted to raise the price," said Thornton, "but that wouldn't have been right. We said that we'd sign with the first team to meet our demands, and Bavasi felt he had to do it. It was a matter of credibility with the fans. My understanding also was that the American League had given the Indians an ultimatum: They told the team that if they wanted to continue to operate in Cleveland, they had to show it. Signing me was one way to do that."

In 1985, Thornton had 22 homers and 88 RBI, but his batting average sunk to .236. In 1986, Thornton dropped to 17 homers, 66 RBI, and a .229 average.

He was thirty-seven years old and was starting to show it. At the end of that season, Bavasi quit, and the Jacobs brothers bought the team and hired Hank Peters. All Peters could see was that he had an aging Thornton, who was a drag on his payroll.

The Final Days

By 1987 it was evident that Thornton was not the team's DH, the job having gone to Pat Tabler. In fact, the Indians had absolutely nothing for him to do, so he sat game after game.

"By the middle of May it was obvious what was happening," said Thornton. "Pat Corrales was the manager, and I told Pat that if the decision had been made to go with the kid, then release me. I told him that if I continued on the team and never played, it would end up being a wedge between myself and the front office. It was about this time when Al Campanis made his remarks [about blacks lacking the necessities to have baseball leadership positions], and minority hiring became an issue. There was a lot of speculation in the media that I'd move into the front office, but I never heard anything. At mid-season, Corrales was fired, and Doc Edwards became the manager. I went to [General Manager] Dan O'Brien and suggested that I could move into the front office, and it would solve a couple of problems at once."

O'Brien talked about Thornton working his way up through the minors.

"I said that I wasn't interested in managing at the big-league level, so I didn't see any reason to go to the minors as a manager or coach," said Thornton. "I wanted to learn the game from the front office, maybe do something like Sal Bando, who worked under [General Manager] Harry Dalton in the Milwaukee front office. But O'Brien didn't seem interested."

So one of the premier players in the history of this franchise wasted away since he never played.

"In his last few years, Andy told me that he wanted to stay in baseball but in the front office," said Mike Hargrove. "This was no secret. The thing about Andy is that he's a rock. Andy is a guy that if you had trouble with something, you could go to him for advice. It may not be the advice you want to hear, but it would be good advice because it was what he truly believed. That's the kind of guy you want in the front office."

The Tribe players watched how the front office bungled the Thornton situation, and most thought exactly as Rick Manning did: "Andy got a raw deal at the end. Not from the fans or the media—they wanted him to go into the front office. When I played with Milwaukee, they did the same thing to Cecil Cooper. Here was this guy who was great for the franchise, and they just buried him on the bench. Everyone respected Andy, especially how he continued to produce on the field after his wife and daughter were killed and when he had other personal problems. He was a true gentleman, and to see him treated like that, well, it wasn't right."

Danny O'Brien never gave Thornton a final answer.

"He just left it hanging," said Thornton. "By making no decision, he made a decision. I had been in baseball for twenty-one years with five organizations. I should have picked up something along the way. I was willing to learn. I was on the payroll anyway, so why not let me try the front office?"

Hank Peters took over as team president in November 1987.

"There was an uproar about Andy still having one more year on his contract, but he never played much," said Peters. "He asked that he not play out the last year of his contract, and that was fine with us. We talked about other jobs. If Andy wanted to coach or manage, we could have found something, especially at the minor league level. But he said he didn't want to travel much and wanted a front office job. Well, there were only so many front office jobs."

Obviously, the Tribe did not want Thornton in the front office.

"I always thought that had Peter Bavasi stayed with the team, he would have hired me," said Thornton. "It would have been the kind of bold move that he would have liked. But the Indians were run by conservative men. There wasn't a lot of imagination. So I walked away. I didn't let them have a day for me. I just figured it was time to move on."

There are still some prominent people in Cleveland who believe that Thornton belongs in the front office.

"This is purely my personal opinion," said Hargrove, "but the franchise should have made a big deal about helping Andy bow out of the game gracefully. But I also think they were afraid of Andy, at least a little bit. He always spoke his mind, and that made some people uneasy."

Nev Chandler carried that one step further: "A lot of baseball people are insecure, and if Andre Thornton were in the front office and learning how to run a team, he would be viewed as a threat," said Chandler. "Instead of realizing what they would gain from having Thornton as one of their point men to the community, what you had was a bunch of guys protecting their own turf."

Today, Thornton does not sound bitter when he discusses his final days with the Tribe. He does an incredible amount of work with inner-city youth through his Christian Outreach center. He also owns a sports marketing firm that represents Albert Belle. His latest interest is in some Applebee's Restaurants in the St. Louis area.

"God gave me a good head for business and the ability to make money," said Thornton. "A lot of my efforts are now in the area of administration and fund-raising so we can keep our charity work going. I'm the guy out front, meeting with business leaders."

Thornton had another major accident, this one in the summer of 1991.

"I was driving about five miles from my home, a street I drive down nearly every day," said Thornton. "I never knew what happened. One second I was driving, the next I was out cold."

What happened was that a tree fell on the roof of his car.

"I later learned that it was an old, rotten tree that just cracked and fell over," said Thornton. "There was no special reason for it to happen that day. The weather was good, no wind or anything. The tree hit the roof of my car, bounced off it, and the car kept going. I was knocked out instantly as the car banged into something and stopped off the road."

A UPS truck driver was coming in the other direction. He saw the accident, turned off the motor of the car, and called for help. Thornton was trapped inside a web of mangled metal.

"When I woke up, I was stuck inside, and they were cutting through, trying to get me," said Thornton. "I prayed, 'Lord, don't let me panic. Don't let me move. Help is coming.' I had a concussion. I had a separated shoulder that needed surgery twice. I was pretty banged up, but if you saw the car, you'd know that there is no reason for me to be living today."

Then Thornton talked about the car in front of him.

"It was a mother with two little children in a convertible," he said. "Just imagine if the tree had fallen on them or if my car had gone off the road and flipped over."

Thornton said he still drives down that same road.

"And I see the same tree, or at least what is left of it. Some people asked me how I could still drive past that tree. I say that I'd go another way if you could guarantee that another tree would never fall on me. But there are a lot of trees in the forest."

Thornton said he never has nightmares from either of his auto accidents.

"I am more aware of sudden destruction than most people. I'll be on an airplane and there will be a storm. . . . I know how quickly things can happen. . . . I wouldn't be paralyzed or trembling, but I also know that the next moment, you could be in eternity, and I ask the Lord to calm me down. I'll see a terrible accident on the TV news, and suddenly I'll feel the people's pain and there will be tears in my eyes.

"But the thing is that I view what has happened to me as what the Lord wanted. After the tree incident, I probably heard every tree story you can imagine. But that also opened doors for me. People would meet me and say, 'Andre Thornton . . . you're the guy the tree fell on.' And that's good. It's a starting point for conversation, and it has helped me get to know more people. Rather than be bitter about things, you take what has happened to you, and you deal with it the best you can. I don't know why things happen or even if I understand all of what has happened to me, but it has given me a sense of urgency, knowing that there is a brevity to life. And that is why I try to live so I can leave a mark."

The Ballpark

They no longer play baseball at Cleveland Stadium, and that's a good thing. The Stadium wasn't a ballpark, it was a mausoleum—too big, too damp, too old, and too cold. At least that was how I felt about it the last few years, especially after having been to nearly every major league stadium.

When I was a kid, naturally it was different. When I was a kid, I knew only one stadium, and I loved it dearly.

It began when my father and I drove into the huge parking lot behind the center field bleachers. We'd see the Wahoo sign, the beleaguered chief standing on one foot, holding a bat above his head, and grinning ear to ear. No wonder he looks like an idiot; he's been standing on one leg for twenty-five years. It had to numb every part of his body, especially his brain.

That mindless smile is reason enough to change the Indians logo; Chief Wahoo has the big nose, the big teeth, and the ruddy face of a guy who drinks Ripple from a bag. Forget the arguments about political correctness; why can't the franchise have an Indian symbol that looks like a warrior, a man with dignity—someone like Crazy Horse or even Sitting Bull? (I particularly like Sitting Bull because he may have been the first man ever to sell his autograph. When he traveled with the Buffalo Bill Cody Wild West Show, he signed autographs for free. But one day he signed something for a woman and she gave him a dollar. To Sitting Bull, that established the price for signing his name, and by the end of his life he was getting $1.50.)

But Chief Wahoo didn't sell his name. And contrary to what some of the

Indian players say, no one sees the chief and thinks of Phil Seghi. Chief Wahoo looks as if he sold his soul for a six-pack, reinforcing all the old stereotypes about Indians and drinking. No wonder the Native Americans are upset when they see Wahoo at the Stadium or on the team's hats.

Like it or not, the first sign of the Stadium was Chief Wahoo. Then there were the bleachers, where kids lined up before the game hoping to be picked to work as vendors, selling hot dogs, peanuts, and popcorn while watching the game as they walked miles through the huge stadium.

Cleveland Stadium was baseball's largest venue, with 6,062 seats, and it had almost mythical bleachers. They were not a good spot to watch the game—too far away in dead center field. But that was also part of the charm. No one ever hit a ball into the center field bleachers on a fly at Cleveland Stadium. The distance is 445 feet from home plate. Players certainly hit the ball that far, but never to dead center—at least not in Cleveland.

But I never sat in the bleachers; when I went to a game, I wanted to see it. When I arrived at the Stadium, I went to the main gate, Gate A. There used to be an old man with a dancing monkey and a German shepherd. You were supposed to drop some money in a cap on the ground because the old man had dressed his monkey like a bell hop.

Not far from the "Monkey Man," as I called him, was the "Scalper." He was an old man with a cane who always had a walking cast on one foot. He wore a nice but tattered brown suit and a cabby hat, looking a little like Burt Lancaster in *Atlantic City*.

One day, I arrived before the Scalper and decided to wait for him. He showed up a few minutes later, coming from downtown across the West Third Street Bridge in a cab. When he got out, the cabby honked, and the Scalper waved as the car pulled away.

I walked to meet him. He was limping. He stopped and pulled out a huge cigar from the inner pocket of his suit coat. Slowly, he unwrapped the cigar, then dramatically bit off the end and spat it on the ground. Now we were ready to do business.

We usually said very little. I asked him what tickets he had. He showed me, and they were usually excellent box seats about ten to fifteen rows from the field, either behind home plate or in back of the third-base dug-out on the visitor's side of the field.

I asked him how much, he told me, and I paid it. That was that. I was in high school and far more interested in seeing the game than finding out the Scalper's life story. But once I did ask him, "Do you ever go to the games?"

"Nah," he said. "I just sell the tickets."

"Even when you have an extra ticket left over?" I asked.

"Never," he said, and he said it as though he meant it.

That was the end of the conversation.

Some people may find it hard to believe that there were any scalpers at Indians' games, especially since the Stadium could hold eighty thousand fans. There weren't many of them, and those who were there sold tickets for *less* than face value. Someone told me that the Scalper knew some guys in downtown Cleveland who had season tickets; they had bought them for their companies and used them only for games with the Yankees or special promotions like bat day. Most of the time the Indians were so bad that the companies couldn't even give the tickets away to their employees, so they sold them to the Scalper for next to nothing, and he sold them for a buck less than you'd pay at the ticket windows.

When I began covering the Indians in 1980, I looked a few times for the Scalper, but he was never there. I figured that he had probably died, and I never thought much about him—until now.

When I think about the Stadium, I start to feel old. Not because the Indians no longer play there. Thank the Lord for that. This team has needed a smaller, state-of-the-art, honest-to-God baseball stadium for decades. But when I was growing up, I never thought of the Stadium as a bad ballpark. Nor do I remember people saying that.

"That's because it wasn't," said Nev Chandler. "In the 1950s, the crowds were big, the team was good, and I remember the groundswell of noise when the Indians would do something. The roar would fill that huge ballpark, and when you were in the middle of it, you had a feeling that the crowd could be heard all over town. You'd walk into the ballpark, see the old guys selling programs, and smell the hot dogs at the concession stands. And there would be a lot of people pouring in. . . . In the 1950s, the Stadium was a special place."

Even in the 1960s it wasn't so bad, according to the players.

"I loved that ballpark," said Rocky Colavito. "Of all the places I played, I never felt more comfortable in than Cleveland Stadium."

The scoreboard unleashed fireworks after a home run—a Bill Veeck idea. It also had horns that appeared on both sides of the scoreboard and blared away whenever an Indian homered.

"One of my favorite things to do, even after I grew up and became a sportscaster, was to get to the park early when I knew there would be a big crowd," said Greg Brinda. "I liked to watch the place fill up, the fans coming down over the West Third Street Bridge and through the gates and then up the ramps to their seats. It amazed me that you could put so many people in a park for a baseball game. That is one thing they'll lose with the new Gateway Stadium."

The Stadium was a Works Progress Administration project designed to bring the 1932 Olympics to Cleveland. That didn't happen, but the biggest stadium in all of baseball became home to the Indians. The size prevented the Indians from immediately moving there. They played at the Stadium in 1932 and 1933, but returned to the much smaller League Park (capacity twenty-three thousand) for most games until Veeck moved them permanently to the Stadium in 1947.

When did the Stadium begin to go bad?

"I never thought it was any good for baseball," said Gabe Paul. "It sits right on that damn Lake Erie, and the wind blows off there—it can chill you to the bone. A mile away, the weather wouldn't be nearly as bad. But on the lake, we had games called for fog, snow, you name it. Also, it's just too barny, too damn big. You can't convince people to buy tickets in advance because they know they can wait until the last minute and still get good seats."

If you ran the Indians as Paul did, you knew it was much better to get the money up front—before the season and before the fans realized how bad the team would be once again.

"Do you know that there are still fifty-two thousand of those original wooden seats from 1932 in that park?" asked Paul. "Those things are museum pieces, but they aren't very comfortable to sit in. Hey, the place is great for eight football games a year (which is why the Browns are staying there), but for eighty-one baseball games, forget it."

As the team began to lose and the fans stopped coming, the Stadium became a bizarre place. The team often played in front of seventy thousand empty seats, and any idiot with a loud mouth and a lame brain could be heard not once but twice because it seemed as if there was an echo.

"The Indians would go through this winter ritual," said Chandler.

"They'd move the fences in or out, as if that made a difference. They even tried to get the fans closer to the players, and that led to one of the biggest mistakes they made. It was in the middle 1970s that they lowered the field eighteen inches to create better sightlines for the fans."

That was when they discovered that the field was built over landfill.

"There were stove tops and parts of bathtubs and kitchen sinks under there," said Paul. "From that time on, we went from having one of the best infields in baseball to one of the worst. You can't put sod on top of that garbage and expect it to grow."

Tons of dirt were trucked in over the years, but the field refused to settle evenly. There were hard spots and mud, and they had to paint the grass so it at least looked green.

A Tribe pitcher named Mike Stanton became so upset with the condition of the mound that he pulled a unique stunt after he was removed from the game. While the next pitcher was warming up, Stanton found a shovel in the dressing room, took it onto the field, and threw it at the mound, his way of protesting what he considered to be shoddy work by the grounds crew.

"I heard people say that the Indians should turn the Stadium into a home field advantage," said Chandler. "How? It was a cold, foreboding, empty place most of the time. No one wanted to play there, and why would they? As a baseball facility, the Stadium had become an embarrassment."

"Obviously, losing had a lot to do with why people looked down on the Cleveland players," said Andre Thornton. "But the Stadium made it worse. In the middle of a game, a guy from another team would ask me how I could stand to play there for eighty-one games a year. They didn't see the Stadium as major league. It was demeaning, at best a slight step above Class AAA."

Thanks to the dampness off Lake Erie, the Stadium was a marvelous breeding ground for insects.

"Some of the best entertainment we had was watching the spiders crawl across the press box windows," said Pete Franklin. "Sometimes millions of gnats would dive-bomb the park, and players spent the whole game swatting in front of their faces just so they could keep the bugs out of their eyes and mouths. When those bugs came in, they always blamed it on Canada. 'It's not our bugs. They came over the lake from Canada,' they'd say. What the hell the poor Canadians had to do with it, I'll never understand. Maybe it's their revenge for our sending them all that acid rain."

Or as former Indian Alan Bannister said, "The worst thing was that spiders fell down from the ceiling on you when you sat at your locker, and the concourse always smelled like spilled beer."

Because the Stadium was used for rock concerts and Browns games, the field took a terrible beating. In the fall you could see the yard markers in the outfield. Occasionally, center fielder Rick Manning would signal for a fair catch when he was settling under a fly ball.

The plumbing often broke, usually in the women's rest rooms.

"After more than one Browns game, Phil Seghi walked into his office the next morning and found a puddle on his desk," said Gabe Paul. "It came from the ladies' room that was right above Phil's office."

The Stadium became a battleground between the Indians and the Browns since Browns owner Art Modell was also in charge of the Stadium. Until 1974 the city of Cleveland owned the park, and it still does. But in 1974 the city had no money to run or make needed major repairs, so Modell paid about $2 million annually in rent to the city and in exchange became the landlord of the facility.

This galled Gabe Paul, who hated the idea that he had to negotiate with a football man and that the football man had the leverage. Paul thought Modell didn't play fair when it came to carving up the concession money. He thought Modell didn't give the Indians a break when it came to taking care of the field. He thought Art Modell was nothing more than a glorified slumlord. The fact that the Browns were usually in the playoffs and a winning franchise—much like the Indians of the 1950s—also annoyed Paul.

As for Modell, he thought Paul was attacking him and the Browns to take attention away from the real problem—the fact that Gabe Paul's Indians were disgraceful.

Members of the Browns organization say that Steve O'Neill asked Paul when the Indians would be a winner. "Not as long as we have a lease with Art Modell," Paul reportedly said. Paul has denied the story. True or not, it reflects the state of mind that was prevalent in the front offices of both franchises.

"After a while they stopped speaking to each other, and Art and Gabe used to be good friends," said Nev Chandler. "I know Gabe took great delight in the Browns' misfortunes. One of Gabe's greatest joys was when the Browns had back-to-back seasons of 4–10 and 3–11 while his team was their usual 70–92."

Then the Indians and Browns settled into legal trench warfare, communicating only through legal counsel. There were suits and countersuits.

"After taking over the Indians [in 1985], one of the first calls I made was to Art Modell," said Peter Bavasi. "I knew that the Indians and Browns had been suing each other for years. In fact, when I was a consultant, I had been hired by Bob Gries [a partner of Modell's] to compare the Indians' lease with other leases in major league baseball. This was in 1984, before I had any idea I'd be in Cleveland, so I had no special interest in the outcome. I found out that the lease probably ranked in the middle of the pack. The problem was that the team wasn't any good and no one came to the park, so concession revenues naturally were down. In 1986, when I was with the Indians and we drew 1.5 million, the lease was fine and everyone made money."

Bavasi said that there was a natural rivalry between Modell and Paul.

"No other baseball team had a football team for a landlord," Bavasi said. "In most leases where the football and baseball teams share the same facility, the baseball team gets the advantage because it has far more home dates. But that won't happen if the football team is also the landlord. So that annoyed Gabe. And Gabe also saw all the attention that the Browns and Modell got from the media—most of it very positive—and that bothered him. Gabe was a fine P.R. man, but Modell is a master with the media. It became a battle of egos and a test of will and nerves."

It also was a waste, according to Bavasi. He opened his initial conversation with Modell with this question: "What do you think these lawsuits have been costing you?"

"About $300,000 in legal fees," said Modell.

"I just checked our records, and we've spent over $350,000 on legal fees," said Bavasi. "We've spent about $700,000 and accomplished nothing except making the lawyers rich."

"That's right," said Modell.

"Let's drop all the litigation and fire all the lawyers," said Bavasi.

"Sounds good to me," said Modell. "Then what?"

"You're going to save $300,000," said Bavasi. "Why not give some of that back to the Indians in lease concessions?"

Modell quickly agreed.

"That was all it took, one phone call," said Bavasi. "Art enriched our lease by $200,000, and if you factor in the legal fees we stopped paying, we saved over $500,000. A great moment occurred during the 1986 season when Gabe Paul and Art Modell found themselves at the same cocktail party. They shook hands, and neither had a lawyer at his side. That was progress."

In the late 1980s and early 1990s, the condition of the infield was no longer a Cleveland joke. The yard markers were still found in the outfield grass during the fall, but the Indians simply ignored them. The war was over because a new stadium was coming.

"The fact was that other teams hated coming to the Stadium, guys hated playing at the Stadium, and even the fans have never really taken to it," said Hank Peters. "You will hear some diehards say, 'It's okay. What's wrong with it?' Well, those people have never been to other parks, or they would know. The place is just too goddamn big, and it lacks the intimacy and comfort you associate with baseball. For football, when you have eighty thousand fans every Sunday, it's great. For baseball, it's a calamity."

Once the Jacobs brothers purchased the Indians for about $45 million in 1987, it became clear that one way or another, there would be a new ballpark.

"The Jacobs are Cleveland guys who have helped redevelop the downtown area," said Bavasi. "They are savvy politically when it comes to putting together deals and getting it done. They bought the team with the idea of being the Indians owners who finally get their own baseball stadium, and they've done it."

The Great Tease

Peter Bavasi had one advantage when he took over the Indians in 1985: He wasn't Gabe Paul. (Gabe had benefited from the same kind of comparison with Frank Lane.) Exactly who he was and what he wanted—well, that was a subject of public debate. He had been the general manager of the San Diego Padres in the middle 1970s, then became president of the expansion Toronto Blue Jays in 1977.

"I left Toronto in 1981," said Bavasi. "A sickness had set in. I was sick of them, and they were sick of me. I had been there too long, or at least that was the opinion of the board of directors."

Bavasi moved to Florida and opened his own consulting firm based in Tampa. "Among my clients were the Yankees and Astros," he said. "They wanted me to evaluate their spring training facilities, their broadcasting deals, things like that, in comparison to what other teams were doing. I also did some work for the Indians."

But Bavasi had another client, the city of St. Petersburg, which wanted a team for its new domed stadium. That was what made Tribe fans nervous: Bavasi's being named the team's president right before the 1985 season.

"I was never going in there with the idea of moving the franchise to Florida," he said. "The team was still owned by the O'Neill family. One of Steve's final wishes was that the team be sold only to owners who would keep it in Cleveland, and his family planned to honor that."

Bavasi was aware of the kind of mistakes that had characterized Indians management. As the Toronto Blue Jays prepared to joined the American

League in 1977, the expansion team was looking for a young catcher, and the guy they liked was Tribe farmhand Rick Cerone. But when the Tribe turned in its protected list, Cerone's name was on it.

"But look at this," said Blue Jays general manager Pat Gillick. The Tribe had not protected Rico Carty, who batted .310 with 83 RBI as the team's DH in 1976.

"What do we need Carty for?" asked Bavasi, the team's president. "He's old, he's got bad knees."

"Rico was Mr. Wahoo," said Gillick.

Bavasi just stared at him.

"Mr. Wahoo," repeated Gillick. "The Indians Man of the Year. Let's take him. In Cleveland, the writers and fans will kill the team if they lose Carty. Then they'll have to trade and get Rico back."

Carty had bad knees, no position in the field, and a birth certificate that showed he was thirty-six. That was why the Indians were convinced Toronto would never take him. But the Blue Jays did, in the first round. And the fans and writers did indeed "put out a real hue and cry," to quote Bavasi.

The Indians found themselves talking trade with Toronto, talking about the guy they wanted to keep, and in the end trading twenty-two-year-old Rick Cerone for the aging, aching Carty.

"The deal worked out great for us," said Bavasi. "Rico played one more year and was done. Cerone caught forever."

So why would Bavasi want to run the Indians?

"Baseball is a game of redemption," said Bavasi. "A guy can strike out three times but still hit a home run in his last at bat to win a game. The best hitters make outs 70 percent of the time. In baseball, failure is built in. But that also leaves a lot of room for redemption. A manager who gets fired by one team wants to manage another one to redeem himself. Well, that was how it was for me. After what happened to me in Toronto, the idea of coming to Cleveland where they had had almost nothing but failure since 1960, that excited me. What's the fun in taking over a team that is already a huge success?

"They were losing money. They were losing games. They were losing fans. And the media hated their guts. Anything I did would be positive."

The son of longtime baseball executive Buzzie Bavasi—who was a close friend of Gabe Paul—Peter Bavasi is a charming con artist with just enough romance in his soul to make you want to believe him.

After he was offered the Tribe's job, he said he paged through the Indians' media guide.

"I saw the names of all their great players," he said, "Feller, Wynn, Doby, Garcia. . . . They had eighteen Hall of Famers. In the 1940s and 1950s they were a powerhouse on the field and an artistic and financial success. I called Bill Veeck, and we talked about 1948. I asked Bill if it could happen again.

"Veeck told me, 'Why can't it be like 1948? The world has changed. But baseball hasn't changed. The town of Cleveland and their fans haven't changed. People still love that team.'

"As Bill talked, I was taking notes. Then he said, 'You know, the Indians . . . that was my team.'

"I wrote that down and it became the motto for my two years there: The Tribe: This is my team!

"I heard all about how downtown was dying and Cleveland was a rust-belt city. But so was Detroit, and the Tigers have always been a great draw. Same for Chicago. Those teams had old downtown stadiums, and it worked. Why not Cleveland? That was a puzzle I wanted to solve."

Bavasi roared into town. He came off like a Madison Avenue advertising executive. As *Cleveland* magazine characterized him, "He wears Ralph Lauren shirts, Brooks Brothers suits, and Gucci loafers."

Right away Bavasi began to sell: "George Steinbrenner says the Yankees are a Mona Lisa. Well, the Indians are a Picasso."

At his first press conference, Bavasi came out with charts like Ross Perot, only this was before Perot had the idea. Bavasi had chain-of-command charts and flow charts with blocks and arrows.

"It went on for forty-five minutes," said Nev Chandler. "I thought, this guy thinks the Indians are General Motors."

Paul was worn down by the team, the losses, the criticism, the never-ending search for an owner. He was nearing eighty, while Bavasi was a relatively young baseball executive bursting with ideas and hope.

"I seized upon the idea of why couldn't the Indians be turned around," he said. "Why couldn't players such as Brett Butler, Andre Thornton, Pat Tabler, and Joe Carter restore this once great franchise? Why leave it to the next generation to do it? I wrote letters to everyone in the organization from the big-league players to the scouts to the kids in rookie ball. Then I followed up with phone calls, and I asked them to join me on this quest to restore the Indians. It was amazing. People were very positive. They said no one from the Indians had ever approached them like this. Their attitude was, 'Yeah, we'll buy a ticket on that.' All but one guy, that is."

That guy was Bert Blyleven, who also happened to be the team's best pitcher, a nineteen-game winner in 1984.

"I met with the entire team in spring training," said Bavasi. "I could see that Blyleven wasn't buying any of it. So afterward I talked to him alone. Bert was very honest. He said, 'I admire what you're trying to do, but I'm not ready to join that bandwagon. If I were you, I'd get me out of here.'

"I liked Bert, and I wanted to keep him. I asked him to become the leader of the team.

"He said, 'I'm burned out here. You'd better move me.'

"So we traded him. I couldn't take a chance on my spending two hours pumping up the players, and then two minutes after I walked out of the dressing room, Blyleven would deflate the whole clubhouse."

The Tribe would have made a good deal for Blyleven if they had been patient. They sent him to Minnesota for four young players: Curt Wardle, Jim Weaver, Rich Yett, and Jay Bell. It looked like the typical blocked-headed Tribe trade, moving a star for four kids who probably wouldn't make it. In the case of Wardle, Yett, and Weaver, that was true. But Bell became an All-Star shortstop. Unfortunately, it was with the Pittsburgh Pirates. Former Tribe manager Doc Edwards complained about Bell's lack of range. Several members of the Hank Peters front office of the late 1980s also thought Bell would be nothing more than an average hitter. He batted only .219 in two seasons covering 118 games with the Tribe. But Bell was only twenty-three when he was traded for slick shortstop Felix Fermin, who has been very solid in the field for the Tribe, but he's no Jay Bell.

Blyleven did make one last contribution to the Indians.

"I was talking to the players about how our uniforms should look," said Bavasi. "I told them that they were going to be involved in the decision-making process, so why not ask them about the uniforms? Carter and Tabler suggested that we put the Chief Wahoo logo on our caps. Tabler said, 'It will sell like crazy,' and he was right."

Bavasi did wonder if it would offend Native American groups.

"But Blyleven told me, 'Nah, it shouldn't. Chief Wahoo really looks like Phil Seghi,' " said Bavasi. "That was the joke among the players, and we never did hear from any Native Americans in the two years I was there."

In 1985 there was nothing different about Bavasi or the Indians. In fact, it was worse as they went 60–102 while Blyleven was a seventeen-game winner for Minnesota.

After the season, Bavasi announced that Pat Corrales would return as manager.

"The reporters asked me how long Pat was signed for," said Bavasi. "I said that I signed him for forever. They looked at me. I said it was a 'perpetual' contract. They started calling him 'Perpetual Pat Corrales.' But all it was was a one-year rollover deal. It meant that Pat always had an extra year to go on his contract. I had the same kind of deal. That way, if you're fired, you are always guaranteed one more year of salary, and no one can ever say that you are in the last year of your contract.

"So I was right. Pat was hired forever, at least until someone decided to fire him."

A very strange thing happened to the Indians in 1986: They won. Not the pennant, but they won eighty-four games, the most since 1968. And the really remarkable aspect was that they improved by twenty-four games despite receiving nothing tangible in the Blyleven deal.

"People said that 1986 was a fluke, but I don't think so," said Bavasi. "Look at our lineup. Few people noticed, but Gabe and Phil made some very good deals for young players toward the end of their time running the team, and it paid off."

They traded a sore-armed Len Barker for Brett Butler and Brook Jacoby, who both became starters.

They traded Rick Sutcliffe and Ron Hassey for Mel Hall and Joe Carter, two starting outfielders.

They traded Jerry Dybzinski for Pat Tabler.

They traded Von Hayes for Julio Franco.

They traded a washed-up Gorman Thomas for Tony Bernazard, a player Paul always called "the Little Gentleman."

Bob Quinn drafted Cory Snyder.

The 1986 Indians had four guys who batted over .300—Bernazard, Franco, Tabler, and Carter—and hit .284 as a team.

They had six guys with at least 17 homers: Carter (29), Snyder (24), Hall (18), Jacoby (17), Bernazard (17), and Andre Thornton (17).

They led the league in runs scored, batting average, stolen bases, and even in triples.

The pitching was shaky with a 4.58 ERA, third highest in the American League. But Tom Candiotti was a sixteen-game winner, forty-five-year-old Phil Niekro won eleven games, and Ernie Camacho had 20 saves.

"A lot of what happened that year did come from sheer emotion," said Bavasi. "The guys started to believe in themselves and what we were doing. They didn't think that the Indians *had* to be a terrible team. We had players coming to the park at 2:00 P.M. for a night game, and they stopped at the front office just to talk. We did little things like putting air-conditioning in the wives' waiting room. That may not sound like much, but it meant a lot to the husbands because it made their wives happy. Several of our players had career years because we had a potent lineup. There was just a feeling of excitement."

As has always been the case when the Indians are respectable, the fans came. The Tribe drew nearly 1.5 million, their second largest gate since 1951. It was especially impressive since the Indians' 102 losses in 1985 meant there was virtually no advance sale for 1986.

"When we had some winning streaks, we were getting forty thousand, even fifty thousand a night," said Bavasi. "Bill Veeck told me that in 1948 he'd look out the window from the upper deck of the Stadium and see these waves of humanity walking on the [West Third Street] bridge and into the park. To see these throngs—and these were real, ticket-buying fans—it gave me an incredible thrill, the same that Veeck described to me."

But 1986 turned out to be nothing more than a tease.

Sports Illustrated put the Tribe's Snyder and Carter on its cover for the 1987 baseball issue. The article was titled: "Indian Uprising. Believe it! Cleveland is the best team in the American League."

Like the 1986 season itself, the cover was something of a ruse.

"The writers on the staff didn't vote the Indians as the best team," said Peter Gammons, one of the writers. "We knew that Cleveland had major pitching problems, that they would be lucky to go .500 with the pitching.

But an editor there thought picking the Indians would be cute, so they went ahead with it."

It was astonishing, even to Cleveland fans who were used to the bottom dropping out of their baseball team. But the 1987 Indians lost *101 games*. The team *Sports Illustrated* declared to be the best in the league proved to be the worst in baseball.

In 1985 the Tribe was 60–102. In 1986 it was 84–78. In 1987 it was back to 61–101. And Perpetual Pat Corrales was fired at mid-season, replaced by Doc Edwards.

What happened?

At the end of the 1986 season, the Jacobs brothers purchased the team. Bavasi resigned to go into private business. One theory was that Bavasi knew he couldn't be the emperor of the team, as he had been when the O'Neill estate owned the franchise. The Jacobs had definite ideas about the future, and those plans may not have been the same as Peter Bavasi's.

Bavasi said it came down to dollars.

"I had a great offer from a company called Telerate," he said. "Bowie Kuhn had recruited me for the job. It paid several times what I earned with the Indians [$150,000]. I had stock options and equity in the company. There was no way baseball could match it. Besides, I felt I had redeemed myself in 1986. I got out of the Indians what I wanted and did all I could."

Some of the players felt otherwise.

When the Jacobs brothers bought the team, they decided to cut the payroll and build with young players. Carter, Candiotti, and Butler weren't old, but they wanted big money and believed they had earned it in 1986.

"Some of the guys did tell me, 'I thought we all were going to stay together and rebuild this thing,' " said Bavasi. "I told them that I didn't play. My leaving should not be a big deal."

But it was. Bavasi had instilled some pride in the team. His slogan, "The Tribe: This is my team," went over well not only with the fans but with the players.

"But money got in the way," said Bavasi. "Instead of the players thinking that they were doing something to tell their grandkids about, they were asking management, 'What's in it for me?' Guys were filing for arbitration. The Jacobs brothers were not going to throw big money around. Trades ended up being made because of dollars. Had I stayed, I doubt that I could have changed it because the Jacobs were going to operate a certain way."

That may all be true, but it can't have helped that the man who sold the players on committing themselves to the team was one of the first to jump ship for monetary reasons. For all his hard sell, Bavasi's slogan proved to be nothing more than "The Tribe: This is my employer."

19

Putting the Pieces Together

In 1987, Peter Bavasi left the Indians with no president. The Jacobs brothers needed someone with experience, someone who would be in charge like Bavasi but maybe not be quite such a center-stage actor.

For the job, they brought Hank Peters back to Cleveland. Peters had been the Indians farm director from 1966 to 1971. He was general manager of the Orioles from 1975 to 1987, helping Baltimore win two pennants. But by 1987 he was tired of working with Orioles owner Edward Bennett Williams, who wanted to spend his money on free agents while Peters stressed the farm system, and so the Orioles did a lousy job in both departments.

"I was sixty-three years old when I came to Cleveland," said Peters. "I had been let go by the Orioles. I could have sat on my duff and got paid by Baltimore for two more years, but the Jacobs brothers immediately contacted me, and the idea of rebuilding an organization revved up my engines. This was going to be my last baseball job, and I knew I wasn't going to be there five to ten years and work myself into the grave. I agreed to stay for at least three years but no more than four. After losing 101 games, the Jacobs knew they had problems. They were successful businessmen, and I could tell right away that they were in this for more than just the tax writeoff. They wanted a winner."

Doesn't every owner?

"But I convinced them that if they really wanted to win, they'd have to wait," said Peters. "We'd have to draw up a plan and stick to it, taking our lumps on the field and in the media. I kept talking player development and scouting. When I arrived in November 1987, Joe Klein was the GM. Jeff Scott was in charge of the farm system and scouting, which is really two jobs. They had the minimum number of farm teams, which was four. You can look back now and ask yourself how many guys from that farm system in the middle 1980s made an impact in the majors—Albert Belle, Steve Olin, not many. Guys they told us were good prospects were not prospects at all.

"To be honest, the franchise was even in worse shape than I'd imagined. We were starting from point zero."

Wait a minute. Weren't the Indians 84–78 just two years earlier, in 1986? How could the team be barren two years later?

"They had a lot of contract problems, letting guys become free agents," said Peters. "My first day with the Indians was November 15, 1987. I asked my secretary to get Brett Butler on the phone because he was a free agent. She said she couldn't; she didn't have his phone number. She told me, 'At the end of the season, Butler refused to give his off-season number to anyone in the front office.' I called Butler's agent, Dick Moss. I told him that I wanted to talk to Brett. He wouldn't give me Brett's phone number, but he said he'd have Brett call me. Butler never did. We got Butler's address, which was a post office box. I sent him a mailgram, telling him to call me collect. I'm still waiting for that call. We matched the offer he received from San Francisco, but his agent told us that if we wanted to keep Brett in Cleveland, we had to give him one more year than the Giants did. That was how a lot of the veterans felt about Cleveland. They wanted to get out."

In his meetings with the Jacobs brothers, Peters realized that the resources were limited, and he decided that most of the money would go to scouting and the farm system even if it meant losing veterans to free agency—or trading them before they became free agents.

Of course, avoiding free agents wasn't always the Indians' choice.

"We had a helluva time trying to get a free agent to sign with us," said Peters. "We needed a shortstop, and Scott Fletcher was available. The kid was from Wadsworth, which is outside of Akron, so he was an area player. It looked like a match made in heaven. We were willing to meet his financial needs, and we figured he'd want to play in his hometown."

Fletcher's agent asked all interested teams to submit a bid.

"I told [owner] Dave Jacobs that if we did sign Fletcher, it would not be a good signing," said Peters. "This confused him. I said Fletcher was a good shortstop and we needed one, but we would have to overpay to get him. Yet I still felt we had to do it. I not only made a bid, I also told his agent that we were willing to exceed by a modest amount any other legitimate offer he received."

Instead, Fletcher's agent called a few days later to say the Tribe was out of the hunt.

"He told me that every time Fletcher came to town with the Texas Rangers, his relatives and friends bothered the hell out of him," said Peters. "He never got any peace or rest. He thought if he played for the Indians, this would go on all season, and he didn't want to go through that."

A stunned Peters hung up the phone.

"I mean, when you can't even sign your hometown players even though you are willing to outbid everyone else, you have problems," said Peters. "Instead, Fletcher signed with the White Sox [in 1990]."

Peters said he offered free agent pitcher Charlie Leibrandt "more money than anyone else, but he re-signed with Kansas City. He played on winning teams with the Royals. We were a loser, and playing at the Stadium added another stigma. We just couldn't get free agents."

Peters's signature on the Tribe is the Joe Carter deal. This really should be called the Carlos Baerga deal, and it just might be the deal that undoes the Indians' curse once and for all.

It was after the 1989 season, after Carter had played in all 162 games and had 35 homers and 105 RBI, though he batted only .243. He had averaged 108 RBI in his last four years with the Tribe.

Carter had been through a couple of contract disputes with the front office, and the 1987 brass, primarily Dan O'Brien, just lowballed him. Carter eventually got his money from the Indians, winning an arbitration case against the team and even getting into a public dispute because team policy would not allow players' wives to travel on the team's charter flights.

Before the 1989 season, Carter rejected a five-year, $9.6 million offer from the Indians, instead pocketing a one-year, $1.6 million deal as a result of his triumphant arbitration case.

"We wanted to keep Carter, but when he turned down the $9 million, his agent told us that he just did not want to stay with the team," said Peters. "His agent said, 'Joe does not want to play in Cleveland. He blames the front office and the media for a lot of his troubles that have turned the fans against him.' Rather than lose him to free agency at the end of the 1990 season, we set out to make the best deal we could for him."

Peters had plenty of teams in the market for Carter, who is a good person and a hardworking player.

"The big question was whether Joe would sign a long-term deal with the teams that wanted him," said Peters. "I went to his agent, who gave me a list. Joe didn't want to play in Canada, Milwaukee, Chicago, Minnesota, or on the East Coast. We came down to four teams: St. Louis, Kansas City, San Diego, and California. In theory, I had twenty teams to trade with, but in reality, it was only four. St. Louis offered Vince Coleman and Willie McGee, but both were going to be free agents at the end of the season, and I didn't want to get into a situation where we could lose the players. Kansas City kept saying it would make an offer, but it never did. The Angels talked, but we wanted Devon White in any deal, and they didn't want to give him up."

"Jack McKeon was the GM in San Diego, and when Trader Jack wanted someone, he was not afraid to be bold and give up some players to make the deal work. We immediately agreed on Sandy Alomar. We needed a catcher, and Sandy was the top catcher in Class AAA. The Padres put him in the package, and they threw in [veteran outfielder] Chris James. The third guy was the sticky point. We had great reports on Carlos Baerga and wanted him badly. He had to be in, or there was no deal."

At the time, Baerga was twenty years old and had hit .275 with 10 homers at Class AAA Las Vegas. Nice numbers but not a real clue as to what was to come from the switch-hitting second baseman.

"We went around and around, but finally they agreed on Carlos," said Peters. "The knock on him was that he could hit but would never be much of a defensive player. But he was so young. He'd signed when he was seventeen, so we knew he had a lot of room to develop."

To seal the deal, Carter signed a three-year, $9.3 million contract with the Padres.

When the trade was announced, Peters told reporters that Baerga was ready for the big leagues "and would be an excellent hitter." But the Indians planned to use him at third base because Jerry Browne was slated to start at second.

"Carlos hits well from both sides of the plate," said John Hart, who was Peters's assistant and heir apparent to the GM job in 1989. "We figured he'll put on ten to fifteen pounds and get stronger, maybe hitting 12 to 15 homers."

The biggest selling point was Alomar, the 1989 Minor League Player of the Year who became the 1990 American League Rookie of the Year for the Indians. But the last three years have been one injury nightmare after another for Alomar—knee, back, arm, fingers, you name it.

Meanwhile, Baerga has emerged as an All-Star, more than adequate defensively at second base because of his rocket arm. At the plate, no second baseman is a more dangerous hitter; not only can Baerga bat .300, he can hit 20-some homers. He plays the game with such zest that the hardened Cleveland fans immediately adopted him as one of their favorites.

The Carter—I mean the Alomar/Baerga—deal may have been the biggest, but sometimes the little deals end up being big, too. So it was when the Tribe traded minor league catcher Eddie Taubensee to Houston for a minor league outfielder named Kenny Lofton in December 1991.

The Indians knew that Lofton was a tremendous athlete, and he had been a basketball player at the University of Arizona. He could run, but could Lofton hit? The Indians had more than enough time to find out. What they discovered was that Lofton is a terrific bunter and may be the fastest runner in the majors. But he is more than a pure athlete: He is bright, he knows his strengths, and he plays to them. He doesn't want to pull the ball and hit homers; he wants to get on base and steal.

In the outfield, it may be possible to hit something over his head, but it seldom happens. After two seasons with the Indians, Lofton is their best leadoff man since Brett Butler, and he has a chance to be one of the best in the history of the franchise.

"What you have is a guy with great natural athletic talent who wants to overachieve," said John Hart. "That is a rare combination."

The Hank Peters regime had no hand in the drafting of Albert (then Joey) Belle, but they do deserve credit for nurturing him to become one of the premier power hitters in baseball. It was former general manager Joe Klein and scouting director Jeff Scott who decided to take Belle in the second round of the 1987 draft from LSU.

"He was one of the top three talents in the draft," said Klein. "They said he had problems in school. Well, they weren't big problems in my mind. The majors are full of guys who had problems like Belle."

At LSU, Belle did things like chase a fan who had been harassing him while he stood in the outfield. Occasionally, he didn't run out a pop-up or ground ball.

"There was a game right before the 1987 College World Series where Belle hit a ball he thought was a home run, and he started to jog to first base," said LSU coach Skip Bertman. "But the ball hit off the wall, and all he got out of it was a single. I had to suspend him for the rest of the season because I'd told him that I would. His family was upset at me because they thought it would hurt him in the draft, but the scouts all knew about him."

Yes, they did. They knew he was a tremendous power hitter, but they wondered what kind of guy is suspended for the College World Series. Klein and Scott did their homework and determined that Belle was a bright person from a decent family who was very emotional and tightly wound. Most of his problems were of the self-destructive kind—putting too much pressure on himself and not coping with failure.

"We didn't have a first-round pick in 1987," said Klein. "Taking Belle was a chance to get an impact player in the second round. In school, he was a very good student. We just had to be patient with him."

Klein and Scott were gone not long after signing Belle to a $65,000 bonus. But it was Peters, John Hart, and farm director Dan O'Dowd who supplied the patience.

"Albert is a deep study," said Peters. "He has his own set of problems. Every day is an emotional challenge for him and some of his problems with his emotions are ongoing, but we've always believed in Albert."

They didn't lose faith in Belle after the Florida Instructional League game when he smacked a line drive that he thought was a single, but an infielder made a leaping catch. He kept running—past first base, down the right-field line, out of the park, and into an nearby orange grove. The team didn't see him until a few hours after the game.

They didn't lose faith through all the bat throwing, helmet heaving, dirt kicking, and other temper tantrums.

They stayed with him (but fined and even suspended him) when he didn't hustle.

They stayed with him when he went into alcohol rehabilitation in 1990.

When he came out, he said that he preferred to be called Albert Belle, his real first name, instead of Joey, a nickname.

They stayed with him when he was kicked out of the Mexican winter league for lack of hustle.

They stayed with him when he threw a ball at a heckling fan at Cleveland Stadium in 1991, hitting the fan in the chest. The fan wasn't hurt, but Belle was suspended for a week.

Belle blamed his troubles on his "perfectionism" and a drinking problem that he said he hid from everyone around him. His coaches and teammates were stunned when Belle went into rehabilitation because he was never considered a heavy drinker by those who knew him.

"My father was an alcoholic," said Andre Thornton. "The difference between Albert and my father was that my father loved to drink. But Albert, he saw drinking as a problem and dealt with it. My father could never take that step."

One of the best aspects of Belle's time at Cleveland Clinic is that he met Thornton in 1990.

"I was working with a football player in rehab, and a nurse asked me to talk to her group," said Thornton. "Albert was one of the group members, and a few weeks later he called me. We became friends, and I feel like a big brother to him. We studied the Bible together. We talk about baseball. He's relaxed with me because he knows that there is nothing I want from him."

While Thornton was known as a man who always had his emotions under control, he said that was not the case early in his career.

"I had 14 home runs in seventeen days in the minors when I was called up by the Cubs in 1973," he said, "but they just stuck me on the bench. I felt this hostility and anger. The frustration had me boiling inside. It got so bad that in batting practice I could hardly hit the ball out of the cage. The anger was sapping my strength. We had players like Ernie Banks and Billy Williams, respected veterans, but I didn't feel comfortable talking to them.

"It was much the same for Albert when he first came to the Indians. He felt there was no one he could trust, and he blew up. Look at the history of the game from Ty Cobb to Rogers Hornsby to Ted Williams to Jose Canseco. There are so many great players with volatile tempers. That's Albert, too."

In the off-season Belle attended Cleveland State and earned a degree in accounting.

"Albert can be a presence in this community, a real star," said Thornton. "He likes the attention. He likes people to like him and cheer for him. He loves to compete. In my mind, it's easier to tone down a guy who is driven and a perfectionist than it is to get a player to turn up the intensity. Albert and I talk about molding his emotions and energy into something positive. That is why he has stayed in Cleveland in the off-season, and why he does as much charity work as anyone on the team. There are still going to be ups and downs. I told Albert, 'I won't let you fall if I can help you. I can steer you through some of the pitfalls because I've been there.' What a dynamic and explosive player he is. I know he isn't always easy to understand, but he is growing up."

Another reason for Tribe fans to feel good about their team is that Mike Hargrove is the manager.

This is what the Tribe should have been doing for years—not just trying to develop players but finding a manager who can cope with baseball in Cleveland, who understands the special problems of the Indians.

That's Hargrove, and that also was the idea of Hank Peters, who developed Hargrove as a manager.

I admit I have a special feeling for Hargrove, dating back to when he played for the Tribe in the 1980s and I covered the team. He was more than a .300 hitter, he was a decent human being, a man who never made excuses and who looked you in the eye when he tried to answer your questions.

But Hargrove can get mad. More than once he asked me, "How in the hell could you write that?" But then he'd listen, sincerely wanting to know. And he would tell you that you were wrong and why, but more in the form of a debate than an argument. Often, we'd just agree to disagree, but Hargrove would make sure that his opinion was heard. And it wasn't always something I had written about him. It was nearly impossible to say anything bad about Hargrove, who was a classic overachiever. Nonetheless, he would take issue with things said about his teammates or the organization if he thought the criticism was out of line.

Hargrove always cared about more than himself. Along with Andre

Thornton, he was one of the few players in my five years covering the Tribe who actually worried about the franchise. They didn't settle for saying, "Hey, I did the best I could, and the hell with everything else."

Occasionally, his patience would run out. There was a hatchet man talk show host who so upset Hargrove that one day Mike said, "I wouldn't piss in that guy's mouth to put out a fire."

Then he laughed. He also meant it.

Paul Dade and Phil Seghi are the men responsible for bringing Hargrove to Cleveland. The year was 1979, and Hargrove was hitting .192 in San Diego. "I had been a good hitter in Texas [1974–78]," said Hargrove. "I got traded to the Padres, and my stroke wasn't for squat. At the end I couldn't even hit in batting practice."

Seghi always liked Hargrove, who hit .300 in three of his five years with Texas. He called the Padres and said he would be glad to take Hargrove off their hands, and he offered a nonentity named Paul Dade. San Diego jumped at the chance; Hargrove's stock had sunk so low that he even cleared National League waivers before joining the Indians in June 1979.

"I had asked the Padres to trade me," said Hargrove. "The day before the June trading deadline, [Manager] Roger Craig told me, 'I'm sorry. We just traded you to Cleveland.' Sorry? I wanted to kiss him. At that point, any place would have been a good change for me. But I figured that Cleveland was struggling, so I'd get a chance to play and be back in the American League. I was excited about the Indians."

That was the difference between Hargrove and most veteran players: They would have gone into a six-month funk had they been traded from sunny San Diego to Cleveland, which was considered baseball's Devil's Island.

"With the Indians, [coaches] Dave Duncan and Joe Nossek worked with me every day for about two weeks right after the trade," said Hargrove. "Suddenly, my stroke came back. Those guys revived my career, as did coming to Cleveland."

Hargrove batted .325 in a hundred games with the Indians in 1979. In 1980, he was a .304 hitter, and he batted .317 in 1981. He played both left field and first base. He was slower than a dead box turtle, but he often led off because his on-base percentage was over .400.

Mike Hargrove walked a lot. And Mike Hargrove drove pitchers crazy—all the time.

"The 'Human Rain Delay,' " he said, remembering the nickname given to him by Joe Tait.

Hargrove led the league in twitches, fidgets, and bizarre gestures, and he performed them before every pitch. Adding the fact that he took a lot of pitches and that his bat control enabled him to foul off a lot of pitches, it often seemed as if a Hargrove at bat lasted longer than the Gerald Ford administration.

"It started when I was in [Class A] Gastonia in 1973," he said. "I had damaged a nerve at the base of my left thumb, and I never could swing the bat after that without a pad on that thumb. If I don't hit the ball perfectly, the vibrations from the bat go right through my thumb and hurt like crazy. We didn't have a trainer back then, so I took some tape and a piece of foam rubber and made my own thumb pad. But the thing was always coming loose, so I learned to screw it down on my thumb after every pitch."

Then Hargrove discovered that when his batting helmet wasn't quite right, he was uncomfortable, so he would press it tightly down on his head. And he would adjust his shirt, his pants, and sometimes his socks.

And he did all this between every pitch.

"Early in my career I'd be at the plate waiting for the pitch, and I would be thinking that my thumb pad was loose or something like that," said Hargrove. "So I decided I'd take a little time and make sure that everything was right. Like practice swings. I'd take one. If that didn't feel good, I'd take another. Then it was three. Finally, it got to where I didn't feel comfortable unless I took three practice swings between each pitch."

I loved Hargrove but hated his routine. It reached the point where I simply didn't watch him bat. I read a newspaper and looked up only when I heard him hit the ball. Otherwise, I'd find myself twitching along with him.

"One time, a woman from the TV show '20/20' approached me," said Hargrove. "She said they were doing a show on obsessive-compulsive behavior and wanted to open it with some film of me batting. I told her to forget it; that was the last thing I needed. I never thought I was obsessive-compulsive. It was just the way I batted."

Given the fact that Hargrove hit quite well and seems very sane in every other aspect of his life, who would disagree with him?

Hargrove's career ended after the 1985 season, when he batted a respectable .285 in 107 games for the Tribe. The Indians went on a youth kick—Pat Tabler was their new first baseman—and they let Hargrove be a free agent. Only Oakland called, with a nonguaranteed contract to try out in spring training. He did and was cut.

The phone never rang again. He was thirty-five years old.

"When they let me go, I felt as if the blood was going to run right out of my fingers, and there was a cold feeling in the pit of my stomach," said Hargrove. "I was part of the 1986 collusion settlement. It was also when the teams all decided to carry twenty-four instead of twenty-five players. So I'll never know if that was why no other teams called. I just felt as if I was being robbed of the last few years of my career. I thought I still should have been playing up to 1989. I'd see guys on TV and know that I was better, even at that late stage of my career, than they were. I felt bitter about it. I felt I was cheated because I could have played two, three more years and because I never had a chance to announce my retirement."

Hargrove had a. 290 batting average and a .400 on-base percentage in twelve major league seasons.

After being released by Oakland in the spring of 1986, Hargrove returned to his home in Perryton, Texas.

"Like most big leaguers, I thought I was ready to manage in the majors the day I quit playing," he said. "What's the big deal? When we played, we all managed the game in our heads at the same time, and we second-guessed our managers, figuring we knew more. One of Cleveland's coaches, Fred Koenig, had to quit at mid-season. I went to [Tribe president] Dan O'Brien to ask for the job. I mean, I could throw batting practice, hit fungos, be a first-base coach. But Dan O'Brien said, 'Under no circumstances will I bring you to the big leagues. If you want to get to the majors as a coach or manager, you have to go through the minors, work your way back up.'"

O'Brien sent Hargrove all the way to the bottom, the Indians' rookie league team in Batavia, New York.

"I was twelve years in the majors, and they're telling me to go to Batavia?" said Hargrove. "But I went. I was the hitting instructor. I also began as a first-base coach and ended up coaching third. I enjoyed working under [Manager] Tom Chandler, but I didn't like Batavia. I didn't like the filthy clubhouse where the lockers were nails in the wall and where the flies were thick in the air. I didn't enjoy the dirty, dingy parks. I thought that I had been through the minors once, why should I have to go back? But I never considered quitting. I knew if I wanted to manage in the big leagues, I had to do this. I had theories about the game, and the minors were the perfect place to try them out."

Hargrove moved up a notch every year in the Tribe farm system. He was a coach in Batavia in 1986, a manager at Class A Kingston in 1987, a manager at Class AA Williamsport in 1988 and at Class AAA Colorado Springs in 1989. He went from earning $450,000 in his last year as a player to $25,000 as a manager. He and his wife, Sharon, packed up their kids and chased the game across the country. He was Manager of the Year in 1987 (Carolina League) and 1989 (Pacific Coast League).

"We were grooming Mike to manage the Indians," said Hank Peters. "In 1990 we were looking for a manager. I interviewed Mike for the job, but I hired John McNamara instead. I wanted an experienced man, so I went with John. But I named Mike to his coaching staff. I wanted Mike to learn from John, and John was a very good teacher."

It was a unique situation. Both McNamara and Hargrove understood what was in the future.

"Johnny Mac would call me into his office and say, 'When you're a manager, this will happen . . .' and he'd explain something to me," said Hargrove. "Hank Peters never told me that I'd be the next manager. He made no promises, but after a while, people were talking about it. I wanted it to happen. I didn't just want to manage in the majors, I wanted to manage the Indians."

McNamara lasted one and a half seasons. He was replaced by Hargrove during the 1991 All-Star break.

"I thought John did a good job in his first year with us, but all the losing and everything was taking a toll in 1991," said Peters. "It was inevitable that Mike would be the new manager in 1992, so why wait? It was painful for me to fire John because I had known him for so long. I called him into my office on a Saturday morning. He looked at me, and he knew what was coming. As I told him that we had to make a change, I had tears in my eyes. Then he had tears in his eyes. We didn't say much."

Hargrove was also told to report to the office on Saturday morning.

"We had been playing terribly, and Johnny Mac was telling me that he felt something was going to happen with him," said Hargrove. "I didn't sleep a wink that night. As I walked into the office, I was wondering, what if they fired Johnny Mac but didn't give me the job? There were no secrets between Johnny Mac and me. He knew that I wanted the job, but when I got it, I felt awful for him."

When Hargrove went into the manager's office for the first time since taking over the team, he found a note from McNamara wishing him luck. It's framed and hangs on the wall over his desk. Next to it is a picture of a grizzled, exhausted cowboy who is asking, "Why did I ever sign on with this outfit?"

It just seemed natural that Hargrove should manage the Indians. Unlike some managers such as Mike Ferraro or Frank Robinson, who came from other organizations, he wasn't overwhelmed by the problems inherent in managing a team that had not been in contention since 1959. And unlike Jeff Torborg, a coach who replaced Robinson, Hargrove had earned his position in the minors. He was forty-one when he took over the Indians in July 1991, and he has a chance to be the team's best manager since Al Lopez, a long-term guy who is comfortable in Cleveland.

"I liked managing immediately," said Hargrove. "There is a lot to be said for being the 'yeller' instead of the 'yellee.' Like anyone else, I like the feeling of power. I also like the responsibility. I get a bigger kick out of watching my team perform well and knowing I had a hand in it than I ever did even in my best days as a player. One of the most satisfying moments in my life was when we won the second-half championship at [Class A] Kingston in 1987. The players were jumping around, they were so happy just to win a Class A title. I felt proud of them and real good about what I did. I've had my doubts, days where I've wondered if I can handle people or run a game as well as I should. There are also days when I screw up so badly and no one notices it, but I know. And there were times in the minors when I wondered if I'd ever get to the majors. I was scared. But anything worth having is worth being scared about."

The Past Meets the Future

As the Indians approached the 1993 season, I never felt better about a Cleveland team—at least not since You Know Who was traded in 1960. Not that these Indians were going to win a pennant or even be serious contenders. At least not in 1993. But I sensed it coming, and coming soon, perhaps in 1994, in the new ballpark.

The Tribe finished the 1992 season with a 76–86 record, a nineteen-game improvement over 1991. But what I really liked was that the 1992 Indians were 62–56 after the first two months of the season.

They have the right manager in Mike Hargrove.

They have a core of inspiring young players all tied to long-term contracts in Albert Belle, Kenny Lofton, Carlos Baerga, Sandy Alomar, and Charles Nagy.

They have an owner in Dick Jacobs who strong-armed the city into building a new, state-of-the-art, forty-two-thousand-seat stadium. Jacobs also wisely invested in scouting and the farm system while giving Hank Peters and then his protégé John Hart time to develop a team.

The 1992 Indians were even picked as the Minor League Organization of the Year by *Baseball America* magazine.

Everything was in place for a terrific 1993. Then came the type of tragedy that can only leave you asking, "What if?"

What if Dick Jacobs didn't own a winter home in Homestead, Florida, and instead was content to let the Indians continue to train in Tucson?

What if Homestead had not been flattened by Hurricane Andrew?

What other team has ever picked a new training site, then had Mother Nature turn it to rubble?

What if the Indians had picked somewhere—anywhere—but Winter Haven as a second choice for spring training?

What if Hargrove had taken up an offer from the Los Angeles Dodgers to play an exhibition game on March 22, instead of giving his team the day off?

What if more Tribe players had taken up Tim Crews's invitation to spend the day off at his new forty-eight-acre ranch on the shore of Little Lake Nellie in Clermont? Or what if fewer players had gone? Would any of it have mattered?

What if Steve Olin had followed his instincts and turned around and headed back to Winter Haven when he became lost while driving to Crews's ranch? What if Olin hadn't promised his three-year-old daughter that she could ride a horse at the ranch of his new friend, Crews? Would he have been in the boat on that fatal night?

What if Olin had followed the advice of his wife, Patti, who suggested he stay onshore because it was getting dark?

What if Tim Crews did not have an alcohol content of 0.14 in his blood, making him legally intoxicated in Florida? Would that have made a difference in how he piloted his eighteen-foot, 150-horsepower boat? The two other pitchers had only a trace of alcohol in their bloodstreams.

When people die tragically, the What Ifs never end.

What happened was that Crews, Olin, and Bobby Ojeda went for a ride at about 7:30 P.M. in Crews's boat, and Crews drove straight into a dock. Crews and Olin were killed instantly. Ojeda lost part of his scalp, injured his pitching shoulder, and carries scars—mental, emotional, and physical—that will never go away.

Ojeda lived only because he was slouching a bit in his chair while his two teammates were sitting straight up. That was the difference between life and death, a few inches.

Crews and Ojeda were in their first year with the Indians. Both had been with the Dodgers in 1992, and both were signed as free agents to bolster the pitching staff. Ojeda would be a left-handed starter, a thirty-five-year-old with eleven years' experience who had won 113 games. Crews was supposed to help out in long relief.

Because he was new to the team, Crews invited the entire bullpen to his home. Olin's best friend, Kevin Wickander, decided to go to Busch Gardens instead. Derek Lilliquist went to his home in Vero Beach. Ted Power and Eric Plunk were tired and rested in Winter Haven.

Starter Mike Bielecki planned to go because Crews said there were a lot of big bass in his lake and Bielecki loves to fish, but his wife isn't thrilled with fishing, so he was a late scratch.

"We never knew what hit us," said Ojeda. "Crews is a great boatsman. The throttle stuck and, *bam,* that was it."

But that wasn't it. The loss meant that there were six children without fathers. It meant that Ojeda went through a period when he contemplated suicide and couldn't bring himself to pitch. It meant that the Indians were without Olin, one of the truly nice men in the clubhouse and a sidearming reliever who had saved twenty-nine games in 1992.

"Olin had the heart of a lion and the guts of a burglar to throw that fringe stuff up there and get people out," said John Hart.

Andre Thornton was flown in from Cleveland to speak at the wake that was held for the team in Winter Haven. After a few days the players' tears had dried, and it was sort of business as usual. Hart and Hargrove found themselves trying to replace three pitchers and find a stopper for the bullpen. But they discovered another problem—Wickander.

Olin was not only Wickander's friend—"The two pitchers could have been joined at the hip," wrote Sheldon Ocker in the *Akron Beacon Journal.* Olin was the steady family man. Wickander was the party guy who landed in alcohol rehabilitation. When he got out, Olin was there. Wickander settled down, married, and grew closer than ever to Olin. For a promotion, they both stuffed seventy-one pieces of bubble gum in their mouths. They drew arrows under the bills of their caps to remind themselves to throw strikes.

Wickander was so stricken with grief that he couldn't pitch effectively for the Indians. Stepping into the clubhouse, he'd automatically look at what was once Olin's locker. In the bullpen he'd miss his best friend. Every day, maybe even every waking hour, he longed to talk just once more with Olin.

Determining that there were just too many reminders of the tragedy in Cleveland for Wickander to handle, the left-handed pitcher was dealt to Cincinnati, perhaps the first trade made to help a player recover from the death of a teammate. So the tragedy actually cost the Tribe four pitchers: Olin, Crews, Ojeda, and Wickander. It was a main reason that the team stumbled early in the season and struggled all year—the shock of the event and the lack of arms.

Then All-Star Charles Nagy came down with, of all things, shingles. That was late in spring training. Early in the season his shoulder required surgery. Suddenly, the Indians were without their ace and seventeen-game winner in 1992.

"If you believe in luck, then you also have to believe in being unlucky," said Duane Kuiper. "We all know about the mistakes the Indians have made over the years, but this has been a truly unlucky franchise. Just look at the boating accident. That is unprecedented in baseball history, but it's just the latest in a long line of tragedies for this team."

By mid-season the Indians began to play decently, thanks primarily to Hargrove's steady hand and the respect he earned from the players. Albert Belle and Carlos Baerga were All-Stars, and it was a true miscarriage of justice that Kenny Lofton didn't join them.

In those three players, there was hope. They can be more than good; they all have a chance to be great.

"Players are like anyone else," said Hargrove. "Give them an excuse, and they will take it. But people with character bounce back. In the past we never had a lot of people with tremendous character, but we do now. No team in baseball ever had to come back from what we faced in the spring of 1993. The fact that we didn't just fold our tents and go home says a lot about the people on this team."

Baseball people began to pay attention to the Indians in 1992. They were impressed with how the team cut its payroll, retooled the farm system, and traded for young players. Then the front office signed the key young players to long-term contracts, protecting the team from the threat of free agency that had forced so many bad trades in the past. At last, the Indians seemed to have a plan.

"I studied the Indians organization going back to the late 1950s," said Hank Peters, the man who kick-started the Tribe in the 1990s. "You can look back over thirty years and see the deterioration of what was once a great farm system. When the owners wanted to save money, they looked at cutting back the scouting and farm system because that was something the public or media couldn't immediately see. The other thing was that every four or five years, the Indians were sold. None of the owners made a long-term commitment. They just wanted to put a Band-Aid on the bleeding at the big-league level. A number of the owners had enough capital to buy the team but not enough to truly rebuild it. There also used to be a lot of tax advantages to owning a team. You could depreciate the players and have other write-offs. When those tax breaks ended, the team was often sold."

Peters makes an excellent point. From 1949 to 1986 no group owned the Indians for more than six years. On the average, the team was sold every four years.

"Trades were made to pay the bills," said Herb Score. "I don't blame the owners. I thought Ted Bonda did a good job running the team. And Gabe Paul—the easiest thing would have been for him to move the franchise. They were on the verge of bankruptcy a few times, but Gabe somehow kept the team afloat and kept it here."

That's true, but it wasn't good enough. It changed in December 1986 when Dick and the late Dave Jacobs purchased the team, hired Peters, and really began building it from the bottom up.

"I love what the Indians are doing because they have a plan," said Frank Robinson. "The organization was bad for so long because of the people who operated it. They weren't truthful. When I was with the Indians, we didn't have a lot of young players, but we traded off Rick Cerone, Pedro Guerrero, and Alfredo Griffin without knowing what we had in them. Each year Phil Seghi was telling the press and the public that we had a chance to win, and I'd say to myself, 'No way.' We didn't have the personnel to do it, and the front office didn't want to make the commitment to get the players. It wasn't until recently that it has changed, and now what is happening in Cleveland is impressive."

Meanwhile, the fans are watching and waiting.

"Cleveland is a baseball town, first and foremost," said Nev Chandler. "The Indians were a charter member of the American League. In the 1940s and 1950s, they had great teams. I've covered all the major sports in Cleveland. I grew up here. Give the town just a representative baseball team, and the excitement generated will dwarf anything Cleveland has seen with the Browns or the Cavaliers. It wouldn't take much from the Indians to make baseball the dominant force in town."

On his sports talk show, Greg Brinda asked the fans, "From your heart, if you could pick one of the Cleveland teams to win a championship, which would it be?

"It wasn't even close," said Brinda. "The fans picked the Indians, 3-to-1, over the Browns or Cavs. That caught me by surprise. I thought that maybe all the lousy baseball over all those years had gotten people down. But through all the generations of bad baseball, there is still a candle of hope waiting to be lit. Fans would call and get choked up, just talking about what it would be like to see their team in the World Series just once before they die."

I wasn't shocked by Brinda's poll. Like most people in Cleveland, I was born after 1954, after the last pennant. I don't even remember a team in contention. That's just it: I want to know what it feels like to be in the midst of a pennant race, and I know I'm not alone when it comes to these emotions.

But are the Indians on the right track? To me, there was only one person to ask.

"I know a lot of people say that the team has been cursed and snakebit ever since they traded me the first time," said Rocky Colavito. "But it seemed like my trade started the whole thing. A whole bunch of bad trades and bad teams followed, getting rid of everyone from Mudcat Grant to Buddy Bell to Dennis Eckersley."

But Rocky, what about the future?

"It seems to me that the Indians are finally trying to do it right," said Colavito. "Lord, I hope so. The fans deserve it."

INDEX

About the Author

Terry Pluto is the typical Cleveland Indians fan. They last won a pennant in 1954; he was born in 1955. His first favorite Tribe player was Rocky Colavito, and he probably has seen over two thousand Indians games at the old Cleveland Stadium. Now a sports columnist for the *Akron Beacon Journal,* Pluto covered the Indians from 1980 to 1984 for the *Cleveland Plain Dealer.* For better or worse, he gave Joe Charboneau the nickname "Super Joe." He also covered the 1979 Baltimore Orioles for the *Baltimore Evening Sun.*

Among his baseball books, Pluto has written *Weaver on Strategy,* with former Orioles manager Earl Weaver, and *Sixty-One,* the story of the 1961 New York Yankees, with Tony Kubek. In his last eight years with the *Akron Beacon Journal,* Pluto has won twenty-eight national and state writing awards and was the 1989 Ohio Sportswriter of the Year.

This is his thirteenth book. His book about the old American Basketball Association, *Loose Balls,* was chosen the best sports book of 1990 by *USA Today.*